Road to Ruin

*An Introduction to Sprawl and
How to Cure It*

DOM NOZZI

Foreword by Victor Dover

PRAEGER

Westport, Connecticut
London

Library of Congress Cataloging-in-Publication Data

Nozzi, Dom.
   Road to ruin : an introduction to sprawl and how to cure it / Dom Nozzi ;
foreword by Victor Dover.
   p. cm.
   Includes bibliographical references and index.
   ISBN 0–275–98129–0 (alk. paper)
      1. Cities and towns—United States—Growth. 2. City planning—United States.
      3. Land Use—United States. 4. Urban transportation—United States. 5. Quality of
      life—United States. I. Title
HT384.U5N68   2003
307.76'09773—dc21   2003045760

British Library Cataloguing in Publication Data is available.

Library of Congress Catalog Card Number: 2003045760
ISBN: 0–275–98129–0

First published in 2003

Praeger Publishers, 88 Post Road West, Westport, CT 06881
An imprint of Greenwood Publishing Group, Inc.
www.praeger.com

Printed in the United States of America

The paper used in this book complies with the
Permanent Paper Standard issued by the National
Information Standards Organization (Z39.48–1984).

10 9 8 7 6 5 4 3 2 1

As roads fill to congestion, we continue to [widen] roads, failing again and again to understand that highways generate their own traffic in a never-ending cycle, or perhaps simply ignoring this reality because road [widening] is good for the economy.

—Stephen B. Goddard, *Getting There*

Contents

Tables and Figures

Acknowledgments

I am indebted to Perry Maull, Maureen Conroy, Mike Byerly, Bobbe Needham, Grant Thrall, Susan Brady, Ed Crawford, and my parents for their inspiration and knowledge, which made this book possible. Special thanks to Ian Lockwood, Dan Burden, Victor Dover, James Howard Kunstler, David Coffey, Walter Kulash, and Andres Duany for opening my eyes and changing my life.

Foreword

This book is about a culture gone mad.

Ours.

It also contains the workable "eight-step program" that will lead to recovery, if we'll admit we have a problem. Our problem is that we're dangerously addicted to driving.

Dom Nozzi looks back at the results of the century when America went car-crazy and makes the case for why we should—and how we can—redirect our civilization toward more sensible and sustainable behavior.

Nozzi's clear voice rises above a chorus of professionals, political leaders, business innovators, environmental advocates, and other thinkers who have begun challenging our auto-oriented systems for land development, regulation, and city management. To get our minds around the predicament of our contemporary cities, we must grasp the ways our support of (and dependence upon) a single mode of transport has rendered those cities dysfunctional. This book explains what every commuter ponders while stuck in traffic: how did cars take over our towns and our lives, what has it cost us, and what happens next?

Nozzi walks to work—lucky him—but he is no anti-car extremist. (I can vouch for the fact that he is a very capable driver; he's taken me on driving tours through some of Florida's more egregious sprawl.) But he convincingly argues that, for more people, using an automobile should be an *option* instead of a requirement for daily survival. This is a practical and attainable vision, not a wild-eyed dream of a car-free utopia.

Like each of us, his point of view is no doubt shaped by his days at the office. Nozzi works in one of those outposts on the front lines in the battle over sprawl and development, the local city planning department. Those halls play host to intense brawls over street design, land use, and neighborhood form. Traffic is issue number one in the daily skirmishes.

There one can hear all the radicalized opinions of rule-bound public works engineers, real estate developers, not-in-my-back-yard insurgents (NIMBYs), expensive lawyers, and volunteer preservationists. In Gainesville's fortunate college-town environment. Each group is equipped with spokespersons more eloquent than usual, and debates start earlier and run for longer than in other American cities. Progress is certainly being made, in Gainesville and elsewhere, but at a glacial pace. I'll bet Dom Nozzi was at work when the need became apparent for a balanced, straightforward text that breaks past the usual shrill rhetoric about cars and traffic.

While it is written for popular readers, *Road to Ruin* also picks up and advances an important scholarly thread stirred by Lewis Mumford, furthered by Jane Jacobs, and more lately coalesced into practice by the New Urbanists and Smart Growthers.

A two-part formula about land use and transportation was associated with twentieth-century city planning in America, especially in the rapidly changing Sun Belt. First, the formula assumed that land uses would remain separate and kept low in their intensity and density. Second, the formula assumed practically all trips from one land use to another would be made by car on a coarse, treelike regional roadway network, usually in a succession of single-occupant trips. That formula still underlies most zoning and highway planning in the United States. It is most astonishing that this formula was applied, rather suddenly, on a continent-wide basis, *without a field test.* No one in human history had ever built cities this way, and naturally not everyone thought it would work.

Since the beginning of the transformation of our cities and our lives around Happy Motoring, critics have complained. Mumford famously wrote, "Forget the damned motorcar and build the cities for lovers and friends," though one wonders if he really expected the leaders of the day to take up this particular idea. He and other critics blasted the emerging car culture and the new highway-building mania even as they scripted their own more cautious propaganda on cities of the future. "Our national flower," groaned Mumford, "is the concrete cloverleaf." However, those early arguments, right as some may have been, were based on forecasts and opinions about what *might* happen as the new automotive way of life unfolded on a larger scale. "A city exists, not for the constant passage of motorcars, but for the care and culture of men," Mumford warned. Few listened.

The Happy Motoring propaganda machine, churning on noisily for a century, eventually just drowned out and overwhelmed the detail-oriented Mumford types. Logic wasn't foremost in the naive first days of

Futurama on wheels; in a blatant example, a 1955 gasoline advertisement in *Colliers* admonished readers, "Drive more—it gets cheaper by the mile."

"Don't honk your horn. Raise your voice," trumpeted newsreels financed by General Motors just after World War II. "We fought, and we won our right-of-way. Write your hometown officials. Postcard your newspaper editors. Demand more highways and parking space. Give yourself the green light." At another point the newsreel's narrator authoritatively lamented, "Today *two miles of roadway are wearing out for every one being built!*" The goal was to inspire voters to demand funding of the interstate highway system, even though, in retrospect, the statistic seems to suggest that fully one-third of the roads in the country were already, at that moment, either being built or ripped up for reconstruction.

Thanks to the enormous investments that followed, many adult Americans alive today grew up during the last years of a golden age of motoring, when the suburbs were newer and many of our cities could still boast of what traffic engineers call "the free-flowing condition." For a time, it probably seemed possible to build our way out of congestion problems; it probably seemed sustainable to believe that wider roads were better roads. It wasn't so.

There is now no doubt that the golden age of motoring is over in our metropolitan areas. The phrase "free-flowing" rarely comes to mind anymore amid the suburban gridlock and road rage that characterize our era. Tailpipe pollution chokes the air, despite technological advances. We all know of shiny new roads in our hometowns that were supposedly built to solve congestion but instead ended up clogged after just a few years. Today transportation planners talk with a straight face about "induced travel demand" to explain how newly expanded roads attract a rise in demand for traffic capacity, overtaking them with new congestion of their own making. It's a phenomenon Mumford foresaw, but in his day there were fewer built-out, long-established examples from which to draw conclusions.

Now, in this book, the argument has been built anew from readily available, checkable facts. *Road to Ruin* is full of empirical data, and this distinguishes it from the earlier polemical critiques of car culture. Nozzi supports his instinctive ideas and personal observations with a treasury of hard evidence about what *has* happened, gathered from our nation's last six or seven decades of experience. I hope we will be hearing quotes from this book at city planning hearings.

This factual book comes at an important moment. A vocal Libertarian backlash against Smart Growth recently got underway; in some circles, adherents of transportation reform are being characterized, at worst, as totalitarian throwbacks (or, at best, as do-gooder, politically correct dummies who are hopelessly trying to take away our cars). Sprawling, car-dependent development is now widely derided, but local governments are uneasy about promoting the alternatives, which involve living closer together and driving less. Violent military conflict and political turmoil in the Middle East continue to raise uncertainty over future control of oil fields. Controversy boils over drilling for petroleum in the Alaskan wildlife preserves. *Road to Ruin* is part of an urgently needed national conversation about car culture and community.

In these pages we are shown how the physical form of our settlements and the details of our streets should matter most to us, rather than the number of lanes or the speed of the cars. Here we are told, let cities be cities, and don't suburbanize them.

Seek a minimum livable density. Connect, physically, so we can reconnect socially. Like much of the book, all this turns conventional wisdom on its head, of course.

It's about time.

Victor Dover, AICP
Dover, Kohl, and Partners

Introduction

A few days ago, someone knocked over one of the concrete monuments that mark the street names in the central-city historic neighborhood where I live. A reckless Saturday-night driver? A truck backing up? It didn't matter. This small sentinel had stood witness to decades of laughing children biking past, senior citizens walking their Scotties and golden retrievers, families headed for the duck pond, moony high schoolers strolling hand in hand. For me, the toppling of the old monument symbolizes what has happened to our streets and neighborhoods over the last 60 years.

Until about 1945, the focus of design for American communities was people—pedestrians, bicyclists, kids. Neighborhood streets were places where people walked, socialized, greeted neighbors sitting on their front porches, places where kids played kick the can and rode their bikes. Compared to most of our neighborhoods today, streets were narrower and connected to each other at almost every block, blocks were shorter, street surfaces were often rougher. Cars parked along the roadside, trees shaded streets and sidewalks—and there *were* sidewalks. In city streets, people ran into friends, exchanged greetings with strangers, conducted business, window shopped, waved to acquaintances through shop and restaurant windows.

In 1990, Roberto Pirzio-Biroli, an Italian architect and city planner, looked down from a skyscraper on the city of Denver. "Where is the city square?" he asked. "Where do the people go to be together? Where is the piazza? . . . Without a piazza, you cannot live!"[1] He could as well have asked, "Where are the *people?* Where is the *life*?"

On a recent trip to Europe, I was struck by the contrast between cities such as Paris, Florence, and Rome and American cities. In Europe, cars, homes, and hotel rooms are modest. But the public realm—the streets, sidewalks, and public parks—are a veritable paradise: ornamental architecture on beautiful buildings, human-scaled streets with buildings snugged up close to the sidewalk to create a comfortable sense of enclosure—an outdoor room—and streets full of sociable people all evidently enjoying themselves. The public realm in European cities is inclusive, welcoming with a powerful sense of community a mix of ages, skills, economic classes, and races.

In *Crabgrass Frontier*, Kenneth Jackson makes similar observations.

Cities, by their very nature, ought to encourage the elevation of the human spirit. Anyone who has ever visited the Piazza San Marco in Venice . . . knows something of the potentialities and varieties of urban experience. They remind one of Samuel Johnson's telling phrase: "When a man is tired of London, he is tired of life." . . .

In the United States . . . what is most significant is not the influence of urban culture, but the general suburban resistance to it. What is striking in the lives of most residents is the frequency with which they choose not to avail themselves of the variety of experiences the metropolis affords, the manner in which they voluntarily restrict their interests and associations to the immediate vicinity, and the way in which they decline contacts with the larger society.[2]

In American cities, we have turned our backs on the public realm and instead made the insides of our *cars and homes* luxurious. Rather than the safe, interesting streets and sidewalks of Europe, our city streets feel unsafe; walking along them, we feel overexposed. I think of those sociable piazzas in Florence and Rome, and I empathize with Pirzio-Biroli—"Without a piazza, you cannot live!"

What changed our vital cities and welcoming communities over those 60 years?

Our ongoing love affair with cars.

Starting in the early twentieth century, American communities set out to make cars happy.

A new theory of street design emerged. We should widen those old narrow streets to carry larger numbers of cars more "safely." We should get rid of trees, buildings, and parked cars alongside streets so that drivers would not crash into them. We should make street corners at intersections larger and more forgiving, increasing visibility left and right, to avoid accidents. Yet unintended consequences arose from wider streets and larger intersections. Motorists were able to drive faster, often faster than they should. Streets no longer invited people to come together to walk or bicycle.

We had begun redesigning streets not for kids or bikes or walkers but for high-speed, high-volume car travel.

We who could afford to moved to the new suburbs, where we built gates and walls and berms to shield and isolate ourselves from traffic noise and crime. We often chose to live on large cul-de-sacs that connected to nothing. In many neighborhoods, parents had to scold their children about playing near the street, much less in it. Residential neighborhoods became "a mass of small, private islands; with the back yard functioning as a wholesome, family-oriented, and reclusive place. There are few places as desolate and lonely as a suburban street on a hot afternoon," Kenneth Jackson suggests. He finds "the evolution of the front porch . . . a microcosm" of this decline. "The front porch was the physical expression of neighborliness and community. With a much-used front porch, one could live on Andy Hardy's street, where doors need not be locked, where everyone was like family, and where the iceman would forever make deliveries. With a front porch, one could live in Brigadoon, Shangri-La, and Camelot, all in one."[3]

Along with our front porches, we gave up walking or bicycling, rather than compete with the raging torrent of cars. Cities and city neighborhoods became places to *get through* on our way to work or shop from homes remote from city centers.

In our cities, we gave up the ornamental detail that lends buildings their character—who notices or cares about detail while speeding by at 45 miles per hour? To escape traffic dangers, fumes, and noise, we set buildings farther and farther back, turn their faces from the street, and add berms. The rare pedestrian in many cities today walks between blank, boring walls too distant to enjoy even if they were interrupted by doors and windows. The front entrances of department stores or public buildings no longer arrest or intrigue the passerby with rich detail and displays. Litter and dumping have become problems. People who once picked up litter during their walks aren't walking, and drivers speeding along unfriendly modern streets have became less concerned about tossing a Coke can or fast-food litter out the car window. We work or do business in buildings that allow us to come and go without ever stepping onto a streetside sidewalk; we simply escape into our private car in a garage or lot. We have willingly traded aesthetics, vibrancy, and socializing for convenience, speed, isolation, and status in our "privatopia."

The more we surrendered our public space—our city squares and shaded streets, our sidewalks and streetside shops—to wider roads and parking lots and cars, the more unpleasant that space became for *people*. And the more people wanted to abandon it and flee from it. The result for many of us: the discovery that the sanitized suburban enclaves where we sought privacy, exclusivity, and prestige proved shallow, empty substitutes for the intimate human connections our parents or grandparents once enjoyed. Meanwhile, our city neighborhoods pay the price in more noise, higher taxes, and less safe streets. The minute we emerge from our lavish suburban homes, we confront a dreadful public realm of speeding cars, an absence of pedestrians, lack of street trees, large parking lots, glaring lights, and noise pollution. Indeed, some observers argue convincingly that a lavish private realm (the interiors of our homes, our offices, our cars) in auto-dependent cities is a manifestation of an effort to compensate for a bleak public realm. The American suburb is the land of private wealth and public impoverishment.[4]

Andres Duany suggests that Americans have confused standard of living with quality of life—that is, we've assumed that a high standard of living would deliver a high quality of life. As Juliet B. Schor pointed out a decade ago: "The American standard of living embodies a level of material comfort unprecedented in human history. The American home is more spacious and luxurious than the dwellings of any other nation." In the years since World War II, she notes, we have enjoyed a "national shopping spree . . . feeding on a steady diet of single-family houses, cars, household appliances, and leisure spending. The average American is consuming, in toto, more than twice as much as he or she did 40 years ago. And this holds not only for the Gucci set but all the way down the income scale."[5]

Yet it is in the public realm that a community's overall quality of life is measured. "Livability is . . . determined by how community members feel when they venture into the public realm."[6] Measured by how much personal free time we have to enjoy a quality public realm sociably with our neighbors, we have paid for our high standard of living in the United States by sacrificing our quality of life.

By 1988, a British study reflected the about-face in our priorities: "The pedestrian remains the largest single obstacle to free traffic movement. . . . For decades, traffic engineers who design roadways actually referred to walkers in the *Highway Capacity Manual* as 'traffic interruptions.' "[7]

Whatever a community makes its main form of transportation profoundly shapes the way it will use its land, not the other way around. Weak land use plans and feeble regulations did not create urban sprawl, for example; pouring money into roads and cars did. And whatever transportation our community chooses—for most of us, cars—also shapes our quality of life. As we have learned over the years, single-mindedly choosing car transportation has dispersed and isolated us and degraded our communities' quality of life, environment, and financial health.

The more convenient we make life for cars, the less livable it becomes for us. We complain about our commute, about congestion, about rush hour, about chauffeuring the kids to soccer, dance lessons, school. We become enraged at other drivers, at whoever designed our terrible road system, at traffic lights and congestion. We blame city officials, overpopulation, those feckless university students in their Porsches, four-lane roads where there should be six lanes.

An alternative exists: the traditional urban model (the way most American towns were built before World War II) that respects and promotes the public realm, that encourages a sense of community and civic pride. This remains the scenario in the increasingly rare communities not dominated by cars. It is just that simple.

And just that difficult, because we Americans love our cars. They're convenient, private, comfortable status symbols, our homes away from home. They take us directly wherever we want to go, effortlessly, safely, and *fast*. They make us feel self-reliant. They're our suits of armor.

The magical and disastrous thing about cars is that they make distance—technically defined as the geography that separates destinations—virtually irrelevant.[8] We think nothing of driving five miles to buy a light bulb. We don't give a second thought to the preposterous idea that our home is 10 miles from where we work. Drive three miles for a cup of coffee? No problem! Seven miles to rent a video? Piece of cake! No culture has ever seen so many miles traveled for so many trivial reasons or, for that matter, for essential daily needs.

So couldn't we make our communities more livable some other way than by cutting down on car travel? Couldn't we just do something about the traffic? How about wider roads, bigger intersections, more free parking space? Let's try electric cars, higher-mileage cars, more "beltways," and more efficiently timed traffic signals.

And right there is another dilemma. Because we are motorists for nearly all our daily travel, we think and see like motorists. We depend on travel by car. As drivers, we equate our needs with the needs of our cars—our needs as drivers. Yet almost always the needs of our cars are at odds with our needs as people. Still, we'll do almost anything not to give up our suits of armor. Most of us cannot imagine life without them.

We have tried a number of tactics to improve our quality of life in our car-oriented world. Paradoxically, the strategies have become obstacles to the real solutions to our land use and transportation problems. For instance, to combat the traffic and pollution created by additional car trips from more and more remote suburbs, our conventional and historical remedy has been to widen roads, create enormous street intersections, and lay down asphalt seas of parking. What's wrong with that? By encouraging more car travel, these solutions in fact *worsen* the traffic and pollution problems they were designed to alleviate and trap us in a vicious cycle.[9] "Ironically enough, most communities are trying to overcome the traffic crisis in ways that actually perpetuate it," wrote D. R. Porter fifteen years ago.[10] Furthermore, we cannot make car travel easier without making other forms of travel—public transit, bicycling, or our two feet—more difficult.[11]

So every "solution" that makes our communities more car friendly not only doesn't work but also makes things worse. All such remedies force us to drive more often; encourage more people and businesses to move from in-town locations; make walking, bicycling, and riding the bus more difficult; degrade our quality of life with noise, hazards, and air pollution; cost us a lot of money; and move our once unique communities closer to becoming Anywhere, USA.

As it has become more clear that auto-oriented urban sprawl puts our quality of life in a downward spiral, people-friendly solutions have started to present themselves again. We could develop vacant, underused in-town property instead of more remote "greenfield" suburbs. We could design more modest, low-speed streets and build fewer enormous parking lots. We could design places where people can park once, then walk—to their workplaces, stores, recreation, and civic activities. Or imagine this: we could live within walking, biking, or transit distance of most places we go every day.

The key to all of these possibilities is designing and redesigning meaningful portions of our communities not for cars, but for pedestrians. We will never have enough money as a society to accomplish all that is necessary and important to improve our lives. Indeed, a number of communities are now nearly bankrupt because of problems described later in this book. In line with the old adage "If you run out of money, you are then forced to think," in an environment of scarce dollars, we need to be able to think smarter. The key is to identify the linchpins, the features we can put in place that will kick into life a positive cycle that will require little or no effort or expenditure of resources.

One of these linchpins, and one of the most important lessons I've learned as a city planner, is that *the pedestrian is the design imperative.* Making pedestrians the focus produces—naturally and inevitably—a number of desirable outcomes without much additional community effort. Examples?

Streets will become much safer because high-speed car travel, a leading cause of injuries and deaths, will be reduced. People unable to drive, such as seniors, children, and the disabled, will regain independence and dignity. Streets will become more attractive: Sign pollution and glaring lights will decline as they are no longer needed to attract occupants of fast-moving cars; street trees, street furniture, building ornamentation, and awnings will reappear. As national chains of car-oriented restaurants and other businesses that thrive in a car-based community give way to locally owned, unique, pedestrian-oriented businesses, community and neighborhood pride will be restored. Local economies will improve—particularly downtown—as property values rise in response to demand created by successful pedestrian-oriented businesses and revived interest in tourism. And by the same token, communities and neighborhoods will be less threatened with abandonment and decay, because sprawl will be less rampant (sprawl is better controlled when there are fewer high-speed, high-capacity streets and more modest parking lots). Finally, the poor will have a better chance to improve their circumstances, because they will not have to own and maintain so many costly cars.

But most people-oriented solutions present a paradox. Across America, the codes that regulate local urban development have made it illegal to improve our communities in these ways, which are summarized in a concept called "smart growth": development is compact, walkable enough to provide transportation choices, close to daily destinations, human scaled, respectful of the environment and the public realm, mixed in land uses, and sociable, with diverse incomes, age groups, and housing choices and a sense of place and community. Here is the problem: "Smart growth may be popular . . . it may result in better places for kids, parents, single people, and senior citizens," as one observer writes, "it may do all that, but it is still illegal across the United States."[12]

Smart-growth developments often require a developer to seek difficult and costly exceptions to local zoning codes that commonly prohibit, for example, designing narrower streets, building closer to the street, mixing homes with stores and offices, including neighborhood-integrated schools that children could walk to, reducing minimum lot widths, and incorporating "granny flats," that is, apartments above or behind homes. "Developers have often complained that the reason sprawling, single-use, car-dominated development occurs is that local zoning ordinances and subdivision regulations inhibit other development forms. . . . Even if a developer was interested in building a pedestrian-oriented, compact development, local regulations would be costly to overcome."[13]

If that were the end of the story, this book would not exist. I would resign myself, along with everyone else, to increasingly unlivable communities, more time trapped in my car on the road, more frustration and isolation, more inescapable congestion, until the economic and social and emotional costs of being car dependent became unbearable for a critical mass of people. Twenty more years? Fifty?

But there is hope. An important subcategory of smart growth is the "New Urbanism," a strategy of community and neighborhood design that uses timeless, traditional development principles at the same time it incorporates contemporary technology and values; the pedestrian, not the car, is the design imperative (see chapters 9 and 10).

As Marvin Harris pointed out in *Cultural Materialism* (1979), it is not ideas that determine our behavior and values, but the environmental and economic conditions we must cope with each day. That is, we learn most easily through noticing what things cost and how available they are, not through the propagation or exhortation of ideas. In my own work and in this book, I apply my own materialist understanding of what tools are effective—and therefore called for—to land use and human behavior. And despite a major theme of the book—that transportation drives (or determines) land use—I am a professional planning practitioner. Therefore I elaborate more thoroughly the details of urban design than the details of transportation engineering.

I love healthy, walkable cities—their energy, vitality, and rich diversity. I wrote this book in large part because I have seen the equivalent of too many monuments like my neighborhood street marker toppled, and because I fear that we are allowing cars to destroy the joys of the traditional city by dissipating their energy, sapping their vitality, and homogenizing their fascinating diversity.

CHAPTER 1

Dire Straits

If we are to have the full use of automobiles, cities must be remade.
—Paul Hoffman, president of the Studebaker Corporation, 1939

The most serious obstacles in our roadbuilding program are not
money, nor engineering problems, not cruel terrain—but PEOPLE.
—James J. Morton, special assistant to the U.S. secretary of
commerce, 1964

As fond as we are of complaining about traffic, auto mechanics, and car problems in general, asking drivers to use their cars less is like asking Floridians to turn down the air conditioning, Texans to eat less barbecue, or Nebraskans to watch less football.

WHY WE LOVE OUR CARS

Sure, we know there's a lot wrong with cars—pollution, crashes, wildlife and environmental issues, expense. But anyone who tried to take our cars away from us would face a battle that would make the French Revolution look like a grade-school scuffle. It *just makes sense* for most of us to drive.

Indeed, we have modified our lives to take advantage of what our cars allow us to do. Our cities have spread out; we have built residential-only neighborhoods; middle-class families drive on vacation to national parks, Disneyworld, beaches, and other far-flung spots; many of us enjoy higher levels of privacy in well-appointed homes remote from cities. It sometimes feels like our civic duty to drive—why else would the government

so heavily subsidize cars with, just for starters, free roads and free parking, inexpensive gas, and emergency police and fire service? Richard Lay-
man points out, for example, that unlike railroads, roads and highways
were built primarily with government funds such as property taxes,
income taxes, and gasoline excise taxes, which is also the case with air-
ports. "Railroads paid for the construction and maintenance of tracks, and
paid for the construction and maintenance of railroad stations," as well as
"property taxes on their rail lines, whereas truckers and airplanes don't
pay property taxes on the roads/air traffic routes that they travel on."[1]

How else could we carry groceries, kids, bikes, and garden supplies, all
in one trip? City busses don't wait in our garages, ready to zip us directly
across town to the video store or a ball game, into the city to work, five
miles to a friend's house, or across the state to visit our sister—in privacy
and comfort, with our favorite music playing. With a car at our command,
we don't have to trudge to the subway, huddle in the rain or snow waiting
for a bus, or simmer in the summer sun sweating our way six miles to
work on a bicycle.

So we're in agreement. We're keeping our Expeditions, F-150s, Blazers,
and Explorers. It is irrational for us not to.

WHAT DO THOSE SUVs COST US?

Of course, we pay a price for all that convenience. Air, water, and noise
pollution. Injury and death. Environmental degradation. Loss of land. Urban
sprawl. Our time. Lots and lots of money. Social and emotional isolation.

Clean Air

Air pollution is an easy place to start, because nearly everyone agrees
that cars cause it—or a large portion of it. Beyond that agreement, the
arguments get murky. Just to make clear the correlation between driving
cars and air pollution . . .

The U.S. Environmental Protection Agency indicated that in 1997,
motor vehicles emitted over 50 million tons of carbon monoxide into the
air, over 7 million tons of nitrogen oxides, over 5 million tons of volatile
organic compounds, 320 tons of sulfur dioxide, and almost 15 million tons
of road dust into the nation's air.

Since 1970, per-mile vehicle emissions have decreased because of
cleaner fuels and better tailpipe technology, but the substantial increase in
vehicle miles traveled is threatening to reverse this trend in the near
future.

In 1991, air pollution from motor vehicles resulted in 50 to 70 million
respiratory-related restricted activity days, over 850 million headaches
caused by carbon monoxide, 20,000 to 46,000 cases of chronic respiratory

illnesses, 530 cases of cancer, and 40,000 premature deaths. Converted to 1999 dollars, motor vehicle air pollution in that year created up to $531 billion in health damage, $5 billion in crop damage, $44 billion in visibility damage, and $365 million in building damage.

Carbon dioxide emissions from transportation in 1984, which was 32 percent of all carbon dioxide into the air, was 379 metric tons in the United States. It rose to 473 million tons by 1997. From 1996 to 2020, carbon emissions are projected to increase by about 48 percent.

One-person-per-car travel creates more air pollution than any other form of travel.[2]

A community's level of air pollution is directly proportional to the average speed of its vehicles.[3] (Think about that one for a minute. The faster cars move, the *more* air pollution.)

Your family only drives about 20 miles a day, you say? Great. But fewer car miles don't always mean less air pollution. What counts is the number of *trips*. The emissions from one "cold start" (the first few minutes of each trip when your engine coughs to a start) approximately equal those produced by a car traveling 45 miles per hour for 22 miles.[4] As much as we all applaud more stringent tailpipe emission standards, we can still count on sprawl-related increases in car travel to make air pollution 30 percent worse in 2010 than in 1989.[5]

Now for the murkier areas. Conventional wisdom, not to mention common sense, tells us that compared to free-flowing traffic, congested traffic causes more air pollution. But look at the car-friendliest cities in the country, those with the most miles of road asphalt per person: Phoenix, Denver, Detroit, or, friendliest of all, Houston. In Houston, recently ranked as among the least densely populated U.S. cities, toxic air emissions in 1998 equaled 90 percent of the total emitted by the entire state of California. The city had 69 ozone health-alert days that year, despite its rigorous emission standards. Schwarzkopf informs us that low concentrations of ground-level ozone can irritate the eyes, nose, and throat. Heavier smog levels can trigger asthma, bronchitis, coughing, and chest pain; increased susceptibility to respiratory infections; and decreased lung function and physical performance. Prolonged exposure can damage lung tissue and contribute to chronic lung disease.[6] On four days, Houston had the highest ground levels of ozone of any city in the nation. (Ground-level ozone, the primary unhealthy ingredient of photochemical smog, is produced by a chemical reaction between two common air pollutants caused mainly by car emissions, hydrocarbons and nitrogen oxides.) In 1999, Houston's smog exceeded federal standards on 52 days.[7]

As hard as it may be to swallow, the more a community tries to reduce traffic congestion in conventional ways, the worse its air quality gets. The California Air Resources Board, for example, has found that congestion is less a factor in creating air pollution than the number of vehicle trips and the length of those trips.[8] And reducing congestion by building wider roads encourages more solo car trips. By the same token, the more dispersed a community's suburbs, producing more car trips and longer trip distances per person, the more air pollution—20 percent to 50 percent more than compact development produces.[9]

Human Lives and Well-Being

Another familiar cost of driving, apart from air pollution, is the highway death and injury toll. We hear the dire predictions before every holiday, but unless someone we know dies or is injured, it's easy not to connect them to real people.

The number of people who die on U.S. highways every year is the equivalent of a fully loaded Boeing 747 aircraft crashing every three days, killing everyone aboard. In 2000, almost 6.5 million motor vehicle crashes killed 41,821 people and injured more than 3 million; 13 percent of those killed were pedestrians, bicyclists, and others not in the vehicles. Every 13 minutes in 2000, someone died in a motor vehicle accident, an average of 115 persons every day.

We have 250 million cars in the United States. Every 450 cars are responsible for one traffic death, every 100 cars for one permanently handicapped person, every 7 cars for an injured person.[10]

Of children 12 years old or younger who die in motor vehicle crashes, 39 percent are killed while walking or bicycling.[11]

Deaths and injuries resulting from motor vehicle crashes are the leading cause of death for persons of every age from 4 through 33 years old (based on 1998 data).[12]

Land

Cars have gobbled up from one-third to one-half of all land in U.S. cities.[13]

We have paved 60,000 square miles of land—2 percent of the total, and 10 percent of all arable land[14]—for "roadways, cloverleafs, parking lots, and service areas—a collective mass about the size of Georgia, . . . 38.4 million acres."[15] By 1995, we had set aside about 3,000 square miles (1.9 million acres) for parking. Roads alone in 1997 covered 11 million acres of land (17,375 square miles), not including shoulders and medians, an amount of land equal to Maryland and Delaware combined.[16]

The average employer provides more room for employee parking than for office space. In Los Angeles, every car requires eight parking spaces: home and work, the grocery store, the doctor's office, various retail shops, restaurants, and other businesses.[17]

The family car consumes about three times more space than the average family home.[18]

A bus can carry 40 passengers with 16 percent of the energy it takes a car to carry one person. A filled 40-foot bus is equivalent to a line of moving cars stretching six city blocks; a filled six-car train is equivalent to a line of moving cars stretching 95 city blocks.[19]

A walking-oriented city allocates less than 10 percent of its land to transportation, while an auto-oriented city must dedicate up to 30 percent of its land to roads and another 20 percent to off-street parking.[20]

Large amounts of asphalt aggravate the urban "heat island effect," which increases community air conditioning costs and energy consumption. Stormwater runoff from large expanses of asphalt is the leading source of surface-water pollution in many cities.

Our Own Money

Our convenient cars cost us, individually, quite a bundle out of our own pockets. Transportation is now the second highest expense category for American households. About 18 percent of all household expenditures go toward travel. Only housing—at 19 percent—costs more for households (travel eats up about 22 percent in more auto-dependent cities such as Houston). Travel costs more for households than food, insurance, utilities, health care, and education.[21] To cover that, an American family works from New Year's Day to March 14. No society in history has worked so much just to be able to get around. (By comparison, at the beginning of the twentieth century, we spent only about 1 or 2 percent on transportation.)[22]

Owning a small car that we drive 15,000 miles a year costs $6,041 annually, according to the American Automobile Association,[23] and delivers little in the way of economic return compared to, say, housing—"$10,000 spent on motor vehicles provides just $910 in equity, compared with $4,730 [in equity] for the same investment in housing."[24]

The average cost of travel by car in 1989 was 78 cents per mile. (Governments and businesses calculate car expenses at 25 to 30 cents per mile.) We spent $1.6 trillion for car travel in 1989, when our gross domestic product was about $5 trillion.[25]

By 1999, government spending hit $117 billion for roads and $29 billion for public transportation. Including private spending, the total annual U.S. transportation tab is about $1 trillion, about 11 percent of our GDP (not including the incidental costs included in the 1989 figure just listed).[26]

U.S. drivers used more than 120 billion gallons of gasoline in 2000, $186 billion worth. If fuel economy does not improve, passenger-vehicle fuel use will go up more than 50 percent by 2020, to almost 190 billion gallons per year, when oil import spending is expected to hit $160 billion, according to the U.S. Department of Energy, up more than 50 percent from the

$106 billion—about $380 per person—we spent to import crude oil and petroleum products in 2000.

Businesses in auto-dependent communities must shoulder higher overhead costs—higher salaries to accommodate the higher cost of living (mostly the result of households' necessary car ownership), parking space, and government taxes to pay for road projects. Free employee parking costs businesses $85 billion a year, and the federal government loses $21 billion a year in taxes because employee parking is not taxed.[27]

Public Money

When the American Petroleum Institute claimed that motorists pay their own way, transportation professionals must have been struck dumb by the absurdity.

All told, U.S. motorists enjoy hidden subsidies of more than $700 billion a year. To boot motorists and truckers off this form of welfare, gas would have to cost from $5.60 to $15.14 per gallon—that includes all of the subsidies and indirect costs not paid by motorists: pollution, health, environmental, protecting oil supplies, tax breaks, and outright motorist subsidies.[28] The 1997 Federal Highway Cost Allocation Study found that vehicle user fees (fuel taxes, registration fees, and road tolls) would need to increase by more than 43 percent to fund all roadway expenses—more, if other motor vehicle externalities such as pollution, congestion, and noise are factored in.[29]

The federal government spends $50 billion a year to maintain U.S. military activities in the Persian Gulf, partly to keep the oil flowing to us. Traffic jams cost some $100 billion a year in lost productivity. Cost of maintaining the strategic petroleum reserve? $1.5 billion. Air pollution and health costs? $9 billion.[30]

If you paid taxes in Minneapolis in the mid-1990s, for example, you paid for road construction and maintenance through property taxes, whether you owned a car or not, and almost 25 percent of Minneapolis residents didn't. Less than half of the $90 million the city spends yearly on driving-related projects comes from user fees such as gas taxes.[31] Seattle motorists in the early 1990s got an annual $792 subsidy from their fellow Seattleites, plus $1,920 in free parking.[32]

The Federal Highway Administration in 1997 estimated that we would need to boost motor vehicle user fees such as gas taxes, registration fees, and road tolls more than 43 percent to cover the road costs that cars impose on society—more if we factor in other costs, such as crashes and pollution.[33]

Instead of griping that gas costs too much, maybe we should pause for a moment of gratitude to those who subsidize our driving, the "millions who pay the $2.25-per-gallon premium through property, sales, and income taxes and higher consumer prices [and] do not even drive—the elderly, cityfolk who rely on public transit, and the poor."[34] We also might remind ourselves that in six major western European countries, gas costs motorists upward of $4 per gallon.

As motorists, we drive our cars to the public trough in a number of ways: "congestion delays imposed on others . . . ; roads and traffic services funded through general taxes; unpriced parking; roadway land value; uncompensated crash damages; air, water and noise pollution; and external costs associated with resource consumption."[35] Each person who chooses to commute by car in Atlanta, for example, "imposes congestion costs of $3,500 per year, or $14 per workday, on other people . . . over and above the costs actually paid by the driver."[36]

Trucks are the worst offenders. Not only does a 13-ton truck cause a thousand times more structural damage to a road than does a car,[37] but truck taxes cover only 14 percent of the maintenance they necessitate in cities and 29 percent of that on intercity roads.[38]

The numbers go on and on.

Waste

In terms of literal waste, not the years of time lost driving or the 90 percent of energy wasted in the gas cars consume,[39] we are overloading our landfills with the detritus of our cars.

American car owners annually discard more than 250 million tires and 20 million dead batteries.[40]

We dump about 10 million car and truck chassis every year.[41]

Housing

Paving a parking space costs a builder about $1,500, on top of the cost of the land.[42]

Because builders must set aside a certain amount of land for parking, fewer homes can be built per acre: cars squeeze out houses. One study found that requiring one off-street parking space per unit cut dwelling units per acre in new multifamily developments by 30 percent and increased construction costs by 18 percent.[43]

A nonprofit development that provides housing at $80,000 per unit needs a $4,000 subsidy if no parking is required, a $12,792 subsidy if one space per unit is required, $26,251 for two spaces, and $51,376 for three. Required space for parking is especially unfair to lower-income households, which usually own fewer cars.[44] But when households—including low-income households—must pay thousands of dollars for a parking space whether they want and need it or not, it becomes a significant incentive to own and use cars.

Peace and Quiet

The top neighborhood annoyance in both the United States and Europe is . . . noise.[45]

The U.S. Environmental Protection Agency reports that motor vehicle travel heads the list of sources of urban noise pollution, and cars en masse make the most noise of any form of travel. Passenger cars typically generate 70 to 90 decibels, which exceeds not only the residential noise limits of many communities but also the 55-decibel threshold above which long-term exposure can cause hearing loss.[46]

Motor vehicle noise can significantly reduce property values near heavily traveled streets, $22 billion annually in the United States, according to one study.[47]

Urban Sprawl

When architect Joel Schwartz in the early 1990s challenged his lecture audience to "name a New Jersey community built in the past 50 years that is a really good place, . . . nobody could name a single location."[48]

Rarely does anyone have a good word to say for sprawl, simply defined as our cities' tendency over the last 50 years to spread like kudzu over more and more land in the form of suburban low-density housing and commercial strips. A Brookings Institute study defines a metropolitan area as "sprawling" if it is consuming land at a higher rate than its population is growing.[49]

Imagine this scenario: A developer announces a new building project in the works, and the entire community applauds and supports the idea. Believe it or not, that's how it was in the United States before World War II. Communities eagerly awaited new developments—homes, churches, retail stores, offices—because they knew each building project would improve the quality of life for everyone. Today, we put every conceivable roadblock in the way of development, from snail darters and spotted owls to small wetlands and historic features. Not that such categories of treasures are expendable. But the real opposition to growth springs from our recent experience: decades of development projects that nearly always *lower* the quality of life. A 2000 Pew Center survey found that of all local concerns, Americans are most troubled about sprawl and traffic—more than crime, jobs, or education.[50]

Almost every no-growth movement in the nation is based on a reaction to traffic problems.[51] Look at the acronyms we've created to refer to groups who oppose growth and development: NIMBY (not in my back yard); NIMTOO (Not in my term of office); CAVE (citizens against virtually everything); BANANA (build absolutely nothing anywhere near anything); NOPE (not on planet earth); NOTE (not over there either). Happily, a new term has emerged for citizens who *want* affordable housing or higher densities in their neighborhood: YIMBY—yes in my back yard.

Such a fearful atmosphere leads to a sort of paralysis, as we no longer trust even informed, conscientious developers, planners, or city officials to deliver on promises that *any* development project will be good for the community. For example, when a neighborhood sees its property values escalate for various reasons, becoming "gentrified," all sides generally agree that a change will be beneficial in the short term, yet the fear of eventual unforeseen problems leads many to seize the moral high ground by proclaiming that gentrifying will "chase away poor people" who might no longer be able to afford to live in the neighborhood. Many of us even fight proposals that would rein in the extravagant use of cars, such as parking restrictions or road narrowings.

But no wonder the no-growthers proliferate. We convert 1.2 to 1.5 million acres of rural land to auto-oriented, unpleasant, horrifying, sprawling development in the United States *every year*.[52]

In many states, natural forests and other wildlife habitats have given way to suburban sprawl. In Florida, for example, sprawl development and the streets needed to support it are "the most serious threat to biological diversity and . . . the primary cause of the present extinction crisis. . . . Collisions with motor vehicles are now known to be the number one source of human-related mortality for all of Florida's large threatened, rare and endangered vertebrates including the panther, black bear, . . . key deer, American crocodile, and even the bald eagle."[53]

Remote low-density sprawl costs 40 to 400 percent more to serve than more centrally located areas and consumes 8 to 44 percent more energy than in-town, higher-density development.[54]

New suburban homebuyers pay "on-site" development costs for sewers and streetlights. But who pays the other sprawl-related costs, such as trunk sewers, water mains, schools, fire stations, wastewater plant expansions, and street widenings? Almost always, the people who already live in the community see their taxes increase to help pay for these "incremental, marginal" costs of system expansion.[55]

And what about the hidden costs of longer drive times? Suburban parents who spend two hours a day (the average) in the car over the 18 years between their child's birth and maturity lose *two years* of parenting time.[56]

But *cars* don't cause sprawl, do they? Where else is the growing population going to go? Sprawl is the inevitable result of population growth, right? In fact, wrong. In Cleveland, for example, population declined between 1970 and 1990; the "urbanization" of Greater Cleveland—the consumption of outlying land—went up 33 percent. The population of Metro New York City, today 60 percent larger in land area than it was 25 years ago, has gone up only 5 percent. See table 1.1.

Table 1.1
Growth Rates: Population versus Land Consumption

Region	Time frame	Increase in population	Increase in land consumption
United States *Source*: Arendt, 1994, p. 19	1974-1984	38%	80%
Puget Sound *Source*: Puget Sound Water Quality Authority, 1992	1970-1990	38%	87%
Los Angeles *Source*: Wood, 1996	1970-1990	45%	300%
New York City *Source*: Pierce, 1994; Center for Urban Transportation Research, 1994.	1970-1994	5%	61%
Cleveland *Source*: Alder, 1995, p. 43	1970-1990	population decline	33%
Chicago *Source*: Northeastern Illinois Planning Commission, 1995	1970-1990	4%	35%
Kansas City	1970-1990	29%	110%

ªSource: Arendt, *Rural by Design*, 19.

ᵇSource: Puget Sound Water Quality Authority, *State of the Sound: 1992 Report.*

ᶜSource: Wood, *Neotraditional Urbanism and Town Planning.*

ᵈSource: Pierce, "The Dawn of 'Civic Environmentalism' "; Center for Urban Transportation Research, *Transportation, Land Use, and Sustainability.*

ᵉSource: Adler, 1995, 43.

ᶠSource: Northeastern Illinois Planning Commission. *1990 Land Use.*

Population growth is less to blame for sprawl than our car-centered lifestyle. When we widen streets and lay down huge asphalt parking lots, we make car travel cheaper, make it easier for people to drive longer distances to their jobs, and thus encourage more of us to live in remote, dispersed areas. We lose "the glue holding the compact city together."[57]

A Sense of Community

Our dispersed, car-oriented lifestyle serves to "separate young from old, home from job, rich from poor, and owner from renter. The car has come to dominate the public realm, extending the private world from garage door to parking lot."[58] This sprawling city design also makes it harder and less practical to bike or walk.

When we're in our cars or our car-oriented developments, we're more isolated from each other. "When it is no longer convenient or pleasant to walk, one of the chief occasions for civilized mingling between neighbors and strangers (the all-important 'serendipity') has been lost. When car life replaces street life, human interaction is reduced to a primitive level: isolated drivers honking at each other, competing for parking spaces, racing for the next light."[59] Instead, we spend most of our free time in our homes—alone—watching TV or "surfing the Web" on our computers.

Many sociologists blame the resulting social isolation for aggravating societal ills such as juvenile delinquency, suicide, depression, road rage, school violence, and many forms of crime.

Apart from the social costs we pay for having car-happy communities, we ante up in terms of aesthetics, particularly in our public architecture. Why is the most recent building always "the worst building"?, asks Fred Kent, president of Project for Public Spaces.[60] The vast sums we pour into asphalt leave little for ornamentation of our public buildings—the architectural details that can inspire civic pride. We often plant our new courthouses, city halls, post offices, and schools on outlying cheap land—boxy throwaways, inconvenient and forgettable. Where among these buildings is our community pride? Is there a "there" there?

Camry Convenience versus Satisfying Communities

Here is an important quandary: How can we keep our convenient Camrys and still have communities we can feel proud of? Does it have to be cars *or* people? When it comes to urban quality of life, the emerging consensus of U.S. researchers and designers is that we must abandon not our cars, but our overdependence on car travel, especially solo car travel. That means, one way or another, we can no longer choose sprawl.

CHAPTER 2

We Have Met the Enemy . . . and It Is We Motorists

The railroads had made it possible for humans to go beyond the horizon linearly, but the automobile's scope was limitless.
—S. B. Goddard, *Getting There*

The suburb fails to be a countryside because it is too dense. It fails to be a city because it is not dense enough.
—Unknown

If critics of sprawl agree on anything, it is on the identity of the factor most inseparably linked with the origin, subsequent spread and current explosion of sprawl: the automobile.
—Lincoln Institute of Land Policy, *Alternatives to Sprawl*

Reid Ewing reports that "some of the hallmarks of sprawl are apparently to the public's liking . . . by [wide margins], people favor 'homogenous neighborhoods' over 'mixed neighborhoods where different types and sizes of houses are in the same general area and where small stores and other commercial activities are nearby.' Survey research in Florida [shows] a preference for low-density suburban and exurban living."[1] In fact, "many Floridians consider low-density, single-use development as the most desirable land use pattern despite growing evidence of its substantial hidden costs."[2]

Another scholar finds that "the most serious flaw in all supply-side responses to traffic congestion [that is, the push to try to widen our way out of congestion] is that they all too often exacerbate the very problem they attempt to solve."[3]

In the decades we have gone for the brass ring—the convenience cars bring us—we have locked ourselves into a leaden by-product: sprawl. Before we became a car-dependent society, sprawl as we know it did not exist.

Over the half-century since World War II, as areas such as south Florida and southern California took thousands of small, apparently innocuous steps to accommodate car travel, people began to wonder how they had let their community become a mass of freeways and interstates, of Wal-Marts and malls and asphalt. We didn't go from walkable towns to $100 billion highways overnight. It was death by a thousand cuts, and our cities have been losing a lot of blood.

The result is our present urban predicament. In a number of recent surveys, Americans have identified the *top* problems of the new millennium as sprawl and traffic congestion.[4] The two are intimately connected, for in the billions we have spent to eliminate congestion, we have inadvertently given birth to sprawl. As the Talking Heads rock band might say, we have embarked on a Road to Nowhere.

Sprawl accommodates—in fact, mandates—car travel.

One way to define sprawl is to look at size: buildings set far back from property lines, large distances between homes, shops, offices, and parks, and big street dimensions.

More specifically, a project qualifies as sprawl, by my definition, when it reflects some of these five characteristics. First, sprawl is characterized by low residential densities. In general, this means not more than three homes per acre—too few people to make public transit viable—with a large distance between facilities such as homes, offices, and stores that makes walking or bicycling impractical. Second, a distinguishing feature of sprawl is that homes are more than three miles from important daily destinations such as jobs, recreation, civic activity, and shopping—the threshold beyond which it is generally impractical to walk, bicycle, or even ride the bus on a daily basis. Without enormously high densities, the law of diminishing returns comes into play: too few people ride the bus, and too few destinations exist beyond three miles of the center of most U.S. cities to economically justify frequent bus service. Third, sprawl features wide, high-speed streets that feed large, free parking lots. Shopping malls, for instance, attract and accommodate huge numbers of cars and load nearby neighborhood streets with traffic. The scale and character of the streets and barren parking lots discourage walking, bicycling, and use of public transit. Fourth, sprawl contains continuous tracts of indistinguishable communities—mile upon mile of residence-only subdivisions not visibly separated by greenbelts or farms. And fifth, sprawl has no unique, local character—it has no distinction. It is an "Anywhere, USA."

Based on these criteria, sprawl can appear as easily with an in-town development project as 10 miles outside the city. If a project feels "suburban," with big, free parking lots, big roads, big setbacks, it qualifies. Any project designed mostly for cars *enables* sprawl, because it creates a market for a lot of people to live conveniently in remote locations. The flip side of the coin is that even in areas remote from an existing town, self-sufficient, walkable new towns designed along traditional neighborhood lines don't deserve to be labeled "sprawl"—they are not detrimental in the ways we find sprawl detrimental.

The questions now are, how did we get in this sad shape, and what price are we paying?

HOW DID WE GET HERE?

It's not as if we didn't have fair warning. "Appalled by the scattershot overbuilding of highways during the depression, [Wilford] Owen had the startling idea that localities needed first to decide how their land should be used most rationally, to harmonize neighborhoods, businesses, and public uses. Only then should they fit highways into that blueprint. Otherwise, he warned, the work of single-minded highway engineers would 'dictate what the plan shall be.' His commentary turned out to be a prophecy. . . . The highwaymen would say [the clustering of housing and businesses around new rail and roads] was simply letting the market forces work, even though where government decided to place the roads determined where people would live and work."[5]

We didn't listen to Owen—or we didn't understand the implications of his suggestion—and we didn't listen either to the country's most important pre–World War II demographer, Homer Hoyt, who sent out a similar message at about the same time. In 1939, Hoyt observed that the form of transportation that dominates during a city's main period of growth will largely determine the city's shape.[6] Fifty-five years later, different experts, same message: "The land use and urban form of cities are . . . fundamentally shaped by priorities in transportation. . . . The essential character of a city's land use comes down to how it manages its transport." And again: "No single force has had a greater impact on the pattern of land development in American cities in this century than highways. . . . Highway transportation improvements abetted other market forces that encouraged increasing numbers of households and firms to pick suburban locations."[7]

We gave veterans home from World War II low-interest FHA mortgages with 25- or 30-year terms; "huge numbers of Americans could realize their dream of a single-family home with a yard—all for $10,000."[8] No wonder we rushed to the suburbs or to another emerging American Dream, a "cabin in the woods."[9] And we of course drove back and forth to work in our 1948 Chryslers and Buick convertibles. Then roads to the suburbs got too crowded.

How to solve the traffic problem? Overpasses, turn lanes . . . interstates! Dwight Eisenhower signed the Federal Highway Act of 1956, which funded a nationwide interstate highway system that now totals 41,000 miles. "The interstates were the cathedrals of the car culture, and their social implications were staggering. Within a decade [of 1956], they would alter beyond recognition where and how Americans lived, worked, played, shopped, and even loved."[10]

Almost immediately, though, even Eisenhower "awoke to unexpected realities of the plan he had pushed. . . . The president noticed a huge gash extending through the northwest section of [Washington, D.C.]. Asking the reason for this massive intrusion of bulldozers, he learned from an aide that this was his interstate highway system. Eisenhower recoiled in horror. His interstate concept, borrowed from the German model, had been to go around cities, not through them. Amazingly, he had been unaware . . . that the only way the interstates could become a reality in this increasingly urban nation was to promise cities enough money to eviscerate themselves." By then toward the end of his term, "Eisenhower concluded that his hands were 'virtually tied,' and he reluctantly gave up, but not without reflecting on the wastefulness of thousands of motorists 'driving into the central area [of cities] and taking all the space required to park cars.' "[11]

Commuting by car had become part of most workdays. "The settlement of American cities has always been limited by how far a family breadwinner is willing to commute to work," transportation specialist Stephen B. Goddard has pointed out, a maxim that in our car-oriented society needs to include not just distance but time.[12] Cross-culturally and throughout history, "consistently people devote on average 1.1 hours per person per day to travel. African villagers, the middle class, and the super rich, who travel by foot, personal automobile, and airplane, respectively, all have similar travel-time budgets. This indicates 'travel homeostasis' where improvements made to reduce travel time result in a compensatory change in behavior to maintain a constant travel time . . . a vicious cycle where an increase in supply places more demand on the network, which triggers transportation professionals to increase the supply."[13] As a city's transportation system expands to allow longer and higher-speed travel, people will disperse in a pattern that in the long run will return to that 1.1-hour round-trip commute equilibrium. Conversely, of course, a slower transportation system (based on walking, transit, or more modest roads) leads to an equilibrium in which the community is more compact and less sprawled.

By designing only for car travel—with huge roads, huge parking lots, and huge subsidies—cities thus blindly locked themselves into a sprawling development pattern. The immediate goal was making motorists happy, and drivers always want less traffic congestion, shorter drive times, fewer traffic signals, higher speed limits. It became a vicious cycle that unintentionally guaranteed cities would experience sprawl and its attendant ills—worse congestion, malls, strip retail stores, asphalt seas of parking lots, billboards, and on and on.

Ideally, when we consider how new regulations will affect our community's development, or when as planners or elected officials we consider a site plan submitted for a new building or how to design a road, we ask, "How do we fashion these regulations or shape this site plan or road so that the quality of life of our community will be improved?" Yet catastrophically, because nearly all of us think of ourselves first as motorists, our answer is shaped by such concerns as Will this regulation work for my Nissan? Is there sufficient parking at this new building for my BMW? Are the trees and benches out of the way of my Hyundai? Will this road let me drive at blinding speeds? And so on. Either implicitly or explicitly, we ask how the design can work not for people, but for our cars. That view is one reason we are so often complicit—in minor, incremental ways—in damaging our own quality of life. We become cheerleaders for our Chevys. We are building a paradise for our Preludes.

Where are the design professionals watching out for pedestrians—the design imperative in cities? Is there a trained pedestrian designer in the city public works department or planning department? Or do we have only "traffic engineers" who understand the needs of cars but have little or no knowledge of what pedestrians require? With our cities so unwalkable, is it any wonder that we see so few pedestrians?

Given this state of affairs, it is unfortunate but not surprising that large numbers of "no-growthers" and blue collars have joined forces with the pro-sprawl lobby on transportation. However loudly such people pay lip service to the idea of fighting sprawl, helping low-income groups, and protecting neighborhoods, by becoming pro-car, they undermine all efforts in these directions. Again, such people are motorists first, growth management advocates second. Car drivers first, social service advocates second.

Here is how it happened then, and how it continues today: Faced with existing or projected congestion, we widen a road from four lanes to six, or enlarge an intersection to the point where it is nearly suicidal for pedestrians to use the crosswalk. Because the bigger road is less safe and less pleasant for people to bike on or walk on or even catch the bus on, more of them choose to drive their own cars and to make more car trips, which puts more cars on the road—the additional car travel *generated by the widened road or enlarged intersection* becomes an after-the-fact justification for the widening. Because the widened road now carries more high-speed traffic, housing values decline along the road, and owner-occupied single-family homes get converted to rental units, offices, and businesses like convenience stores and pawn shops. Now, too, for a time, driving is even more pleasant and fast, so people feel able to live in even more remote areas and commute to the city, while still being able to maintain their 1.1-hour commute times.[14]

We find ourselves in a vicious cycle of sprawl, created in large part by those wide roads we asked for. It is crucial for us to recognize that big roads, big parking lots, and big public subsidies create substantial "market distortions" in our local economies—"market failures" in which there is a *artificially* high demand by "consumers" (you and me) for lifestyle "choices" (remote, low-density subdivisions and extreme car dependence). These market failures artificially promote more lower-density housing demand than would be the case in a free market without such distortions. In combination with the artificially high demand for car travel, these distortions lead to the destruction of neighborhood vitality and in-town commercial viability, because the distortions enable us to flee to outlying sprawl locations at the fringes of cities for homes, for schools, for recreation, and for shopping. In our neighborhoods, the corner grocers supporting a walking community have incrementally been replaced by gas stations supporting an auto-dependent community. "Sprawl is not a natural response to market forces," according to Ewing,[15] "but a product of subsidies and other market imperfections."

We have developed a "momentum . . . which is very hard to stop. The obvious response to the failure of freeways to cope with traffic congestion is to suggest that still further roads are urgently needed. The [widened] roads are then justified again on technical grounds in terms of time, fuel and other perceived savings to the community from eliminating the congestion. This sets in motion a vicious circle (of congestion, road building, sprawl, congestion and more road building)."[16]

Speaking first as motorists and only secondarily as engineers and advocates, elected officials hear staff and citizens solemnly warn that "we must widen the road or babies will die in burning buildings when fire equipment can't reach them." Or "If we don't widen, poor people won't be able to drive to their jobs." So we give in to a bigger road and cross our fingers that our problems will be solved. But the last 50 years show that when we give engineers an inch, they deliver an Atlanta mile—in the name of easing congestion and improving public safety. Road engineers have become our de facto city planners. We need everything we can muster to resist the pro-car temptation they so often sanctimoniously urge.

SELLSCAPES

Naturally, K-Mart and Cosco and the other "Big Box" retailers, along with the developers of today's gigantic shopping malls, saw the potential in this enormous stream of motorists, every one a prospective customer. "While profits plummeted, few [small local business] could afford to move near interstate exits, where land prices had increased sometimes twenty-five fold. But for nationwide chains . . . the interstate exits would concentrate their customers wonderfully."[17]

And not just interstates. As bigger in-town roads carry immense numbers of cars past their property, business people cannot resist putting enormous pressure on city staffs and elected officials to rezone that property to retail to take advantage of all those potential customers. This is why so many Big Box retailers clamor for sites at major intersections. (In the planning department I work in, we get calls all the time from people who want to rezone from residential to office or retail along major arterial roads, and at major intersections.) Except in large, high-density cities, high-volume Big Box retailers are not viable without our subsidizing them via such roads and without our allowing them to build enormous, free, surface parking lots.

All the widened, high-speed arteries leading out of our cities became ripe not only for these retailers but for strip commerce in general.

The packaging of 50,000 daily vehicles . . . into a single arterial street leads inevitably to the irresistible urge to sell things to this population, and creates a sell-scape along the street, . . . a gift-wrapped, gold-plated, gift to strip development. . . . Think about it—we bundle together 50,000 vehicles with 60,000–70,000 occupants into a captive market. We make sure we don't give them any other route. We ruin the roadscape, by the size of it, for anything else. And then we, in theory, expect strip commercial to stay off? Get serious. . . . The presence of 70,000 persons daily passing along a road sets off a strong, almost unstoppable series of development actions ("sell them something").[18]

So a city's choice of transport shapes not only the city's residential and retail development but also the character of its streets. The higher the speed for which a street is designed (its "design speed") and the greater its traffic volume, the more unpleasant it will become for anyone but motorists—customers. To attract the attention of the relatively high-speed motorists, retailers must out-shout their competitors in a never-ending arms race of more glaring lights and giant, Day-Glo signs. High-intensity lighting and bright building colors let retailers evade those pesky sign ordinances by turning their entire building into a sign at night. Chain retailers use "icon architecture" and fluorescent colors to transform their building into signs during the day.[19] Buildings increasingly adopt gigantic features and blank walls—the only architecture we can take in at 50 miles an hour, forgoing streetside windows and building ornamentation. A number of newer gas stations blast glaring lights under their canopies, turning them into what James Kunstler calls UFO landing strips that can be seen for miles around.

The design of our streets—not regulations, zoning, land use plans, or elected officials—determines their nature and the use of the land around them.

THE GRUESOME THREESOME

Cars, sprawl, and widened roads—a symbiotic threesome. Once we have widened our streets and increased their design speed, the war against sprawl and strip commercial development is over. Planners and elected officials may win a few battles, but road widening sets in motion an irreversible, inevitable, incremental slide toward more sprawl, more strip commercial development, more conversion of houses to offices, retail, and rental, and less walking, bicycling or public transit use.

"Sprawl and the auto enjoy a truly symbiotic relationship: auto dominance in urban travel encourages low-density sprawl, and the growth in sprawl, in turn, virtually ensures that the automobile will remain the only form of transportation that 'works' in a sprawl-type setting."[20]

Thirty years ago, Stephen Plowden noted that "[widened] roads will also encourage people to live further from their work or from other places of activity, which means that their journeys become longer and are less easily catered for by public transport." Development then tends "to take place either along the lines of new roads or at least in places convenient to them."[21]

The reasons that wider streets encourage sprawl and strip commerce are fairly easy to grasp. But wider streets also *increase* traffic congestion. Hard to believe. Hard to understand. But true.

"Between 1982 and 1997, metro areas that were aggressive in expanding the amount of road space per person fared no better in terms of rush-hour congestion than those that did the least to add new road space; in fact, they did slightly worse" because of the additional traffic generated by the wider roads.[22]

CONGESTION

Those who understood the consequences of transportation predicted today's traffic congestion, just as they predicted today's urban sprawl. Early in the twentieth century, an American road engineer named Mac-Donald, already concerned with the country's obsession with urban roads over rails, called for an end to "the preferential use of private automobiles" in cities and urged officials to "promote the patronage of mass transit. . . . Unless this reversal can be accomplished, indeed, the traffic problems of the larger cities may become well nigh insoluble."[23]

Sure enough, "resentment against being stuck in traffic is a prime cause of anti-sprawl attitudes." All those people who moved farther out "to 'get away from it all' are discovering that 'it all' has followed them."[24]

Many of us in the suburbs, dissatisfied with what Kunstler calls our "National Automobile Slum," react by fleeing to even more remote locations, which makes us depend even more on car travel, spend even more time in our cars, and so on. In fact, drivers spent "43 more hours per year in their cars in 1995 than they did in 1990. . . . Americans are now driving 88 percent farther than they did in 1969 to go shopping and an overwhelming 137 percent farther to accomplish family and personal errands."[25] Table 3.2 in chapter 3 vividly illustrates the growing car dependency in the United States because of this vicious cycle—a dependence that is far outstripping the rate of population growth.

Here's an all too familiar scenario: I'm late for an appointment and I need to get into the city fast. First, I'm stuck at the entrance to my subdivision by rush-hour traffic crawling past. Then I get behind two cars side by side, both irritatingly driving the speed limit. I'm impatient, and so is everyone behind me. When I finally squeeze past, I race to make up for the slowdown. In my rearview mirror, I see the guy behind me gesturing rudely at the law-abiding drivers as he rockets past. When I get to my appointment, I curse as I careen around the parking lot in search of a space. Is this road rage? No, just an average commuting day. Clearly, we need to six-lane that road so the loafers can have their own lane, and this parking lot needs to be bigger. I need to call my county commissioner and tell her to start earning those big bucks we pay her.

And all this frustration doesn't come cheap. The irony is that lower-income households feel the pinch more. Households with incomes of under $12,000 spend 36 percent on transportation; households with incomes of at least $60,500 spend 14 percent.[26] A decade ago, it was estimated that congestion was costing us $168 billion annually in wasted time; it is unlikely that it is costing us less today.[27]

Besides driving up our blood pressure and emptying government coffers, congestion purportedly leads to poor energy efficiency, higher gasoline consumption, and more air pollution. It is clearly a Bad Thing. Or is it?

A study of 32 cities nearly 15 years ago concluded this conventional wisdom needed another look.[28] On one hand, congestion creates more air pollution at the *microlevel*. (It also encourages us to build more and wider roads, which is fine if we want communities that look like one big parking lot.) On the other hand, people who live in higher-density, more "traffic-congested" areas (where transportation choice is high) produce much less air pollution and consume much less gasoline than those who live in remote locations with more "free-flowing" traffic conditions who can use only cars for travel.

Congestion has gotten a bad rap, in my opinion. Indeed, traffic-congested conditions can move us *toward* more livable communities. For example, such conditions reduce regional air pollution from cars. They discourage "low-value" car trips (figure 2.1) and car dependency and so increase bus trips, walking, and bicycling, encouraging public transit and transportation choice in general, largely because strong political pressure is directed at elected officials to improve alternatives to car travel. Congestion reduces the average driving speed, as well as citywide fuel con-

Figure 2.1
Relative Value of Trips

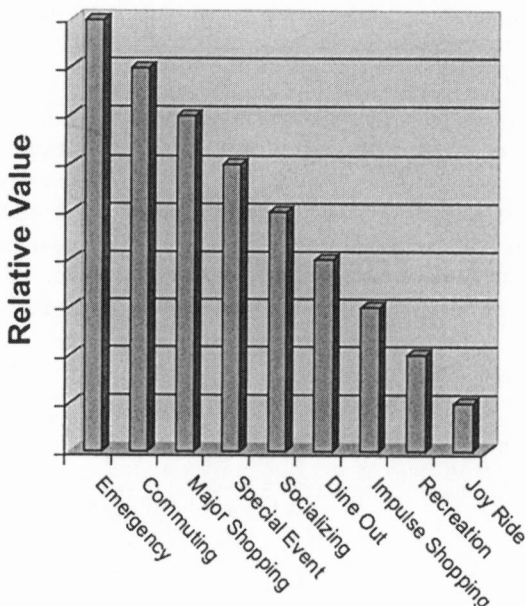

Source: Based on Litman, "Transportation Elasticities."

sumption. As downtowns become not just places to "drive through," these areas become more pleasant for pedestrians, businesses, and homes. Finally, congested conditions promote compact development and infill and discourage sprawl; given the 1.1-hour commute-time average, people want to live closer to their destinations in the face of congestion (an important reason why land values are so high in the core areas of big cities).

Many planners agree with T. T. Jackson that "traffic congestion plays a normal and necessary role in the evolution of major cities. Congestion actually reflects efficient use of our highway resource and is the only effective growth management tool available to encourage high-density development in downtown areas and activity centers, which will in turn encourage public transit usage." Therefore, "we must allow some level of congestion to exist within cities, if cities are to mature into active, exciting, culturally full communities with a strong sense of place."[29]

Congestion is one sign of a healthy city. Without congestion, there is little motivation for a community to be more compact, or to provide a healthy supply of transportation choices.[30]

But won't we hit permanent gridlock? No. Congestion does not increasingly and endlessly worsen if we do nothing about it. Cars do not back up for 2 miles one year, 5 miles the next year, and 15 miles the next when we don't try to resolve congestion by widening roads.[31] Left alone, congestion *regulates itself* as motorists reach a level of intolerance. Frustrated by increased congestion, those who can start driving alternate routes to get to their destinations, or start driving at non-rush-hour times, or take to public transit, bikes, or their feet.

In the university town where I live, drivers often complain that traffic congestion is unbearably worse during the first week of a new semester. Thereafter, congestion near the campus eases. Why? Students and staff start finding new routes to campus. Many avoid going to campus during rush hour. Others become bus riders, bicyclists, or pedestrians. Because of the "time and frustration tax" that congestion imposes during the first week, only those who feel they *must* drive a car to campus on major routes during rush hour continue to do so. This same congestion reversal occurs in every community once drivers reach a threshold of intolerance— unless, of course, the self-regulation is temporarily short-circuited by road widening.

Almost no other country pours as much of its national wealth as does the United States into widening roads or paving over the landscape for parking. The congestion U.S. travelers complain about in Paris or Hong Kong or Rome is the result of governments that do comparatively little for cars and drivers. In fact, their congested cities have helped ensure that driving and car ownership are significantly lower in Europe and Asia than in the United States. In 1995, there were 647 million motor vehicles on the planet. Per 1,000 people, the breakdown is this: United States, 767; Canada, 598; Australia, 590; Italy, 566; Germany, 529; Japan, 523; France, 501; Sweden, 487; United Kingdom, 428; Denmark, 387; Ireland, 309; Greece, 291; Israel, 246; Argentina, 170; Singapore, 151; Brazil, 64; India, 6; China, 5. Other countries are following the pattern of increasing car use faster than the U.S. twentieth-century rate, and the number of vehicles in other countries grew 2.7 times faster than the number of people between 1980 and 1995. If the rest of the world eventually matches the U.S. rate of vehicle ownership, there will be 4.4 billion cars on earth. Typical parking lots hold about 130 cars per acre. At that parking density, we would need a paved area the size of France or Spain to park the world's cars.[32]

As we might surmise, however, Europe's congestion is actually very good news for Europe. "Free-flowing traffic" is the worst thing a city can aspire to, primarily because it creates a "drive-*through*" instead of a "drive-*to*" atmosphere, reduces urban quality of life, encourages excessive driving, and results in a more dispersed, spread-out community that, overall, requires more community fuel consumption because of the greater number of motor vehicle trips. Cities with the highest average traffic speeds have the highest per capita gasoline consumption; cities with the most constrained traffic flows have the lowest.[33] In a free-flowing traffic stream, the increase in community-wide per-person vehicle trips overwhelms any benefits obtained by the efficiency of *individual vehicles* in terms of air pollution.

FREE FLOW, FUEL, AND POLLUTION

Here is another finding that goes against common sense and conventional wisdom: Widening roads to reduce congestion *increases* air pollution and energy consumption, even if the traffic becomes more free-flowing—because motorists will do a lot more driving.

The self-defeating progression goes like this: We add lanes to a congested highway. More people drive on the newly widened road, and traffic immediately eats up 20 to 50 percent of the new road capacity—a *net increase* in traffic and in total emissions of 10 to 25 percent. But let's assume that, for whatever reason, people choose not to make more trips on this road. Even with this unrealistic assumption, emissions either remain constant or increase—until the average speed of traffic exceeds 50 to 60 miles per hour. At that point, emissions go up significantly as a result of acceleration under high engine loads. After about four years, traffic increases to create almost as much congestion as before the widening, with a net emissions increase of almost 50 percent.[34]

Also, apparently against all logic, more free-flowing conditions in outlying areas pump up both fuel consumption and air pollution. A study in Perth, Australia, showed that congestion is understandably lower as we move away from a city core area. "[Average speeds improve 54 percent] and vehicle fuel consumption improves, [which means that] actual per capita fuel use increases significantly. Vehicles in central areas have 19 percent lower fuel efficiency than the Perth average because of congestion, but the central area residents use 22 percent less actual fuel; and conversely, congestion-free outer suburban driving is 12 percent more fuel efficient than average, but residents use 29 percent more actual fuel."[35]

So while *individual* cars get better gas mileage in free-flowing traffic [per mile], the overall *collective* increase in the number [and length] of car trips community wide, due to free-flowing conditions—even fuel-efficient car trips—swamps any benefits. More low-density residential development in outlying areas means more and longer car trips, which use far more gas than the gas saved by reducing congestion. Consequently, when the average vehicle speed in a region increases, air pollution goes up.

ANYWHERE, USA?

At this point, it should come as no surprise that "the root cause of the suburban transportation dilemma is not inadequate highways or polluting vehicles; the real problem is land use sprawl."[36]

Let's assume that you live in the suburbs, not a remarkable assumption when a survey at the beginning of the twenty-first century found that when Americans move, some 42 percent choose suburban or rural settings, 33 percent who are already there stay there when they move, and only 12 percent move to or stay in in-town settings. (The other 13 percent move from rural to suburban areas.)[37] Who wants to live in an unsafe, litter-strewn, crime-ridden city when all those nice government-subsidized roads make it relatively easy not to? Still, all that driving eats up a lot of income. The farms and forests you used to drive past on your commute are mostly gone, and rush-hour traffic is terrible. They're *expanding* the mall. Several of your neighbors have been robbed. You hear about drug busts at the high school. You know people—or maybe you are one of them—who keep trying unsuccessfully to transform your lifeless, boring, sterile residential subdivision into a real community.

Many people have become disenchanted with suburban life, and not just because of their unpleasant daily commute. The town manager of Gorham's Bluff, Alabama, a "new town" in the Appalachians, posted comments on the Internet on October 29, 2002, titled "Dying on a Cul-de-Sac." "For the past year I have rented a house in a horribly designed conventional suburban development," wrote Nathan R. Norris. "This past week I was walking with my three year old son down the cul-de-sac which is closest to our house. From a distance I saw a group of people in front of one of the yards—a rare sight in our neighborhood unless there are parents watching over a group of kids playing." When he stopped to say hello, the group "informed me that the 54 year old man who lived directly across the street had died of a heart attack in the middle of the night. I did not know the man. The moment was exceptionally depressing when I heard the comments of his neighbors—no one knew him. All they remember doing is waving hello while he was driving his riding lawn-mower."[38]

Perhaps Norris's reaction echoes an innate human longing for a sense of place and a sense of community—neither is common in car-dependent suburbs. There is "no there there," as Gertrude Stein once observed about Oakland. "In the 1980s, when the New York Islanders hockey team won the Stanley Cup four years in a row, the team's triumphant motorcade was reduced to circling around the suburban Nassau Coliseum parking lot as loyal fans cheered them on. There was nowhere else to go."[39] A recent study found "an inverse relationship between the level of automobile dominance in a neighborhood and the level of social ties found there"—that is, the more dependent people were on cars for travel, the fewer social ties they had.[40]

Yet letting go of that particular American dream is tough, especially for a generation convinced that flight from the cities to the leafy, fresh-air suburbs was healthier for them and their kids. Widespread acceptance of the virtues of suburban life remains, and many advocate retrofitting our cities to make them more like suburbs. What could be wrong with more land-scaping, more trees, more *space*, lower density? Put differently, what's wrong with making our cities nicer places for cars, drivers, and Bambi?

What's wrong is that the features of residential suburbs, often perfectly acceptable in outlying areas, destroy the greatest virtue of livable cities—walkability. These include (and the list may seem familiar) segregation, homogenization, and isolation of land uses (miles and miles of nothing but residences); dead-ends and cul-de-sacs; few or no sidewalks; street blocks too long for easy walking; and densities too low for public transit or utilitarian walking. Walkability-destructive features in the retail and office areas of suburbs include: wide, high-speed roads; buildings set far back from streets and adjacent buildings; lots of off-street surface parking for cars—usually in front of buildings; large, landscaped buffers, often vine-tangled; randomly placed clumps of trees; one-story "icon architec-ture" buildings and lots of drive-throughs; glaring, high-intensity lighting on tall, highway-oriented light poles; and lots of signs—big ones.

Most of us—because we usually think of ourselves first as motorists—never stop to realize that many suburban features are designed for the benefit of drivers, and that these same features usually harm our overall quality of life. They are what turn so many suburbs into Anywhere, USA. Features that rob locations of a sense of place.

Let's look at just one example: billboards. The field of motorists' vision is substantially reduced at higher speeds (figure 2.2). This not only increases the danger for pedestrians and bicyclists, but also encourages businesses along the street to "shout" with glaring lights and signs that attract the speeding motorists' attention. Sign size increases, as we would expect, as the average vehicle speed on a street increases.[41] According to the Institute of Transportation Engineers,

A highway billboard beside a 55 mph highway is a good example of vehicular scale. In order to attract attention, such a sign must be very large (typically 15' x 40' or more), with lettering large enough to be noticed, and read, by a motorist pass-ing by at 81 feet per second (55 mph). A pedestrian, on the other hand, typically walks at only 3.5 to 4 feet per second, and small details are more noticed than are larger ones. A pedestrian walking next to a billboard likely would not feel com-fortable next to that billboard—simply attempting to get the perspective needed to even read it would be very difficult.[42]

If Toronto planning director Paul Bedford is right, and "suburbaniza-tion is the biggest threat to cities in North America,"[43] should we get rid of suburbs? Not at all. Many of us enjoy the privacy and beauty of our sub-urban and rural homes, and they expand our choices of where to live. But shouldn't our communities stop encouraging them with subsidies?

Figure 2.2
Field of Vision at Various Speeds

15 mph

20 mph

25 mph

30 mph

WELFARE FOR SPRAWL HOUSING

What's wrong with this picture? In Tallahassee, Florida, capital costs for sewer hookups in central-city neighborhoods are about $4,450, compared to $11,450 in remote, low-density, car-dependent neighborhoods, yet everyone pays the same hookup fee. "The poor families living near the sewer plant not only have to endure its odor, but also have to pay far more for their sewer hookup than it actually costs government to serve them. Meanwhile, affluent lobbyists and politicians, who typically reside in distant suburbs on the north end of town, escape both the odors and the full bill for their waste treatment."[44]

Dispersed, auto-dependent development in Loudoun County, Virginia, is a net loss to the tax base of $700 to $2,200 per dwelling unit. In San Jose, California, planners figured out that such development would create annual deficits of $4.5 million compared to a $2 million surplus if future development is compact—that is, located so that not every trip must be by car.[45] A 2001 U.S. Department of Agriculture study found that public infrastructure costs for low-density, remote residential development were at least 5 percent higher and in some cases 25 percent higher than for compact, in-town development. Other recent research shows that even modest increases in residential density can reduce total public capital costs by 25 to 60 percent for roads and 15 to 40 percent for water and sewer service.[46]

When we build new developments in areas remote from water plants, wastewater plants, and schools, we create higher incremental costs for adding new capacity to these services than do new developments near such services.

No wonder the market demand for dispersed, car-dependent residential property is artificially high. Suburbanites get heavy income tax subsidies for owner-occupied homes, federally funded wastewater systems, and subsidized police, fire, postal, and garbage services, as well as road and parking subsidies. At least one state has put its collective foot down: Maryland governor Parris N. Glendening has cut off state tax revenue to projects that promote urban sprawl. "We told communities that they're still free to build sprawl," he said. "We're just not going to subsidize them anymore."[47]

HIGH-DENSITY PHOBIA

Two of the features that draw many of us to residential suburbs, low density and the design of the streets, serve as good examples of the ways designing for cars makes life less satisfying for human beings.

You open your paper one morning in your suburban kitchen and see that your city's planners, in their wisdom, are calling for developments with higher densities near your neighborhood—more houses or living units per acre. Your probable reaction? NIMBY—not in my back yard! You envision loud parties, litter, a broken-down car up on blocks in every yard, drug deals on every corner. And the traffic! Higher-density suburbs? Are they crazy? You can almost see your property value plummet as you reach for the Yellow Pages to find a home security specialist or a good civil attorney to fight this evil idea.

Before you put your house on the market or bars on all your windows, look at a few facts. Yes, there is an association between social problems and density measured in people per residential room—crowding, an indication of poverty—but no such association with density measured in residents per acre.[48] That many higher-density urban neighborhoods have higher rates of crime and poverty than lower-density suburban neighborhoods suggests that the association between density and social problems reflects the tendency of distressed households to concentrate in higher-density urban neighborhoods, not that higher-density development causes social problems.

Furthermore, when we complain of crowded cities where we expect to feel "packed in like sardines," it is seldom that the buildings are too close or that there are too many people, but the claustrophobia of being stuck in traffic. The obvious solution? Minimize the number of newcomers to the city by fighting for low densities, to reduce the number of people and cars. Yet "higher-density development does not necessarily increase congestion. Suburban residents tend to spend more time delayed in traffic than residents of dense cities such as New York and Chicago. . . . High density areas tend to have the slowest traffic speeds, but suburban areas have the greatest per capita traffic delay because residents must drive more miles. . . . Travel distances are shorter [in cities] and travelers have options that bypass traffic congestion."[49]

CUL-DE-SACS

"Lucky you," we say to a friend who lives on a suburban cul-de-sac, "no speeding traffic, no weird people passing through, no one who doesn't belong here. How great for your kids!" Cul-de-sacs, on rare occasions, can benefit the public too, by protecting environmental features that would otherwise be encroached upon by streets and homes in a development project, for example, such as lakes, steep slopes, or wetlands.

But that privacy and safety charges high interest in our kids' intellectual and social growth, in driving time, and in—you guessed it—traffic congestion.

If they're lucky, the kids in our cul-de-sac neighborhoods have friends on the same block to play basketball or ride bikes with. It's comforting for parents to know they're safely insulated from traffic, strangers, and other (often exaggerated) dangers associated with cities. But they are nevertheless deprived.

Much childhood education occurs not in school but in experiences throughout the community. Although children benefit from the safety of the cul-de-sac subdivision when they are small, they cannot live their whole lives there. They have to extend themselves. In older suburbs with fully connected networks of streets, youngsters can get to know their own block, then the block around the corner, then another, and so on. They can test their environment incrementally, ranging steadily further from home.... The traditional street system draws youngsters out, pretty much at their own pace.... No one speaks of 'cul-de-sac' smarts. Youngsters in a cul-de-sac have a hard time getting to know their community or the communities that lie beyond.... A modern [cul-de-sac] subdivision is an instrument for making people stupid.[50]

A study 10 years ago found that Vermont's small-town 10-year-olds have three times as many places they could get to on their own compared to kids in cul-de-sac intensive Orange County, California. (And Orange County kids watched four times as much TV.)[51]

Given the popularity of cul-de-sac neighborhoods, no wonder "the number of trips children take by foot or bicycle has been declining steadily, from 15.8 percent of all trips in 1977 to 14.1 percent in 1990, and 9.9 percent in 1995.... Since 1990, the number of kids walking to school has gone down 23 percent."[52]

Once kids leave their own cul-de-sac, they often leave safety behind. "Whereas more than half of all kids walked or bicycled to school in the 1950s, that number has now fallen below 10 percent as streets have become more dangerous due to traffic.... An estimated 20–25 percent of rush hour traffic on local streets ... is now attributable to the school commute."[53] Further, living in auto-dependent suburbs means that kids face a greater likelihood of injury or death than other children, simply because they must spend more time in cars.

For pedestrians and bicyclists, cul-de-sacs—particularly those greater than 500 feet long—create substantial travel barriers. And while motorists may not pay much attention to the extra distance, that extra 500 or 1,000 feet can be inconvenient, if not daunting, for a walker or bicyclist.

Here are three hypothetical young boys (figure 2.3.) Billy lives 150 feet as the crow flies from his friends Bobby and Jeff. He probably cannot walk directly to his friends because today he is likely to encounter "no trespassing" signs or even barbed wire or chain-link fences. In the likely event that his direct route is blocked, he must use the street. But by street, he needs to travel 3,400 feet (almost three-quarters of a mile) to see Bobby. And if Billy wants to see Jeff, it's 8,400 feet by street (over one and one-half miles). Billy must either ride his bike on dangerous streets or ask his mom for a ride. And it usually is Mom. "Part of the reason mothers drive so many places is that they are often the sole transportation provider for children and elderly parents, who cannot drive and have few other options.... Whether they work or not, married women with school-aged

Figure 2.3
Cul-de-sac Kids

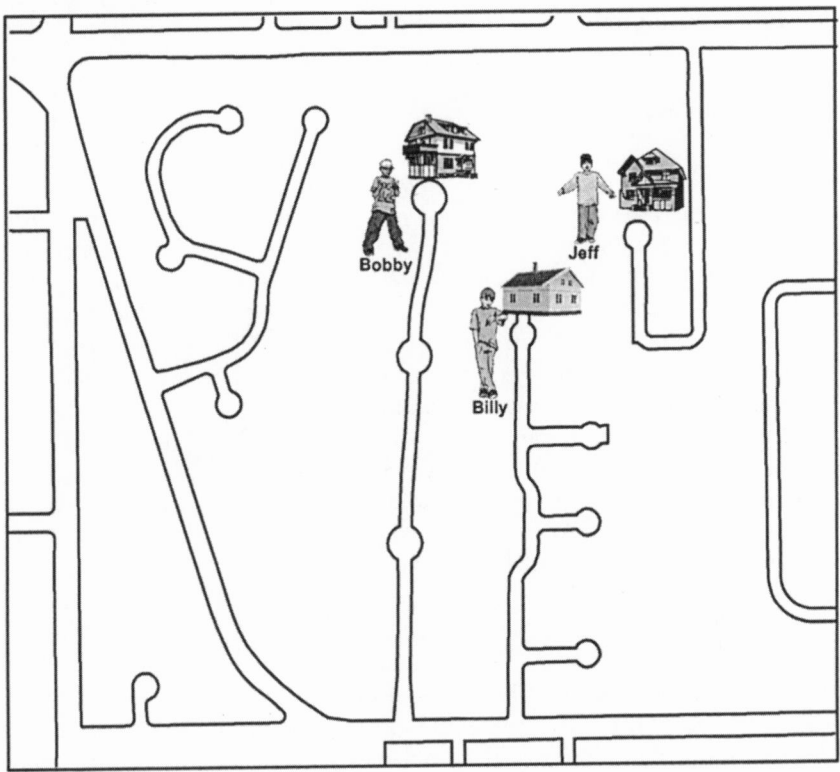

children now make more than five trips [and spend] 66 minutes per day in the driving . . . almost 17 solid days in the car, . . . more time than the average American spends in conversation or participating in sports."[54]

While we drive at higher average speeds in cul-de-sac neighborhoods, our average trip time is longer, as those mothers have probably figured out. Partly because cul-de-sacs often require traveling in the opposite direction of where we want to go, cul-de-sac street networks generate 50 percent more vehicle travel miles than would a network of connected streets.

Those chauffeur moms (or dads) also certainly know that cul-de-sacs reduce the number of "real-time" trip route choices. There is only one way out of a cul-de-sac, and often only one way out of a cul-de-sac neighborhood—no change of scenery that alternate routes would offer, a monotony that deadens the life of many in our contemporary subdivisions. More seriously, emergency vehicles have no choice of routes if they come up against slow or halted traffic or a fallen tree, a lack that can cost lives. This absence of trip choice also substantially increases the service cost for postal delivery, garbage collection, and school buses, because such services are forced to backtrack over streets already covered. (As suburbanites, we can take part of the blame for the ongoing increase in the price of postal stamps.)

Figure 2.4
Power of the Grid

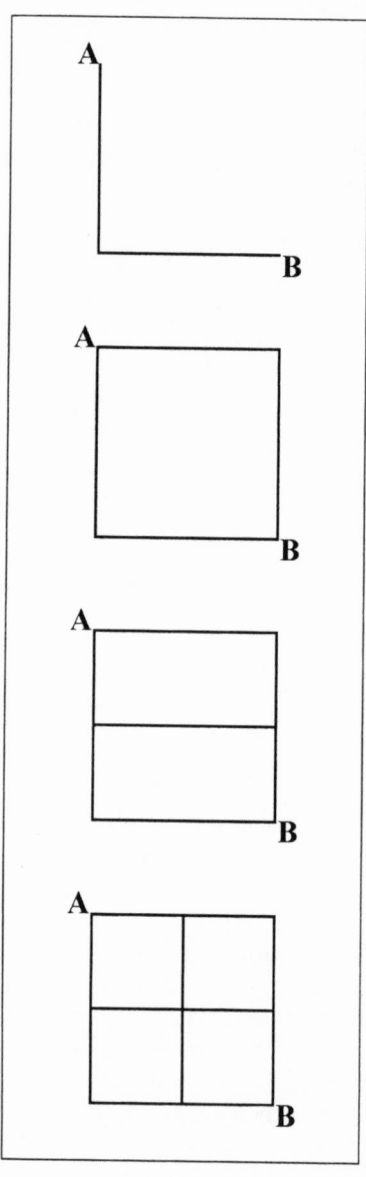

Cul-de-sac neighborhoods create a sparse road network, which funnels cars and trucks onto a few major roadways—one reason we run into congestion even when residential or commercial densities are very low. Unlike a network of connected streets, cul-de-sacs mean that trips cannot be distributed equally on multiple routes—that is, cul-de-sac neighborhoods are not "well-ventilated" street patterns.

To illustrate this matter of route choice, let's look at four different street connections between origin "A," say, a house, and destination "B," say, an office (figure 2.4). The first provides one route choice (the cul-de-sac scenario); the second has two choices; the third has three choices; and the fourth has six choices.

What happens on a connected grid of 10 streets by 10 avenues (figure 2.5)? To get from point A to point B, a person has 184,000 routes to choose

Figure 2.5
Power of the 10 × 10 Grid

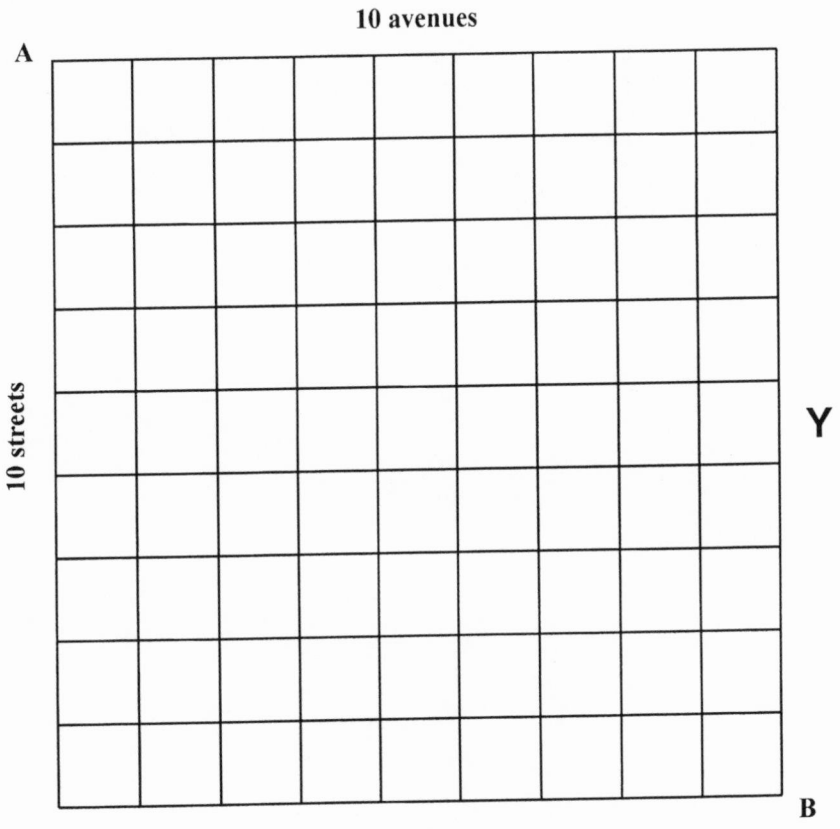

from—the formula to determine the number of route choices is: $(X + Y)!/X!Y!$ In other words, this grid can carry a tremendous load of car trips without becoming congested, because the network can distribute trips equitably on the many available routes. By contrast, the disconnected cul-de-sac neighborhood gets congested even with a tiny development density. Walter Kulash has observed that certain intersections with poor street connections (as in low-density cul-de-sac suburbs) can become congested even though one or more of the parcels on the corners of the intersection are still rural and undeveloped.[55]

The connected street system also inherently results in slower, more neighborhood-friendly car speeds because the numerous street intersections oblige motorists to slow down.

Concerning cul-de-sacs, there is also a fairness issue. Cul-de-sac residents increase the traffic in neighborhoods without cul-de-sacs, because living in a cul-de-sac requires us to get in our cars more often than on a bus, our bikes, or our feet. While our cul-de-sac remains insulated from traffic, we impose a disproportionately large number of car trips on other neighborhoods.

Cul-de-sacs and suburbs have unfortunate consequences, and the fight against higher densities is often counterproductive. Are there battles we can fight that will improve the condition of our community, or are many of these, too, misguided?

CHAPTER 3

Fighting the Wrong Battles

This could be a very short chapter. Overpopulation, misguided elected officials, weak environmental regulations, urban ugliness, and pollution are not the main villains behind urban sprawl. And no-growth advocates, proponents of lower-density housing and clean fuel, and dedicated environmentalists, while often heroic in their efforts, cannot save us either. We have spent two chapters understanding that the main cause of sprawl and lower quality of life in and around our cities is that we have designed our communities to be car dependent. End of chapter.

But because I worry that misunderstanding or misidentifying the causes of our community problems can lead to advocating tactics that actually worsen our condition, I want to clarify how we often fight the wrong battles.

What stuns and scares me about so many policies we hear citizens recommending these days is that they will produce precisely the *opposite* of what we—and they—really want: a better quality of life. Such policies call for the lowest possible densities, almost no in-town development, no mixed-use development, *huge* setbacks, *huge* parking lots, wide roads, aggressive regulatory protection of small, degraded wooded areas, and so on. Such strategies will *ensure* the ruin of neighborhood quality of life and guarantee sky-high taxes, financially strapped families, and overburdened police forces. These are the sorts of "solutions" that Atlanta, Miami, Orlando, Houston, Los Angeles, Phoenix, and Detroit have already tried. Excuse me, but is there some reason these strategies sprawled those cities but will revitalize ours?

We desperately need high-quality, on-the-ground models so that people can see, with their own eyes, that quality urban design delivers a pleasant outcome—that such design, as the above "solutions" exemplify, is not a future to fight against.

Curiously, there is the disingenuous argument that the walkable urban-ist design tools I and others advocate will "chase people from the city" and therefore promote sprawl. If true, why do millions happily vacation in Charleston and Savannah, in European cities, and other walkable towns, as growing millions across the nation flee the suburbia that boasts the elements our misguided NIMBYs seek: big roads, big parking lots, big setbacks, low densities, no mixed use, no transit, no neighborhood socia-bility, no nightlife, no sidewalks, no bicycle paths?

Is sprawling, suburban Atlanta the model our NIMBYs aspire to, or is it Charleston? How many of our NIMBYs vacation in Detroit to enjoy the quality of life of that city?

Here's an example of this kind of misunderstanding and misdirected advocacy. The point is often made that places like southern California are "overcrowded" and "growing too fast." The obvious solution? Advocate the lowest possible residential densities. But wait a minute. Lower densi-ties will in fact further lock the community into overdependence on cars, which as we now know is the main scoundrel giving birth to sprawl.

Our perception of our cities or suburbs as overcrowded, with exces-sive densities, is skewed by the amount of space cars require. When we look at statistics for European cities, our urban densities are compara-tively low. As the accompanying photos show (figure 3.1), 40 people spaced as if on a bus (upper left), on foot and bicycles (upper right), or on chairs spaced as if in cars (lower left) take up very little street space. Put those people behind the wheel of 40 cars (lower right), and they overcrowd the same space. "We're packed in like sardines! Put a mora-torium on growth!"

Measured in terms of human beings, the problem is not "overcrowd-ing." Not too many people, but too many people *in cars*.

BUT WHAT ABOUT POPULATION GROWTH?

If we would just halt population growth (never mind how), we could put an end to "overdevelopment" and traffic congestion—a common belief, and another misguided one. The growth rates of car travel and land consumption (residential subdivisions sprouting up at the undeveloped fringes of the city), and of cars and fuel use, continue to far outdistance population growth.

This country's population increased 39 percent between 1960 and 1990; vehicle miles traveled increased 198 percent. Portland and the states of Col-orado, California, Washington, and Maine saw similar disparities (table 3.1).

Figure 3.1
Forty People

Source: Beamguard, J. "Packing Pavement," *The Tampa Tribune*, 18 July 1999.

From 1983 to 1995, the U.S. population grew 12 percent; vehicle miles traveled, home-to-work trips, shopping trips, and vehicle trips grew substantially more. From 1980 to 1997, as the population increased by about 1 percent a year, miles driven increased by more than 3 percent per year. From 1970 to 1997, total vehicle miles traveled more than doubled and, over the next 20 years, is predicted to grow another 53 percent. More people of driving age and more working women account for only one-third of this growth; vehicle trip length and number of vehicle trips made account for the rest.[1]

From 1983 to 1995, households with no vehicles decreased by 31 percent; 40 percent more households became two-vehicle homes (table 3.2). In 1999, when about 201 million Americans were of driving age, 132 million cars and 83 million trucks traveled American roads.[2]

The American housewife now averages 14 car trips per day.[3]

When the Texas Transportation Institute (TTI) looked at population growth in relation to traffic congestion for the 15 years from 1982 to 1997, they found that "population growth is only a minor factor in the recent rise in congestion" in the metro areas they looked at. While population grew by 22 percent, "the delay experienced by drivers grew by 235 percent in the

Table 3.1
Growth Rates: Population versus Vehicle Miles Traveled

Region	Time frame	Increase in population	Increase in vehicle miles traveled
United States *Source:* U.S. Dept of Energy, 2001	1960-1990	39%	198%
Washington *Source:* Energy Outreach Center, 1994	1970-1990	40%	121%
Seattle *Source:* Arrington, 1996	1970-1990	38%	136%
Colorado *Source:* Yuhnke, 1997, p. 20	1970-1995	64%	140%
California *Source:* Alder, 1993, p. 43	1980-1990	40%	100%
Maine *Source:* Maine State Planning Office	1980-1990	10%	57%
Portland, Oregon *Source:* Metro Planning Department, 1996, p. 7	1985-1995	25%	46%

[a]*Source:* U.S. Department of Energy.

[b]*Source:* Energy Outreach Center, 3.

[c]*Source:* Arrington, *Beyond the Field of Dreams.*

[d]*Source:* Yuhnke, "Take a Deep Breath," 20.

[e]*Source:* Adler, 1993, 43.

[f]*Source:* Maine State Planning Office, *The Costs of Sprawl.*

[g]*Source:* Metro Planning Department, *Creating Better Communities,* 7.

same period." Why? "In large part, . . . [it is] the increase in driving in these areas. Actual population growth in these areas totaled almost 22 million people over this period, but the Surface Transportation Policy Project [STPP] calculates that the increase in driving by each resident makes it feel as if about 70 million more drivers have been added to the highways. This 'perceived population growth' experienced by motorists helps explain the widespread feeling that our metro areas are 'growing too fast' or 'bursting at the seams.' "[4]

Population growth accounted for only 13 percent of the growth in driving in the areas they studied. "In other words, most of the growth in driving comes not from new drivers, but from more driving by the people already on the road. . . . Americans are each driving more every year in large part because of the increasingly spread out nature of our metro areas." STPP's analysis of TTI's data "found that the spread of our metro areas is directly contributing to the increase in driving."[5]

Another easy-to-buy idea is that population growth is to blame for sprawl. Sprawl, it is often pointed out, is substantially worse in a community experiencing population growth than in a community with a static

Table 3.2
Growing U.S. Car Dependency, 1983 to 1995

Measure	1983	1995	Percent increase
U.S. Population	234,307,000	263,082,000	12%
Average Annual Vehicle Miles Traveled (VMT)	11,739	20,895	78%
Average Number of Home to Work Trips	3,538	6,492	83%
Average Annual VMT for Shopping Trips	1,567	2,807	79%
Average Number of Shopping Trips	297	501	69%
Total Vehicle Trips	126,874,000,000	229,745,000,000	81%
Average Annual Vehicle Trips	1,486	2,321	56%
Households with No Vehicles	11,548,000	7,989,000	-31%
Households with Two Vehicles	28,632,000	40,024,000	40%
Vehicle Miles Traveled	1,002,139,000,000	2,068,368,000,000	106%
Person Miles of Travel	1,946,662,000,000	3,411,122,000,000	75%
Cars per Household	1.68	1.78	6%
Daily Vehicle Miles per Driver	18.68	32.14	72%
Average Vehicle Occupancy	1.75	1.59	-9%

Source: U.S. Census. *Statistical Abstract of the United States: 2000,* 120th ed. National Personal Transportation Survey, Table No. 1033, p. 631. Washington, D.C.: U.S. Bureau of the Census, 2000.

population. But how do we explain that our urban areas are expanding at about twice the rate that the population is growing?

The metro New York area grew 50 percent between World War II and 1990, with no significant rise in population.[6] A study of 213 urbanized areas for the years between 1960 and 1990 found a population increase of 47 percent (from 95 to 140 million) and an urban land increase of 107 percent (from 25,000 to 51,000 square miles).[7]

From 1950 to 1990, Pittsburgh's urban area grew 21 times faster than its population; the 24 metropolitan areas with over 1 million in population urbanized land 2.65 times as fast as their populations grew during that same period. So not only are we fleeing the city by living in more remote locations, but we are eating up more land when we get there, largely because of how much we travel by car. In the 1950s, we used about one-fifth of an acre per person for residential and commercial development. By 1988, that had risen to almost two-thirds of an acre.[8]

Our land consumption is increasing exponentially: In the 5 years between 1992 and 1997, we developed more land (16 million acres) than in the 10 years from 1982 to 1992 (13 million acres).[9]

A number of cities are experiencing substantial sprawl despite zero or negative population growth. It is safe to conclude that our land-consuming development patterns now play a more important role than population growth in causing urban sprawl.

THE BALLOT BOX

If the problem were only development patterns, then why wouldn't electing people dedicated to no growth be the obvious answer? The citizens of Boulder, Santa Cruz, San Diego, and Petaluma, like many of us, believed that, with enough political will, their communities could solve all their growth problems. They found the political will all right, but restrictions on development became so tortuous as a result of the new draconian laws, and property values skyrocketed so painfully, that voters replaced many of those no-growth proponents with anything-goes officials.

So even communities who manage to put heroic no-growthers in office and to get antigrowth ordinances passed find their no-growth zeal usually lasts through only one or two voting cycles.[10] Community-wide resentment and frustration soon become so powerful that voters not only reverse the no-growth efforts but often end up with communities in worse shape than before.

Residents of fast-growing urban areas (say, 2 or 3 percent a year) have a choice. They can wring their hands and clamor for elected officials to stop growth. "Stopping growth" so simply means in-town locations continue to stagnate. Such efforts to establish growth moratoria instead typically bring to these communities a great deal of remote, low-quality development that destroys major natural areas in their outlying areas.

Or the community can make the tough changes by establishing quality urban regulations and street design standards that will create a community more rich in transportation and lifestyle choices.

SAVING BAMBI

Here is another example of misdirected energy by concerned citizens. "Developers are destroying the environment," we say. "Let's at least save *some* beauty in our city. Let's preserve some pocket woodlands right here in town."

Often, the unintended outcome of our effort to save low-value pockets of trees or wetlands is to drive up the cost of an in-town development project. The result: We chase development projects to outlying areas, where they not only create more sprawl but harm larger, more valuable ecosystems. Because, over the past few decades, sprawling places such as South Florida had enough road-widening dollars and a strong desire to accept and promote car dependence, these communities lost the important battle: retaining walkable, human-scaled neighborhoods amid untouched natural areas—even though environmentalists occasionally won a skirmish to save a tree or wetland, or stop a development project.

Certainly we want to establish and protect the superb tree canopies and woodlands at the edges of our communities. The mistake is when we struggle to save degraded, small, low-value woodlots in such a way that a beneficial, walkable development project is chased into outlying (more environmentally important) areas, or require a site design that must use dimensions that are not human-scaled.

Frequently, we strive to protect or promote our in-town quality of life, or simply to avert a future of costly sprawl, by misguidedly urging the lowest possible in-town residential densities, strong in-town environmental conservation plans and regulations (protecting even low-value natural areas), or, often, less in-town traffic congestion.

Low-density zoning or land-use designations inside a growing city will not slow or stop growth but simply make more likely the continued spread of development thinly across the regional landscape. Battles against in-town higher density are based on the usually unvoiced belief that such development will deliver crime and safety problems, another auto-oriented "slum" with big parking lots, speeding cars, noise, and—worst of all—more traffic congestion. Take, for example, the "Eastward Ho!" initiative in South Florida. That effort seeks to encourage infill for new growth instead of further encroachment into the Everglades. During one year, however, in one city under this initiative where 27 separate infill projects were proposed, not one was approved.[11]

But developers simply find areas that have less-effective no-growth strategies and little or no resistance to building low-density, unwalkable, auto-oriented subdivisions in outlying areas.

Furthermore, in most cases, the rare developer who sticks it out to build in town ends up being forced to compromise on design. Lower-than-intended residential in-town density is commonly the result, most painfully in community locations that would benefit from higher densities. Lower in-town density typically counteracts community efforts to protect the environment. By stopping the construction of higher residential densities in town, we minimize the number of residences near retail areas, schools, parks, jobs, or civic destinations. Such a "solution" increases the likelihood of more residences in remote locations, resulting in more per capita auto dependence and more damage to outlying larger, more sensitive, viable ecosystems.

We can expect similar outcomes from environmental regulations as stringent in central city areas as in regional forest preservation areas: more regional environmental harm in outlying, usually more sensitive and important areas, where developers can find more and cheaper land. More land to work with reduces development costs even when environmental regulations are stronger. Which means we simply encourage more development in outlying areas when our environmental regulations do not distinguish between in-town and important peripheral natural areas. Given market distortions and subsidies that excessively promote residential sprawl, the last thing we should be doing is discouraging in-town development with environmental regulations that are as tough for weedy city lots as high-quality out-of-town wildlife habitats.

What, then? No regulations to ensure environmental conservation in our cities? Not at all. Even mediocre landscape regulations ensure adequate amounts of vegetation on a site. And some of the most worthwhile citizen efforts today are fighting for sustainable environmental conservation. But even the national Sierra Club has recently started to focus on the "big picture" problem responsible for threatening our ecosystems and neighborhoods: auto-dependent urban sprawl.

The most sensible approach is a discriminating one, shifting our environmental priorities as the habitat moves from a mostly human place to a mostly wildlife place. In town (the "human place"), we need to make the quality of the human habitat the imperative. There, the needs of humans should come first, and the needs of Bambi should come second. Environmental regulations and concerns should grow stricter as, in the outlying areas, the imperative moves toward protecting the habitat for Bambi. We need to let the city be a city, and let nature be nature.

I went through a phase common to young idealists when I believed that creating a more livable, healthy city meant that we should encourage vegetation to "sprout through the pavement." No more. When designing for *wildlife* habitat, I learned in school that it is generally detrimental in sensitive, high-quality wildlife sanctuaries to design for intrusive human activity—so that humans feel comfortable in a marsh, rather than, say, wading birds.

But over the years as a professional planner, I've come to understand the opposite, neglected side of the coin: designing a walkable urban, in-town location for sensitive wildlife is a recipe detrimental to the *human* habitat. Distances become too long to comfortably walk. Surfaces are less smooth and sure to stroll. Thorns and insects become a nuisance. Hostile animals potentially lurk. There is certainly a time and a place for mosquitoes and spongy marshes. But it is assuredly not when we seek to walk to an opera in high heels and tuxedo.

The virtues of the city—what makes the city wonderful for the lover of the city—are those that emphasize the human habitat: walkability, sociability, cultural richness, vibrancy, safety. It is telling that we have thousands of people with Ph.D.'s in creating pristine wildlife habitat. Where are the designers with Ph.D.'s in creating the pristine human habitat?

Certainly, we have an obligation not to compromise the quality of natural features—flowing creeks, air sheds, wildlife—as they move through and then out of a city habitat. We need to be sure that creeks and rivers don't deliver polluted water to our outlying ecosystems, but if large, unwalkable creek and river buffers are necessary, such creeks and rivers need to be at the periphery of the neighborhood. By the same token, we should not build a large asphalt parking lot in the middle of a marsh at the periphery of our neighborhood.

I do not advocate banishing nature from the city, for we need modest parks and squares within walking distance of our homes as occasional refuges from the hustle and bustle. But such spaces should not be so enormous that they compromise the walkability of our neighborhoods.

We need to let the city be a city and let the marsh be a marsh. Otherwise, both are compromised and threaten the survival and quality of the other.

ABOUT STREET TREES

Street trees are a delicate topic, particularly among environmentalists, but even the neighborhood curmudgeon may get sentimental about them. Here is something to think about: none of the most popular, famous streets in the world are loved for their tree canopy. Are the most popular tourist destinations the cities with streets lined with oaks? Nope. They are the cities with narrow, largely treeless streets—think of Florence, Salzburg, Venice, Copenhagen, Amsterdam, Siena, Munich. Why? Because trees, while nearly always essential for a quality street, are not enough. The top priorities for creating a great street are high residential density; a mix of residences, offices, and shops; modest lot widths; and modest building setbacks.

Proper street design is essential, so let us be more precise. The first things a great street needs are these three Ds: density, diversity, dimensions. With these requirements rightly met, we can then, and only then, worry about installing those elegant, shady street trees (and maybe more ample sidewalks). Actually, there are several elements for designing a quality street. In order of priority, great streets have building facades abutting (or very, very close to) the streetside sidewalk, with entrances on the sidewalk. They have relatively high residential density on or near the street, or both. Great streets have a mix of residential and nonresidential development on or near the street, or both. They have on-street parking and shading street trees—limbed up, formally aligned, and spaced so as to avoid blocking the view of at least the first floor building facades. Well-designed streets have short blocks, modest turn radii, no more than three lanes of two-way street (the third lane is landscaped median with pocket turn lanes), and prominent crosswalks. They have verticality—buildings fronting such streets are at least two stories high—and building facades are aligned. The best streets have street lights and traffic signals that are modest in height. They are supplemented with alleys, and the lots that front them are narrow in width. Great streets feature "transparency" on building façades—adequate windows at eye level—implicit here is an absence of excessive blank wall horizontally. They are graced with streetscaping—street furniture, wastebaskets, public art, etc. And finally, they have ample sidewalk width—wide enough for sidewalk cafes, couples to comfortably walk side-by-side, street furniture.

When we take off in the other direction, as cities all over America have done, we give our streets too much space, we prohibit density, and we separate homes from offices and shops. Then we wonder why streetscape tactics such as street furniture, street trees, and wide sidewalks don't "fix" our streets. Unless we install the three Ds up front, street trees and wide sidewalks are just big Band-Aids for a terminally ill patient.

Although "in local debates, the most commonly cited concern is the environment," preserving the urban natural environment will not be the motivating factor that brings us livable cities.[12] At best, when most efforts go into saving trees, the payoff is usually a change in the community land-development codes that preserves larger trees in parking lots of sprawling, strip-commercial shopping malls. Steve Hach, a doctoral student in the History Department at the University of Florida wrote in June 2000: "I was doing research in Miami recently and I was struck by the tone of articles in the paper down there from the 1960s. They knew even then that they were ruining their homes and their environment and yet we all know what happened. Developers were making the same profit-protecting arguments then as they are now. The people weren't stupid, they knew what was going on. I read tons of letters in the files of Everglades National Park from people who were concerned about the environment and run-away development in Dade County."[13]

In other words, a great deal of historic effort by local environmentalists did little, if anything, to protect south Florida from its ruinous fate. The environmentalists may have saved a few trees in their towns. But their region is so degraded that growing numbers are fleeing south Florida. No, south Florida did not find that pitched battles to salvage an in-town wetland was the linchpin to their salvation. They may have saved a tree, but that tree is surrounded by thousands of acres of asphalt parking and countless miles of hostile, depressing, stressful multilane roads. In short, they fought the wrong battles.

Nearly all U.S. communities now have stringent protective policies in place for the direct, obvious, easy-to-recognize sources of environmental degradation, tough regulations that ensure that smokestacks, sewer pipes, toxic waste dumps, and environmentally hazardous products do not harm our environment. Environmentalists fought hard against these direct sources of pollution in the 1960s, 1970s, and 1980s and *have largely won* at the national, state, and local levels of environmental protection.

But all that strong regulation of the direct forms of environmental pollution and policies to protect neighborhoods did *not* deliver us a pristine, sustainable ecosystem, or quiet, stable neighborhoods. In fact, evidence in the form of global warming, species extinction, air pollution, water and groundwater pollution, loss of ecosystems, and loss of quiet neighborhood character bombards us with the message that we are, more than ever, losing the battle to save our environment and our neighborhoods.

If we fight too single-mindedly for in-town habitat viability for oaks or large mammals and forget how to design streets for people, our cities will only become less livable and more of us will continue to run from the city to the suburbs—the pastoral, naturalistic, low-density outlying areas that promise clean air, green space, privacy, good schools, and no traffic congestion (never mind that this siren song lures us into Atlanta-style sprawl). Some developers still operate along lines that make some planners call them "highwaymen," and they know "the hot buttons that [will] sell the public on their program: 'talk of privacy, of private property, of individualism.' "[14]

To come out the victors in the substantial environmental battles that remain to be fought, we need to direct our time and energy away from the usual suspects (evil developers, corrupt politicians, unsympathetic planners, and polluting smokestacks) and toward much more difficult and seemingly intractable environmental threats, such as stormwater runoff from roads and parking lots, emissions from car tailpipes, and new developments that are the primary origin of runaway runoff and tailpipe emission problems: the sprawling into our outlying (and more sensitive and important) areas—the widespread, less obvious sources of pollution embedded in our auto-based, suburban sprawl lifestyles.

It seems to me that the priority for both environmentalists and quality-of-life advocates should be to determine the most effective strategies to slow sprawl to outlying areas and to create cities with a wealth of transportation choices and a human-centered quality of life so enticing that people will lose their desire to flee the city (and relocate in new subdivisions in sensitive, outlying ecosystems). An effective way to accomplish this end is to return to the age of designing in-town locations primarily for people instead of cars.

NIMBY ONE-UPMANSHIP

A particularly noxious brand of NIMBYs is the group disguised as environmentalists. Within the city, they fight to save every blade of grass or small tree or raccoon in hopes of stopping a proposed development project, or at least forcing the project to lower its density to suburban, cow-town density.

They can often be identified by their public demonstrations that they are "holier than thou" with regard to protecting nature in what is in reality a destructive game of environmental one-upmanship.

"You believe we should have a 30-foot setback from wetlands in order to protect them from development? I want a 300-foot setback!"

"Oh, yeah? Well, I think we should have a 900-foot setback and protect both wetlands AND weedy vacant lots in the city!"

"I think to REALLY protect the environment we should prohibit ALL future development in the city!"

This sort of hysterical one-upmanship not only is counterproductive but also promotes destructive sprawl. When sprawl and congestion "happen" in an American city, everyone is up in arms. The reaction is environmental zealotry, passionate folks fighting like strident extremists to stop all development. End result: South Florida. Atlanta. Southern California.

UGLINESS

There is a common mistake made about sprawl. Many see ugly parking lots and unsightly eight-lane arterials and conclude that we should fight sprawl by becoming champions of beautification. But the problem with sprawl is not ugliness. Indeed, the sterile, shiny new, picturesquely landscaped developments in sprawl locations tend to be *more* attractive than the gritty and diverse character found in our traditional, in-town, walkable areas.

We will not slow urban sprawl or resolve traffic problems by cleaning up litter, reducing sign pollution, or requiring more attractive landscaping. We can't control roadside bottles and cans, billboards, and ugly parking lots until—that old familiar refrain—we redesign our transportation system to put the needs of people over cars.

The problem with sprawl is much more deep-seated, engrained, complex, and difficult than appearance—where, as noted, sprawl tends to be comparatively excellent in any event. Sure, parking lots and roads can be more attractive when landscaped, but the costly, quality-of-life-destroying consequences of sprawl require that we not build monster parking lots and roads in the first place, that we instead design a modestly scaled and diverse community—a rich, sociable public realm.

Drive to a remote suburb: the newer buildings seem brighter, the newer streets have fresher paint and fewer potholes, the generous setbacks provide ample room for lush landscaping. The problem with sprawl is not that it is ugly. Sprawl is a problem because the dysfunctional design and location forces us to make so many car trips, reduces public safety, is unsustainable, and is the cause of many other woes catalogued in this book. As conservationist Edward Abbey once said, "It's not the beer cans I mind, it's the roads."

Similarly, the jungle of garish signs is often less of a problem in the land of suburban sprawl. Billboards blare and lights flash on and off mainly on commercial strips and other high-speed, high-capacity streets—on the way to and from suburban neighborhoods, but safely away from them.

We will have gained nothing if, in the end, we have required developers to build attractive yet enormous surface parking lots—even if those lots are well-endowed with trees. Or charming drive-throughs. Or beautifully landscaped six-lane roads. It is still costly sprawl, even if it is free of litter.

AIR POLLUTION

What? Air pollution is not a battle we need to fight?

Pollution from cars burning fossil fuels is, of course, an enormous problem, but it is not *the* problem. And the view that clean fuels will go a long way toward our sprawl-related problems continues to serve as an apology for socially, financially, and environmentally destructive travel behavior. The salvation from most or all of our transportation sins, we would like to believe, will drive right up to us in the form of clean-fuel cars, such as battery-operated, solar, hydrogen, or fuel-cell-powered cars. All our problems will be solved if we just convert our cars to clean fuels. Americans are technological optimists: we like the idea of a technological fix. But clean fuels are nothing more than a "magic bullet"—and are no more reliable.

We can't afford to divert all our resources toward a magic bullet. Clean fuels are only one of several objectives to aim for, and in my view, we should not give them top priority. I applaud the promotion of clean forms of energy for transportation. Such an approach is long overdue. In particular, we need to convert public transit to clean fuels, in part to improve their public image.

So let's reduce the car-generated air pollution, but let's not fool ourselves that clean fuels will solve our transportation and community design troubles. Even if we could magically transform every vehicle to clean fuel today, we would have done nothing to reduce road fatalities and injuries caused by car crashes. We would still have to face the enormous problems associated with acres of asphalt parking lots and their associated problems, such as stormwater pollution, the urban "heat-island effect," loss of urban vibrancy, and loss of space for buildings and vegetation. Land-eating, costly sprawl and strip commercial development would continue. Dead wildlife would still litter our highways. Big Box retailers would continue to expand and displace smaller, locally owned businesses. Downtowns would continue to decline. Seniors and children who cannot drive would continue to rely on others to get around. And so on.

Dirty air is only a symptom of the real problem: designing only for cars.

SCAPEGOATS

Much of what has been described in this chapter are counterproductive "solutions"—cherished by many—that in fact aggravate the problem.

For example, NIMBYs focus on solving an environmental or traffic problem in their neighborhood. But their campaign generally *worsens* these problems citywide. It is terribly ironic that those who yell the loudest for, say, low densities are usually doing so because they are fed up with traffic congestion—yet the low densities they fight for will deliver *more* car trips per capita (not to mention consume substantially more natural areas as low-density subdivisions spread).

Adopting such counterproductive strategies locks us into an accelerating downward spiral. Presumably, their misguided advocates would be appalled to wake up one day and behold what they have wrought. (Be careful what you ask for, as you might get it.) But it is certain that they would find scapegoats for the mess. There will always be *others* to blame: planning staff, developers, politicians, immigrants.

Scapegoating is a great way to escape the terrifying thought that we good guys might in any way be to blame. Can't be us! We're wearing white hats!

I have a theory that such misguided souls lived in southern California and south Florida several decades ago, that a natural urge arises to try to fight what is misperceived as the problem. They naively fight the wrong battle (saving a few squirrels in the city, and failing to see that the real threat is auto-dependent urban sprawl). We see the inevitable result today in Miami, Atlanta, Houston, and Los Angeles.

We have met the enemy and we are it.

BATTLE SCARS

In sum, it is easy to label "rapid population growth" the enemy instead of considering our own values and lifestyle. We elect "no-growth" officials and end up with "anything-goes" politicians. We save a few trees in our city and discover our forests have been clear-cut in outlying areas, or salvation appears in the form of "beautification" regulations, until we realize that pretty parking lots and strong sign regulations still leave us with miles and miles of Anywhere, USA, strip commercial development. Finally, we battle against "dirty fuels," but an exponential increase in clean-fuels driving still delivers stress, crashes, sprawl, throw-away communities and bankruptcy.

Before we get to what the tough solutions are, we need to look at what hasn't worked.

CHAPTER 4

Misguided Solutions: The Tendency to Foul Our Own Nest

We have limited resources to direct toward reducing social problems (and only limited time to solve some of them), so we have a pressing need to understand how to get at the root of these problems to solve them cost effectively. While the crises in transportation and land use continue to grow, we can't afford the questionable luxury of misidentifying causes or misjudging solutions.

As we have seen, such mistakes can lead us to advocate tactics that actually make our communities worse. For example, many who believe that overcrowding poses an important problem in places such as southern California tout the "obvious" solution: the lowest possible residential densities. By failing to realize that what they perceive as too many people is in fact largely the consequence of our car-based lifestyle, successful advocates for lower density actually strap their communities into greater car dependence—which aggravates the perception of overcrowding.

HIGHER GAS PRICES OR FREE PUBLIC TRANSIT

In the 1950s, cigarettes cost 25 cents a pack. Today, if you're lucky, you can buy a brand-name pack for under four dollars—a more than 12-fold increase. The cost of gas, by comparison, is only about four or five times its 1950s price; adjusting for inflation, gas has never been cheaper. That's because the price of gas is subsidized by the government in the United States. Americans who visit Europe are shocked by how much it costs to drive there. Not only that, they may tell you, the busses and subways are crowded and not that clean. And the traffic is awful, worse than New York! You're also likely to hear that the cities themselves are exciting, fun, full of life, fascinating places to be. That a connection may exist among these conditions is worth considering.

If sprawl is partly the result of the cheap, long-distance car travel that shaped our cities' low-density, dispersed design, "then increases in fuel price may not in themselves lead to much [of a reduction in car use, for] high car use is built-in to the structure of the city. People will just tend to put more of their income into fuel and less in other areas"[1] (what economists call "inelastic demand"). Despite the conventional wisdom, a high gas cost or even free public transit will not significantly reduce car travel, because it is still more convenient and obligatory to drive a car in and around most U.S. cities. It's also not rational to let that big expensive chunk of metal sit in your driveway and depreciate unused.

Can passes for free bus rides outweigh all the reasons why we choose to drive a car? Even with gas at three or four dollars a gallon? We'd still have plenty of free or cheap parking and free roads, we'd still have the kids to chauffeur around, and on and on.

MORE DOWNTOWN PARKING

Perhaps the most common "solution" planners hear for revitalizing a downtown is "more parking." It is a seductive suggestion. Few among us have not vied for a downtown parking space or appreciated the outlying shopping mall, its lot still half empty in spite of the thousands of parked cars. How tempting to apply the suburban recipe for success to our failing downtown. Build a lot of parking! Customers will flock to downtown because they won't be discouraged by a lack of parking! Retailers will be healthy!

Oddly, in many cities where these cries go up, the downtown already has a rather abundant supply of parking. Indeed, many downtowns devote more space to parking than to buildings, plazas, and squares. When we hear the claim that there is "not enough parking downtown," what we are really hearing is that there is "not enough *free* parking *a few feet* from where I want to go."

To demand such an impossible supply of parking is to ask a downtown to compete with outlying suburbs *on suburban terms,* that is, asking the impossible. The suburbs can draw on an enormous supply of low-cost land and provide high-speed, multilane roads, which a land-scarce downtown simply cannot offer. The downtown must compete by relying on its strengths: walkable, compact, vibrant, romantic ambiance, the very qualities destroyed by futile efforts to compete with suburbia via "more parking."

We forget that in nearly every city, at least one annual event—a festival, a ball game, a community celebration—draws enormous numbers of people downtown. *Despite* the lack of downtown parking. We forget the simple maxim, to paraphrase *Field of Dreams,* that if we build it [community attractions, that is, not parking], people will come. People will find a way to get to a highly attractive downtown event or shopping experience, be it by bus, arriving early, carpooling, walking, bicycling, or finding parking a few blocks away. (The more attractive the destination, the farther we are willing to walk from a parking space.)

Conversely, the most deadly miscalculation of those who argue that more parking will revitalize downtown is that the result is too often the reverse: adding parking destroys the attractiveness of a center city. Huge asphalt parking lots and sterile parking garages create dead zones. People begin to complain that nothing is happening downtown, and anyway, walking downtown seems unsafe. And inconvenient. It no longer feels comfortable or romantic.

See for yourself. Visit any one of countless American cities—Detroit, Houston, Jacksonville—that have opted for "more parking" as the key to downtown revitalization and spent ungodly sums of public dollars to build incalculable numbers of additional spaces, in the process often demolishing priceless historical buildings. Today their downtowns are windswept, dangerous, weed- and litter-strewn "no man's-lands" full of vacant buildings and despair.

All the free parking spaces in the world will remain empty if nothing nearby attracts us. As Denver mayor Wellington Webb has pointed out, a downtown that is more than one-third parking lots has lost its character and sense of place,[2] and a great many American cities exceed that kind of allocation to dead-zone parking.

When a place is sufficiently attractive, it is impossible to provide enough free parking a few feet away. And when it is that attractive, it is impossible to keep large numbers of people from finding a way to get there, even without "enough" parking.

REZONING AND LAND USE PLANS

When we talk about sprawl, we're talking about how we're using our land. Reminder: land use follows transportation, that is, what will happen to a piece of property over time is determined by the design of the road it stands on and the traffic the road encourages.

In general, [transportation] modeling has assumed that land use is "handed down" by land use planners and that transport planners are merely shaping the appropriate transport system to meet the needs of the land use forecast. This is not the case. One of the major reasons why freeways around the world have failed to cope with demand is that transport infrastructure has a profound feedback effect on land use, encouraging and promoting new development wherever the best facilities are provided (or are planned).[3]

This means that in terms of affecting the ultimate use or condition of a property, whether planners designate a site for retail or single-family residential use makes no difference—unless this new designation corresponds to what is happening on the road the property fronts. Otherwise, the land use will eventually be rezoned to something suitable for the road, or the land will be abandoned.

To put it another way, we cannot modify the conditions of a property by changing its land use or zoning designation but only by ensuring that the street is designed for the property use we want. For example, we can't "force" a single-family residential designation on a property that fronts a hostile, high-speed road.

Clearly, it is much easier to predict the future of land uses along a street if we look at the street design than to predict what will happen to the street based on the land use designations we've assigned to the properties along that street. Similarly, we can more accurately predict whether there will be a sprawled, dispersed, low-density community if we know, in advance, what the street system and form of travel will be than we can figure out whether sprawl will occur based on what the current land uses (or land use plans) are. For example, land use in West Palm Beach, Florida, changed dramatically soon after the city redesigned its streets: removing travel lanes, calming traffic, and adding substantial streetscaping.[4] This revolution followed the street changes; it had nothing to do with a new land use plan.

Land use plans and maps for a mostly built-out city are almost never proactive visions of what the planners believe the city needs for a better future. They are rarely "plans" at all. They simply record *what is there already.*

While we would have a tough time, politically, unilaterally changing the land use designation of private property without the consent of the owner, we *can* change transportation, which nearly all occurs on public rights of way. If we design the street network for modest car speeds, modest street widths, connections to nearby streets, and access by not only cars but bicycles and pedestrians, we will find ourselves with viable public transit, bicycling, walking, and neighborhood retail and mixed uses (not to mention higher densities, compact development, and a lockout on more sprawl). High-speed, high-capacity roads will give us the reverse, *regardless* of what the land use "plan" (or our zoning map) says.

Many of us, along with our elected officials, have come to believe that widening roads and extending utilities are technical issues and therefore nonpolitical. "We're protecting public health and safety," we say, or "providing jobs for poor people," or "helping the economy." In fact, such decisions are not only profoundly political but are the most powerful factors behind sprawl, economic decline, environmental destruction, and so forth. Whenever we widen roads and build huge parking lots, we make critical land use and quality-of-life decisions—decisions that are *exceptionally* political.

We often comfort ourselves by adopting anti-sprawl land use plans that discourage sprawl or environmental destruction. We may even have a long-range community plan that clearly states that "strip commercial development shall not be allowed," and we shall "protect residential properties along our major, high-speed, high-capacity streets"—but who would want to live in such a home? It is unfair *not* to grant the rezoning to commercial use in such a case. Rezoning petitions from people who have a single-family house along a widened, unlivable street shower the planning departments of communities across America. Naturally, the house of the owner asking for the rezoning from residential to office or retail now has much more value as an office or retail building; when rezonings are granted, we take a step toward more strip commercial. Should the rezoning be denied, the usual alternative is that owner lets the home decline, or abandons the woefully located home. The community pays only lip service to an anti-sprawl stance when community plans prohibit sprawl and strip commercial from speedways already in place—speedways that ensure a sprawling, strip commercial future in spite of what the community plans may say.

Adding anti-sprawl language to our land use plans—such as: "The City shall not allow sprawl"; "The City shall create a greenbelt"; or "The City shall create large-lot zoning"—can save us only if we provide a community foundation that will make such a future feasible. That is, we strongly intervene in the marketplace with infrastructure (roads, utilities, schools) decisions we make as a community. Implicit here is that the community plan *start off* with stated objectives that "road capacity shall not be added to community roads," but it takes enlightened politicians with leadership and courage to adopt such policies.

For one thing, politicians must battle the traffic engineers, who often claim that designated land uses force them to call for wider highways.[5] This sounds sensible, until you remember that the market will eventually press for changes in zoning along the widened highway that becomes hostile for residences. A courageous community true to its principles might be able to delay the rezoning for a few years, until the quality of life becomes too miserable for homeowners or the farmer can make millions by selling the land for a shopping center or subdivision.

There is thus little hope that our long-range *land use* plan can, by itself, help us achieve quality-of-life objectives. Elected officials and planning staffs tend to be too timid and are eventually worn down by property owners and developers urged on by a marketplace profoundly shaped by roads. And to the extent that we are a democracy, we are a reactive society inclined to take action only when a serious crisis emerges.

Forty years from now, if we do not restore major streets to make them more livable, we will, though incremental zoning changes, find those streets lined with offices, multifamily apartments, and retail stores. And over those 40 years, a bundle of planners, citizens, and officials will burn out on fighting rezoning battles. In the long term, as Walter Kulash has pointed out, no force, not even a city council made up entirely of "no-growthers," can stop that incremental change after we have designed a street for high-speed, high-volume traffic.[6]

No community in the United States has succeeded in controlling sprawl with land use plans or land use designations alone. When we create and construct a transportation plan, we establish—indirectly and often unintentionally—future land use plans and patterns, not vice versa. Once a street is widened and car traffic is speeded up, the war to fight more sprawl and strip commercial development has been lost.

WIDER ROADS: NO WAY OUT

To put it simply: widening roads does not ease congestion for any meaningful period of time. Wider roads will not help us build our way out of congestion, not at any cost.

In Houston, Atlanta, and Dallas–Ft. Worth—relatively sprawling cities that have devoted the most money to road widening—people now pay more for transportation than for housing. In these three cities, per capita miles of road lane increased 18 percent from 1986 to 1997; household spending on transportation rose 22 percent. By contrast, in Honolulu, New York, and Baltimore—more compactly built cities rich in transportation choice—household transportation expenses dropped by 9 percent.[7]

When we widen a road in an urban area already experiencing traffic growth or congestion, three things inevitably happen, a phenomenon Anthony Downs calls the "triple convergence" (figure 4.1).[8]

First, motorists who had discovered less-congested routes flock back to the widened road. Roads are "free," and gas is the cheapest it's ever been (one-fourth the price it was in 1929). Widen roads by adding travel lanes and you get more car trips, not lasting congestion relief.

Second, rush-hour motorists who had been avoiding the congested road now return to it, for it is temporarily less congested.

Third, people who were riding the bus, bicycling, or walking get back in their cars. The wider road temporarily makes driving more pleasant, and other forms of travel less comfortable, convenient, and safe. (Planners and economists sometimes call this discouraging of noncar travel the "barrier effect.").

In the long run, widening our roads will not make them less congested, but it *will* shape the geographic spread of our communities (figure 4.2). If most of our community's major streets are two lanes wide, the community

Figure 4.1
The Triple Convergence

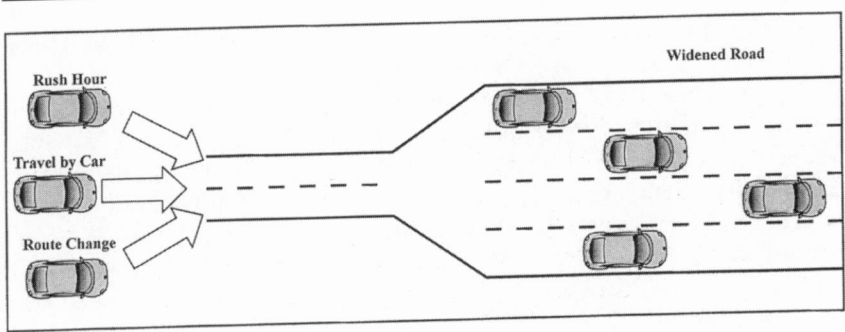

will be much smaller than if the main streets are four and six lanes wide. The width of roads determines how far people can live from the city and still commute to work in a reasonable amount of time. As the number of lanes increases, reasonable travel times extend farther and farther from the city or employment centers. That is, when roads are widened, people return to that 1.1-hour travel time budget equilibrium by living in more remote locations.

Cases in point are areas such as south Florida and southern California, which have poured huge sums of public dollars into creating enormously wide roads in a counterproductive effort to alleviate congestion; they not

Figure 4.2
Two-Lane, Four-Lane, Six-Lane Town?

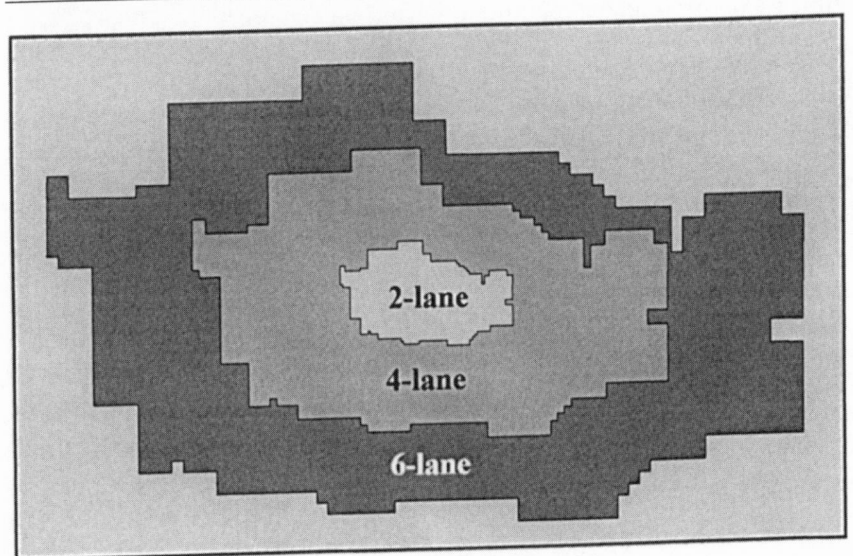

only still have unbearable congestion but also have assured themselves a future of sprawl, lower quality of life, and massive public and private costs. "The concept of human scale implies 2 or 4 travel lanes, not more. It is hard to find a 6-lane street that is easy to cross, pleasant to walk along, or comfortable to wait along when using [public] transit."[9]

In a growing city, if we have a congested two-lane road, our choice is retaining that congested two-laner; or instead, at great public expense, widening that road to become a congested four-lane road; or widening still further to six lanes, which simply provides us with a congested six-lane road. What flavor of congestion does the community prefer?[10] A community can never build streets wide enough to get rid of congestion or enlarge parking lots enough to eliminate parking shortages, no matter how much we spend.

For decades, even the motor vehicle industry has admitted that road widening is a self-perpetuating vicious cycle. In 1967, the *Asphalt Institute Quarterly* reported:

Every new mile tacked onto the paved road and street system is accompanied by the consumption of about 50,000 additional gallons of motor fuel a year. That's a total of 2.25 billion additional gallons of fuel use, accounted for by the added 45,000 miles of new roads built each year. . . . In short, we have a self-perpetuating cycle, the key element of which is new paved roads. The 45,000 new miles added to the road network each year accommodate motor vehicle travel, generate fuel consumption, produce road building revenue. Scratch the new roads and the cycle ceases to function."[11]

A long history of congressional hearings acknowledges the self-perpetuating economic bind the road-building and car construction industries have led us into. "Texas highway booster Representative Brady Gentry[12] asked [Francis] DuPont: 'But is it not true that the highway system needs of the United States of America are almost without limit, and will they not be almost without limit on and on?' DuPont—the Delaware highway builder, GM's director, and a holder of millions of dollars' worth of GM stock—replied, without irony: 'I hope so.' "[13] "General Motors' president, William Durant, recalled years later the beginnings of the American highway lobby: 'The whole network taken for granted in later generations was woven in these years—the highways, the fuel and service stations, the mechanisms of registration, insurance and policing—all simply enlarged upon and refined in the following half-century. (To the industrialists, who were now selling glass, rubber, steel, concrete and their end products in numbers beyond their wildest dreams, whatever needed to be done to sustain the boom and to build pressure for good roads simply had to [be] accomplished.' "[14]

A 1999 study by the Surface Transportation Policy Project shows that the most common way to ease congestion—adding and widening roads—

has had little effect on the growth of motor vehicle traffic congestion in major urban areas in the last 15 years.[15] A comparison of urban areas that have added extensive new road capacity with those that have not found no significant difference in the rise in traffic congestion.[16]

The urban areas that added more new lanes spent roughly $22 billion more on construction, yet it didn't keep drivers from being stuck in traffic any more effectively than cities who spent little. Congestion delays are not made up for by time savings due to the widenings, because the savings are either small in comparison to the delays or they result in more time lost because of "generated traffic," an issue we've already discussed.

Specifically, in 30 California counties, every 1 percent increase in lane miles generated a 0.9 percent increase in motor vehicle traffic within five years—so much for the congestion-easing effect of wider roads. In the long run, generated traffic can consume from 50 to 90 percent of added capacity due to road widenings.[17]

The Southern California Association of Governments estimated some years back that even if a state car club realized its desire to have 19 new expressways built in southern California, traffic in 20 years will still move at an average speed of 25 mph, less than the current speed of 31 mph.[18]

Widening roads bumps into "Parkinson's Law of Traffic: Traffic expands to fill the available road space."[19] Moore and Thorsnes make the point that "no rational concert promoter would decide how big to build a stadium based on the number of people who would come to see the Grateful Dead if the tickets were free. But that is often how transportation planners decide how [big to build a road]: they estimate how many trips would be made on an unpriced [free] facility, then try to build a [road] big enough to accommodate that number of trips."[20]

Often, we justify the "need" for wider roads by pointing to gas savings and air emissions reductions. Yet study after study has shown this received wisdom to be false. For instance, one study of U.S. cities showed that reducing congestion along a road would lead a certain percentage of people currently using public transit to start driving instead. Even if only half of this transfer occurred, the fuel consumed by the added car trips would exceed the fuel-efficiency benefits from more free-flowing traffic. The same study found that residents of outlying areas generate more carbon monoxide and hydrocarbons per capita than city dwellers, because of their longer car trip distances and the lower use of walking, bicycling, or public transit. Again and again, we have seen that after we spend the millions to "improve" our roads, we have bought not only more fuel consumption and air pollution, but also a more sprawled community, worse traffic congestion, and a poorer quality of life.

So widening streets is not just expensive but ineffective—at best. Conventional transportation models overestimate the congestion produced by removing travel lanes and fail to predict that new lanes added to a congested system will quickly generate new motor vehicle traffic and become congested. Conventional transportation models typically ignore human reactions to time costs and prices. They assume transportation infrastructure will not affect the construction of new subdivisions or commercial areas—that if you build a freeway out into cattle pasture, the farmers won't sell out to developers, and that high-speed roads will not discourage walking, bicycling, or bus use.

Yet a transportation system that is designed almost exclusively for car travel creates a positive feedback loop because it is an intimidating system that discourages people from traveling by means other than car. The hostile environment created by the infrastructure needed for car travel continuously recruits new motorists who were formerly using public transit, bicycling, or walking but are now dissuaded by the danger and inconvenience of the car infrastructure. People without access to a car find their educational and employment opportunities (as well as their ability to engage in many other life activities) severely limited in car-oriented areas. They experience a profound loss of personal independence, as they must depend on others to get around. (A large percentage of our population is unable to drive a motor vehicle—in Florida, the Federal Highway Administration reports that 37 percent of the residents cannot legally drive.)[21] Evidence of generated traffic is rarely used in travel modeling, where it would have a substantial impact on deciding whether a road widening project should be constructed.[22]

ADDING TURN LANES

Ominously, to carry larger volumes of traffic, it is *far* more effective to increase road capacity by expanding the size of an intersection than by widening the road. The intersection is the choke point for how much traffic the road can handle. As Stephen Burrington pointed out not long ago in a law journal article, "Restoring the Rule of Law and Respect for Communities in Transportation": "In some European nations, . . . speed limits and levels of driving convenience are set on the basis of what is considered desirable from the perspective of the entire community rather than from that of the motorist. . . . While transportation agencies generally assume that high levels of service must be provided to more and more motorists, they pursue no corresponding objectives for pedestrians, bicyclists, or transit users. . . . If [motorists] have to wait an average of a minute or longer, the intersection [has a failed level of service]. But if a pedestrian must wait [one or two minutes], that fact has no particular significance from an engineer's point of view."[23]

Conversely, one of the most effective ways to create a human-scaled, wonderful, village-like sense of place is to keep intersections modest in size. Think of the small towns we love. Their main intersection is small and usually has the buildings pulled up to the sidewalk and street. It feels cozy. The cities we dislike usually have enormous intersections that ensure the loss of any sense of place. Building a big intersection is the most effective way I can think of to create an Anywhere, USA, atmosphere.

Like adding travel lanes, turn lanes (particularly multiple turn lanes) can also have undesirable land use and transportation impacts. When we hear that turn lanes increase safety, the question should be Safety for whom? The answer is For the motorist who gets frustrated waiting behind a left-turning car, or the unfortunate driver heading the opposite way. What about pedestrians? Adding a turn lane increases both pedestrian exposure time to moving motor vehicles as they cross a street with no refuge island *and* the average speed of those motor vehicles, which endangers everyone not in a car. Turn lanes also tend to make the motorist less attentive to pedestrians and bicyclists.

By adding motor vehicle traffic volume capacity, turn lanes can indirectly promote land use sprawl, strip commercial, and Big Box retail. Further, installing a turn lane often leaves too little right-of-way either to retain sidewalks or bicycle lanes along that portion of the road (so they are removed), or to install them later. By adding motor vehicle traffic volume capacity and making travel less safe for other forms of travel (remember the "barrier effect"?), turn lanes encourage more trips by motor vehicle than would have otherwise occurred. The result: more traffic.

Turn lanes should be added only when their addition does not discourage pedestrian, bicycle, or transit trips; special pedestrian safety features are installed; the turn lane will allow the removal of travel lanes or avoid their addition; or some combination of these. The upshot of all this is that in a walkable commercial area (or a commercial area aspiring to *be* walkable), a turn lane can be acceptable only when added as a turn "pocket" on a two-lane street—in this design, the left-turning vehicle avoids blocking all traffic in a through lane.

Our communities should also evaluate our turn lanes to determine whether we can remove some that, on balance, discourage transportation choice.

ROAD "SIMULTANEITY"

Applied to new development, the idea of public facilities and services being simultaneous with a development (a concept planners call "concurrency") means communities can say to developers, "Either you certify that your new shopping center or subdivision will not lower service standards—water, wastewater, roads, solid waste collection, stormwater management, recreation, public transit—or . . . no development." That is, developers must guarantee that adequate public facilities will be available "concurrent" (simultaneously) with the impacts of any new development. What could make better sense? What could be more fair?

Ask Florida, where concurrency provided the "teeth" for the Florida Growth Management Act that took effect in 1985, billed as the antidote to the state's uncontrolled and explosive population growth problems. Sure enough, the Act "was hailed around the country as a model of enlightened land use regulation."[24] But almost 20 years later, Florida is more plagued than ever with sprawling, low-density, suburban growth, a proliferation of citizen no-growth and "property rights" movements seeking to cut through new red tape, higher taxes, worsened services, new seas of asphalt, mile upon mile of new commercial strips, and near-gridlock traffic congestion. "There is a virtual consensus . . . that the 28-year old growth management laws . . . are failing. Growth management 'really hasn't adequately protected natural resources or stopped urban sprawl.' "[25]

Among growth-management tools that *can* work are *location-sensitive* impact fees. Impact fees appropriately seek to recover from new developments the relatively high costs they impose on an existing community. Such fees need to be tailored carefully so as to not discourage socially beneficial in-town development. Charging higher fees for developments in outlying areas is justifiable because of market distortions such as road subsidies. These distortions are especially unfair because they primarily benefit outlying developments. When those higher costs can be clearly documented, outlying developments can be fairly assessed a higher impact fee. By doing this, we help level the playing field.

So while the concurrency approach makes sense for most public services, it works against community improvement when it is applied to roads. First, most available road capacity exists in remote Sprawlsville locations where development will cause environmental and social problems and place excessive service demands on local governments. Second, road concurrency is the only growth management standard in which providing more of the facility creates more demand, as we have seen.

That partly explains why a growing number of transportation agencies—among them the California, New Jersey, and federal departments of transportation—can no longer justify the astronomical costs of widening roads to try to meet motorists' demands. The governmental response to traffic congestion is increasingly shifting from increasing road supply to a much cheaper and socially beneficial strategy: "managing demand."[26] In Florida, a committee of planners, engineers, and elected officials selected to evaluate the state's 1985 Growth Management Act found that "Florida's land use and transportation system is failing. . . . Few communities offer viable alternative transportation modes to the automobile. Florida leads the nation in automobile-related deaths each year among both pedestrians and bicyclists, . . . elders over 75 years of age are becoming increasingly homebound and isolated. . . . Lower income persons unable to afford a car are increasingly isolated from entry level jobs." The committee suggested that because "no amount of funding will allow enough highways to be built to end congestion, . . . local governments [should] pursue planning goals that assign a lower priority to automobile mobility, and a higher priority to pedestrian and alternative transit modes. . . . Such a policy means designing communities to make pedestrian movement and public transit attractive to residents in areas, even at the expense of vehicular mobility. In other words, vehicular congestion may increase for a time . . . when other community goals are given priority. . . . [Efforts to assure regional auto] mobility, . . . especially road widenings, [can] run counter to the preferences of the local community [regarding livability]."[27]

CHAPTER 5

Putting the Brakes on Sprawl

In a quality city, a person should be able to live their entire life without a car, and not feel deprived.
—Paul Bedford, City of Toronto Planning Director

Most people would be unwilling to live in low-density, outlying, sprawling areas—or drive a car for *every* trip—without roads designed for high speeds and high volumes, and free and abundant parking. "Stopping sprawl requires a simultaneous process of changing the investment in highways that take people out of the city to greenfield sites. . . . It is almost impossible to stop new sprawl through zoning alone if high-speed roads are still being built. They are like a loaded gun pointed at rural land in their vicinity."[1]

Why are U.S. cities so much less walkable and compact than, for example, European cities? Do Europeans simply appreciate the merits of walkable communities more? Are they too poor to own cars? The reason is that most European urban areas developed before the auto age, whereas U.S. cities developed and grew *after* the emergence of cars. It is no coincidence that cities across Europe, since entering the auto age, have begun to see U.S.-style sprawl.

As long as we design our roads to encourage sprawl, we will be afflicted by sprawl. Sprawl is *enabled* by car travel (through near universal ownership of reasonably affordable cars, free and abundant parking, and high-capacity urban roads). A different path is to strive to make *people* the quality-of-life design imperative in our cities, and *ecosystems* the imperative in outlying areas. If we insist on a walkable, high quality of life in our communities—even at the cost of some city squirrels and raccoons—fewer people will hop in their cars to live in remote subdivisions that have replaced outlying ecosystems. So as we stop widening roads, we must also adopt development regulations focused on human-scaled, people-oriented urban qualities.

To succeed in curtailing sprawl, economic conditions must be ripe. The encouraging news is that, around the country, the costs of gasoline, parking, and road widenings are increasing noticeably—giving us motivation and hope for a successful campaign against sprawl.

California offers a perfect case in point. Governor George Deukmejian, who started his term in 1983, strongly supported bigger freeways as an antidote to congestion. Governor Jerry Brown, whose term preceded Deukmejian's, strongly advocated transportation choice and opposed bigger freeways. Yet "more than twice as many new miles of freeways were built during the eight years of the 'antifreeway' Brown administration . . . as during the 'profreeway' Deukmejian administration." During this period in California, the cost of freeway widening skyrocketed during the 1960s when Ronald Reagan was elected governor and continued to be prohibitively high during the Brown and Deukmejian administrations. Deukmejian widened fewer freeways than Brown not because he opposed bigger freeways and Brown supported them—indeed, the opposite was the case. Instead, freeway widening was determined by finances, not ideology. While both Brown and Deukmejian had insufficient freeway construction dollars, Deukmejian's dollars were substantially more insufficient than Brown's. Freeway widening in California had much more to do with economic conditions than with the ideas or values of the state's governors. "Freeways were not stopped by policy shifts, by urban planners heading highway departments, or by changed plans [but] by rising costs and lagging revenues."[2]

AVOIDING THE ALL-TOO-PREDICTABLE FUTURE

The average maximum reasonable walking distance from point A to point B for trips made daily ranges from one-quarter mile to one mile. By contrast, the distance by bus or bicycle is about 3 miles, and by car, about 10 miles (figure 5.1).[3] If we assume that a public transit- and bicycle-based community is more sustainable and less sprawl prone than a car-based community, we can conclude that a community reaches its "sprawl threshold" when it grows to the maximum reasonable distance people are willing to travel by public transit or bicycle—a radius of about three miles, which is a community of about 30 square miles in size.

By looking at how a fairly typical small U.S. city has grown, we can see that this travel-distance theory seems to have been confirmed (figure 5.2). Until about 1930, Gainesville, Florida, was still mostly a walking commu-

Figure 5.1
Travel Distance Theory

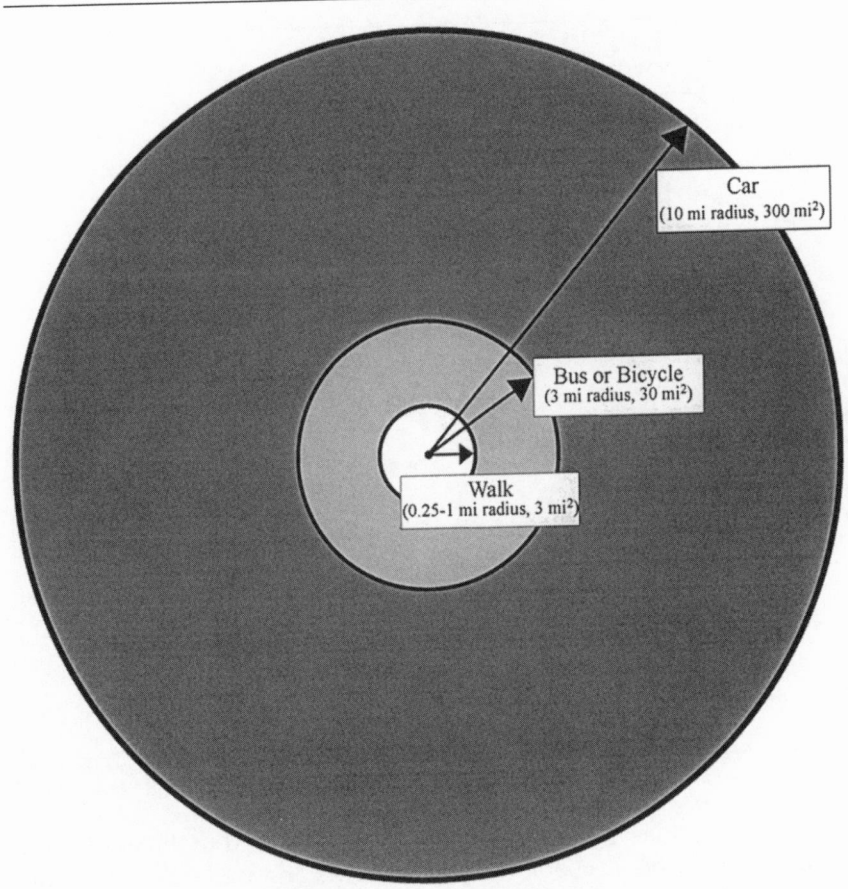

nity, corresponding to a reasonable walking distance of about one mile in radius. As we would expect, urbanization in Gainesville during this walking period had reached out about one mile (zone A). Over the next 30 years, until about 1960, the city was still mostly a public transit community with an urbanized three-mile transit radius from the heart of the downtown (zone B). From 1960 until today, over a period of substantial urban area street conversions from two-lane streets to four- or six-lane roads, the city has developed into a car-based community. Urbanization now extends in a seven-mile radius from downtown (zone C). Gainesville now covers 50 square miles in area. (San Francisco, with 630,000 more people, is 47 square miles. Boulder, Colorado, with a population nearly the same as Gainesville's, was 24 square miles as of the late 1990s.)[4]

Figure 5.2
Urbanization in Gainesville, Florida: Historic and Projected

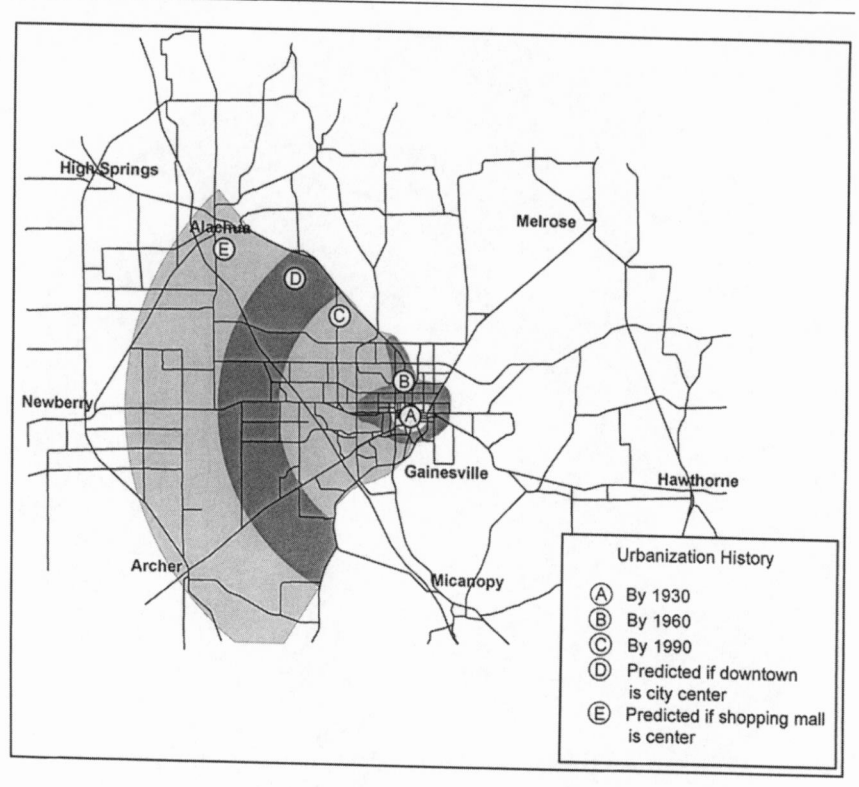

Note that Gainesville urbanization has not occurred to the north, east, or south largely because of low traffic volumes and wetlands constraints.

From 1930 to 1990, there was a sevenfold increase in Gainesville's population. Nationally, a relatively rapid rate for a city of Gainesville's size. But there was a 23-fold increase in urbanized land in the Gainesville area for this same time period.[5]

I don't need to be a fortune-teller to predict, with some confidence, that if the status quo is maintained—that is, if Gainesville continues to widen roads, maintain high-capacity roads, and provide free and abundant parking—urbanization will eventually extend 10 miles from downtown (zone D); if we take the large regional shopping mall on the western edge of the city as a city subcenter of shopping and employment, Gainesville will eventually urbanize 10 miles beyond the mall (zone E).

The status quo of designing nearly exclusively for cars will inevitably subject cities like Gainesville to 10-mile urbanization arcs—growth arcs that radiate out 10 miles from downtown and another 10 miles from subcenters.

URBAN GROWTH BOUNDARIES

"A development area without defined limits encourages sprawl by enabling landowners on the developed fringe to repeatedly propose new projects that are not linked, in significant ways, with the existing community."[6] Urban growth boundaries (UGBs) discourage or prohibit residential, commercial, and school development in areas more than a modest distance from downtown. To succeed, areas within the boundary should have minimum residential densities of six to eight dwelling units per acre; new development with lower densities—particularly in or near neighborhood centers—must be denied.[7] One way to increase development densities is to revoke land development policies that reduce them, such as minimum lot-size zoning and minimum parking requirements.[8]

Portland, Oregon's UGB, for example, has created not only a strong, healthy, vibrant downtown, but also "a compact, livable region while preserving farmland and protecting the environment. The UGB has not slowed Portland's economic development, nor is it responsible for the region's current affordable housing problems. In fact, Oregon's UGBs are progrowth because they allow developers to intensely develop land inside the boundary, free from the NIMBY obstacles they often face elsewhere."[9] The area outside the boundary has seen only a tiny percentage of the area's residential development (mostly adjacent to the boundary) and "no significant industrial or commercial development." Boulder, Colorado's effective UGB includes an urban area (where city services are provided), a reserve area, and an open-space area.[10]

By increasing urban density, a UGB limits most trip distances to the space within the boundary, makes noncar travel more feasible, and thus reduces transportation costs.[11]

UGBs are often stopgap measures, however. Nearly all U.S. communities now have excessive road capacities that lead inexorably to dispersed urban sprawl. The UGB can serve the interim purpose of quickly curbing the strong market forces these big roads have created that push communities into a sprawled pattern. Ultimately, we will need to narrow the big roads to reduce the sprawl pressure, but since such work takes decades, UGBs can step in to slow sprawl in the meantime. I believe UGBs are not sustainable over the long term, because of the enormous pressure landowners just outside the boundary apply on their elected officials to extend the UGB to include them.

BUILDING ON THE STRENGTHS OF THE CITY

We can best fight unsustainable sprawl and the flight from the city if we protect and promote the city as a place that we and our children, as lovers of the city, *want* to live in, shop in, go to school in, work in, and be entertained in.

The preponderance of suburbs in most small- and medium-sized cities and, therefore, the growth in suburban and motorist values, ratchets up the threat of suburbanizing the small remaining slivers of traditional, walkable portions of towns. There is a real danger that we who enjoy quality neighborhoods and cities will soon lose that lifestyle choice. And even if we decided to suburbanize the walkable portions of the city as well as the suburbs—which would clearly be a mistake from the point of view of maintaining lifestyle choices—the suburbs will always be seen as more attractive. The city cannot compete on suburban terms by attempting to incorporate features that can nearly always be done cheaper, easier, and better in the suburbs. The antidote is not to suburbanize the remaining remnants of walkability. To do so is akin to destroying the city to save it.

Because so many cities have been harmed by suburban features, there is a substantial, untapped market for the strengths that make the city livable. Among these are walkability, unique character, sociability, ambiance, vibrancy, diversity, civic pride, transportation choice, and buildings and streets scaled for people instead of cars. To attract investment, houses, jobs, and retail back to the traditional city, we need to build on the inherent leverage of a city, those things that make it distinct from the suburbs and distinctly satisfying as a locus of community life.

Let's recap what I've already outlined about the strengths of a city—strengths that when protected and promoted, deliver us cities with a healthy future. In a livable city, retail buildings are pulled up to, and face, the street and sidewalk, so the buildings give their vitality to the sidewalk and thereby make walking safe, pleasant, and interesting. As in public realms we admire in Charleston, Savannah, San Francisco, Annapolis, and the many walkable European cities, these buildings and street trees lined up along and near the street form a pleasant "outdoor room." We have alleys that serve buildings so that vehicles, driveways, dumpsters, service vehicles, utilities, and garages can be moved away from the sidewalk. In this walkable portion of a city, street vistas are often terminated with important buildings, serendipitously delighting us with the splendor of the many picturesque views these terminations provide.

In such a city, we can walk, bicycle, or use public transit to get from home to a job, city parks, retailers, the public library, and other public buildings. Such proximity among our destinations gives us a *choice* about how we will travel, whereas distance *forces* us to drive a car to get anywhere. The livable city has modest street sizes and parking lots, equitably priced car travel, and other strategies to ensure that cars are not a nuisance and safety hazard to residences, pedestrians, or bicyclists. Cars become optional, not a necessity.

The downtown here is vibrant, romantic, people-scaled, unique, and diverse, bustling with pedestrian activity. In this city, we find on-street parking, so that walking is safe and enjoyable, our small retailers see more customers, and cars do not speed.

In our livable city, we find a mix of housing types and household incomes so that we do not live in a homogenized upper-income or low-income enclave. In this neighborhood, we can "retire in place" instead of being warehoused in a retirement village when we are older and can no longer drive a car. As our car-based travel requirements no longer make it possible for seniors to retire in their neighborhood once they lose the ability to drive (a large percentage of us will eventually reach an age at which we will be unable to drive), they must find a living arrangement that does not require car travel, often today a retirement village, from which they are ferried to destinations in a van. They thus lose a significant amount of independence in a car-based culture.

But can we get there from here?

STRATEGIES

Communities determined to protect, create, or restore livability, sociability, and walkability can make a fundamental strategic choice: they can establish or preserve compact, walkable, mixed-use development and higher residential densities.

Mixing land uses means integrating various kinds of housing with offices or stores. (When these are combined in the same building, such a mixture is known as *vertical mixed use*; dissimilar uses not in the same building but within walking distance of one another are called *horizontal mixed use*.) Over the last 50 years, we have come to view dissimilar uses of land—residences, offices, public buildings—as conflicting, a problem we have often resolved by putting distance between them (which travel by car makes possible). We've built single-family homes only near other single-family homes, apartments with apartments, offices with offices, and so on. One obvious result has been to put us behind the wheel every time we go from one place to another, reducing the livability of our communities.[12]

Distance is the reason most people give for not walking more often, and compact, mixed land use exponentially reduces trip length, so that not only walking but bicycling and public transit become more viable. Residents in older, more traditional, compact, in-town neighborhoods make up to 5.5 times as many shopping trips by walking than do residents of more auto-centric sprawl neighborhoods.[13] Such a land use design also makes it easier for us to combine several errands in a single trip—we can walk to the park, say, as well as shop and go to the dentist. Mixed-use developments also make us more likely to carpool, significantly reducing not only car trips but parking needed in the development. Instead of Thomas, Harold, and Richard driving separately to the grocery, barber, and accountant, they can ride together to one mixed-use location. By the same token, suburban office workers can conveniently run both midday and after-work errands when their office park includes restaurants, banks, and shops.[14] In one mixed-use Seattle neighborhood, for example, more than 12 percent of all trips are made by nonmotorized means, versus 4 percent in the residence-only areas.[15]

We have increasingly segregated our downtown areas over the years, so that today most downtowns in U.S. cities have a very high proportion of workplaces and very few residences, a scenario sure to encourage excessive car use. (European downtowns have a much better balance between workplaces and residences.) Concentrating jobs downtown has little effect on reducing car dependence, whereas a balanced mix of jobs and housing downtown results in much less car use.[16] Some cities now require developers to provide a certain amount of residential housing in conjunction with downtown office development.

Apart from urban downtowns, the highest rates of bicycling and walking occur in neighborhood centers with a jobs and housing balance. (Well-designed "neighborhood centers," which usually occur at major street intersections, are walkable shopping areas mixed with housing.) Adding retail shops to office-oriented areas further promotes walking, bicycling, ridesharing, and use of public transit by those who live near their work and near the commingled retail and service outlets.[17]

Here are some persuasive statistics: compared to a development in a remote, sprawled location, new in-town development can reduce vehicle miles traveled by up to 52 percent and reduce emissions of nitrogen oxide by up to 81 percent and of volatile organic compounds by up to 316 percent. (At the location where these numbers were achieved, 27 percent of all work trips were by transit, compared to the area's average of only 8 percent.)[18]

Yet even when communities encourage mixed-use development, a shift from car trips to public transit, bicycling, and walking does not begin to occur until the area reaches a certain threshold of housing[19]—roughly five to eight houses per acre.[20] Below that threshold, household car ownership goes up, gas consumption increases exponentially, and bus service and walking decline. For purposes of comparison, the "ideal" density for auto-based travel has been set at a very modest two to four net residential dwelling units per acre, 2,500 persons per square mile.[21] (Gainesville, Florida, where I live, for example, has a citywide density of 3.42 units per acre.)

With higher densities, each person needs less impervious surface (surfaces which cannot be penetrated by water and therefore create flooding and water pollution problems during rainstorms, and aggravate "heat island" effects). Higher densities also require less land be devoted, per person, to transportation. Per-person costs go down for public services (police, fire, etc.) and parks, roads, and stormwater. Finally, crime drops as police can more effectively monitor criminal behavior, and we are more likely to pitch in with citizen surveillance—keeping an eye out for bad behavior from our kitchen or storefront window.

Paying lip service to higher densities (for example, by calling for higher-density residential development in our long-range community plans) will not get us there. We need instead to redesign our transportation system so that drivers consider travel times from remote locations excessive, parking is considered expensive and scarce, or both, which usually means that we must avoid draining cities and lowering densities with big urban highways and parking lots. "Modest" needs to become our watchword: modest-sized streets and parking designed for modest travel speeds and modest parking supply are currently the most effective ways to create strong markets for higher densities—not just strong words in our planning documents urging high densities. Put even more simply, over the long run, higher densities evolve when we have traffic congestion, because congestion increases travel times and therefore reduces the distance people are willing to commute. Higher densities are almost never the result of public-sector efforts that preemptively rezone land because a planning document calls for such efforts, unless there is a market demand for those densities (largely created by transportation conditions).

When it comes to transit use, however, density is less important than location. Residences near downtown generate much more demand for transit than residences with the same densities farther from downtown. And residences within 2,000 feet of a transit stop demand much higher amounts of transit than residences farther from the stop. This means we want to cluster higher residential densities near walkably designed transit stops in close proximity of shops and offices.

What if in-town development is not served by transit? Air pollution is still less than for a remote, sprawl development because centrally located sites require shorter average trip distances,[22] which means that fewer of those trips are by car.

Another way to promote transit use is to prevent transit-supporting land uses such as multifamily housing and important, community-serving offices from dispersing into unwalkable, low-density, single-use areas.

DENSITY MATTERS

Flying in the face of everything we think we know about density, higher densities can benefit our neighborhoods in a number of ways when designed correctly. Indeed, the complaints often raised against higher densities—too much traffic, too little parking, too much noise—are caused not by too many people but too many cars (and too much design focus on cars).

Among the advantages of higher densities, we can count on dramatically lower car use per household.[23] Only when densities exceed approximately 13 residential dwelling units per acre do mixed land uses and shorter travel distances become predominant enough to reduce car dependence significantly.[24] Such development is also much more likely to recruit motorists to bicycling than other incentives, such as better facilities for bicycling, congestion fees, or fuel price increases.[25]

Increasing residential densities from 5 to 20 dwelling units per acre will reduce vehicle miles traveled and household car expenses by at least 40 percent.[26] For example, in-town San Francisco households, compared to remote, sprawled households, spent $14,000 less on cars each year; each resident used 339 gallons less gas.[27] A significant reduction in per capita gasoline consumption occurs when population density rises from 1.7 dwelling units per acre to 5.1 to 6.8 units per acre. When densities are less than 7 units per acre, however, we rarely choose to use public transit. At 7 to 15 units per acre, moderately convenient service by trains, buses, and taxis can be supported.

Simply doubling residential densities can reduce vehicle miles traveled by up to 30 percent. Compared to sprawling suburban development, compact, mixed-use development generates about half as much vehicle travel.[28] If the population of an area doubles because of infill development, vehicle miles traveled will probably increase by only 40 to 60 percent rather than the 100 percent they would increase if the population increase occurred in dispersed suburbs.[29] In contrast, doubling an area's population in the conventional, low-density sprawl pattern of most of our suburbs can increase auto miles traveled by up to 186 percent. Even when we take into account household income, vehicle ownership and trips made by car decline as the neighborhood density increases.[30]

We also see less air pollution with higher densities: motorists who live in town emit 14 kg less hydrocarbons, 12 kg less nitrogen oxides, and 98 kg less carbon monoxide each year.[31] We find more viable public transit at higher densities,[32] more convenient neighborhood retail, and lower per capita energy consumption.[33] We see, of course, much lower consumption of land for a given number of people, but also much less land devoted to transportation.[34] Residential development that averages 14 dwelling units per acre requires half as many miles of road as development that averages 3.5 dwelling units per acre.[35]

Lower public service and infrastructure costs also accompany higher densities.[36] So do lower water pollution and less water runoff. A New Jersey study found that its compact development plan would produce 40 percent less water pollution than dispersed development, and 30 percent less runoff. In fact, low-density sprawl development can create 50 percent more storm runoff than compact development.[37]

High densities mean better policing, safer neighborhoods, and less crime;[38] studies show that if we lump together homicides and traffic fatalities, city residents are noticeably safer than suburban residents, since traffic fatalities are so much higher in the suburbs.[39] Finally, with higher densities, bird species abundance and diversity increase, compared with lower-density development of the same number of units sprawled over the same area.[40]

Where Higher Density Works Best

In general, as we have seen, the best places for higher residential densities are areas surrounding commercial neighborhood centers, major bus stops, and downtowns. Households in pedestrian-friendly Portland, Oregon, drive a car 50 percent fewer miles and make 33 percent fewer car trips than those in the suburbs.[41]

Increasingly, higher-density mixed-use urban developments are becoming attractive because of easy access to urban services and facilities and the more interesting, convivial, and active community they provide. The city becomes safer and more "defensible" (because of an increase in citizen watching and citizen caring) with much less space abandoned at night to criminals and gangs.[42]

While public transit, walking, and bicycling work best when density is relatively high, car travel works best at low densities and becomes burdensome as densities increase.[43] As motorists, we are happiest when there are no other cars on the road, a testament to the anti-community nature of the car; as pedestrians, by telling contrast, we are happiest when there are large numbers of other people walking at the same time in, say, a plaza.[44] My own experiences when walking or bicycling confirm this. When I am walking or bicycling, I find that wherever I go, I exchange friendly, serendipitous verbal and hand-waving greetings to friends I encounter along the way. But when encased inside the metal and glass box of my car, those experiences are lost. Inside my car, I pass people too quickly to be able to recognize whether they are friends. And even in those rare instances where there is recognition, we have no time to greet each other and discuss pleasantries. And even if we did have time inside our cars, the metal and glass prevents us from hearing each other. If we are lucky, there is an instant of distant eye contact, or a nod. Hardly the sort of exchange that builds human interaction.

In terms of new growth, when we are striving to reduce car trips it is much more important to prevent new growth at very low densities than to make sure it occurs at very high densities. Low average densities in any part of the urban area generate long average commuting distances. There is a much bigger payoff—in terms of reducing average commuting distances and energy consumption—when we increase average gross densities from 1,000 to 5,000 people per square mile (1.25 dwelling units per net acre to 6.25 units per acre) than when we increase them from 5,000 to 10,000 people per square mile (6.25 units per acre to 12.5 units per acre).[45]

Is there any available land left in our crowded cities for infill or density increases? Absolutely. In 1995 there were up to 450,000 abandoned, idle, or underused industrial and commercial facilities that are restricted from being used more fully because of environmental problems such as a toxic dump.[46] In addition to these opportunity sites are the endless number of commercial strip shopping center areas across the nation—places with tiny densities, huge, vacant parking lots and, often, vacated buildings.

MANIPULATING MARKET SIGNALS

The forces driving sprawl include, in important ways, market signals experienced by individuals—the cost of purchasing a car, the cost of purchasing a home in a remote location instead of in town, the cost of parking, the time cost of traffic delays, and the quality of a neighborhood and nearby schools. Only in trivial ways is sprawl controlled by plans, politicians, or planners. Even the strongest plans and politicians tend to be overwhelmed by the sheer power of the ubiquitous market economy (created, in crucial ways, by our road system). Yet planners and politicians have an important role to play in eliminating undesirable "externalities" in the economy that distort market signals in a way that hinders achieving various societal objectives.

Many market signals that we can manipulate to reduce the strong market pressure leading to more costly sprawl are discussed in this chapter and elsewhere in the book. Three additional examples are detailed here.

In-Town Public Schools

Unfortunately, in-town schools frequently compare poorly to new schools in remote locations. We need to ensure that in-town schools not only receive equitable funding but are easy to bicycle or walk to from nearby neighborhoods.

Schools are often being chased to outlying areas because of public school requirements for large, space-intensive play fields, usually too large to fit into in-town locations. Similarly, public schools often move to outlying areas having cheaper land to provide the expansive parking lots necessitated by the school's very remoteness, which cannot be reached except by motor vehicle. And school districts, like other developers, often find that it is less expensive to comply with contemporary building codes by building new schools instead of renovating old ones.

What is needed are public school play area and building code requirements that are flexible enough to accommodate older, in-town schools.

Location-Efficient Mortgages

Mortgage lenders typically do not consider the financial burden of commuting and other transportation costs for a family living in a remote, residence-only suburban area.[47] One 2000 study found that households in sprawl regions devote more than 20 percent of household expenditures to surface transportation (more than $8,500 annually), while those in communities with more efficient land use spend less than 17 percent (less than $5,500 annually).[48] Research by the National Resources Defense Council has shown that a family living in a central location in Oakland, California, drives only half as much as a similar family living in a remote location. The savings were measured at about $750 per month. Higher overall payments (travel and mortgage) make the more remote home more risky to the mortgage lender than a comparable loan in a more central location.

For location-efficient mortgages (LEMs), banks and mortgage lenders recognize the transportation savings of an access-rich central location. The key correlates for location efficiency are relatively high residential density; good access to public transit; good access to shopping, services, cultural amenities, and schools; good pedestrian friendliness of sidewalks, bikeways, benches, lighting, and plantings.

A portion of these savings can be used by such institutions to stretch the standard income-to-expenses ratios that are part of the mortgage application process. The lending formula can be changed so that a dollar a month saved on transportation can be applied to a dollar a month higher loan payment. As a result, families who want to buy a home in a more location-efficient area could qualify for a higher mortgage than a family purchasing a remote, less location-efficient home.

Of course, this concept is a powerful affordable-housing tool as well. A lower-income household could qualify for housing that would be too expensive under conventional lending rules.

To spell this out, Litman shows how LEMs can be an important way to provide affordable housing. In a more auto-dependent suburban location, a family of four might need two cars—each driven 15,000 miles per year—resulting in an annual transportation cost of $10,000. If this family lived in a location with transportation choices, it could hypothetically shed at least one car, would need less parking, and could have an annual transportation expense of only $4,000 per year. This savings could finance up to $100,000 in additional housing expenses. These more walkable, in-town locations, rich in transportation choices, "tend to have high housing costs but lower transportation costs." Unfortunately, traditional mortgage lenders "only consider housing costs, and treat car ownership "as a financial asset rather than a liability, encouraging homebuyers to choose automobile-dependent housing locations. LEM creates a more neutral housing market."[49]

Fannie Mae, the largest source of home loan funds in the US, supports the development of LEMs.

Distance-Based Car Insurance

Car insurance can be more equitable and discourage auto dependence, if it changes based on distance traveled, usually not the case today.[50]

Because distance traveled probably correlates with increased crash rates, those who drive less often pay the same rate as those who drive more, in effect, subsidizing them.

HOW TO MAKE IT HAPPEN

Despite the strategies I've mentioned to reduce overreliance on car trips—in particular, higher densities and proximity between trip origins and destinations—we still see that enormous majorities continue to travel by car for all of their trips, often despite living in a higher density neighborhood or living only a few blocks from where they want to go. Doesn't this prove that we are permanently wedded to our cars and that nothing can talk us out of them for any reason?

In my opinion, this sort of reliance on car trips, even when the grocery store is only two blocks away, is perfectly understandable. As I've pointed out elsewhere, we've been very good at providing compelling incentives for always driving a car. Who can resist multilane roads and gigantic parking lots when they are almost always provided to us "free of charge"? Why not drive, even when the drugstore is only a block away?

But over the long run, when communities become more dense, parking lots and roads inevitably become more crowded. As cities become denser in population and jobs, several changes start to occur. Growing numbers of us choose to travel more by means other than our cars.[51] Our communities tend to devote less money to increasing road capacity. And the city concentrates development around a strong downtown core area. Crowded roads and parking lots start adding a "time tax" and an "inconvenience tax" to our car trips.

At the same time, local governments can use a wide variety of land use, urban design, regulatory, infrastructure, and pricing tactics to encourage us to walk, bike, or use public transit, and to discourage single-occupant car use. In general, these tactics not only cut public subsidies that make us want to jump into our cars, but also level the playing field by making walking, bicycling, and transit use more convenient, pleasant, and safe (see chapters 7 and 8).

Certainly we will not see majorities of trips made by means other than car overnight, even if we take the steps I recommend here. But should we expect that? After all, we built a car-friendly nation over the course of several decades. It took us more than "overnight" to get where we are today. Shouldn't we expect that it will be more than overnight for us to return to a more sustainable pattern of travel?

CHAPTER 6

Properly Designing Streets

Enter through the narrow gate. For wide is the gate and broad is the road that leads to destruction, and many enter through it. But small is the gate and narrow the road that leads to life, and only a few find it.
—Matthew 7:13–14

The role of the street is social as well as utilitarian.

—Andres Duany

If our goal is pedestrian-friendly communities, we need streets that entice pedestrians (and those who ride a bicycle or bus). That means, among other things, that most of us need to use our car less promiscuously, and we need to design our streets to obligate more modest speeds when we *do* use our car.

One of the main ways communities can discourage us from driving so much and so fast, apart from congestion, is to plan for and encourage walking, bicycling, and public transit as viable, rational forms of transport and to implement "traffic calming" strategies, primarily by redesigning streets for lower, safer speeds—speeds that are less stop and go, and more smooth, slow, and continuous.

CUTTING BACK ON CAR TRIPS

How can we reduce the negative impact of private car trips on our communities? One important way is to cut down on their number—particularly "low value" car trips.

All metropolitan communities in the United States, by federal law, must establish a metropolitan transportation planning organization in which elected officials make regional transportation planning decisions. Among other goals, these plans almost always establish objectives for the ratio of the number of urban-area trips by car compared to other forms of transportation (what traffic engineers call a "modal split"). In the mid 1990s, for example, about 3 percent of all trips in the Gainesville, Florida, urban area were by bicycle, foot, bus, or private vehicles occupied by two or more people. The city's Metropolitan Transportation Planning Organization set a goal of increasing this to at least 15 percent, a target that would deliver enormous benefits without "banning all cars" (a red herring often trotted out by naysayers). Achieving that target would mean 65,000 fewer car trips each day; 4,021,000 fewer gallons of gas consumed each year; and 39,217,000 fewer kg of carbon dioxide, 93,000 fewer kg of nitrogen oxides, and 256,000 fewer kg of volatile organic compounds emitted into the air each year.[1]

We don't need to prohibit low-value, rush-hour car trips on our community's public roads; we can just stop publicly subsidizing and encouraging such car travel with free roads, free parking, free emergency services, and free road widening and street repair. (After all, if we are trying to drive to work or must rush to the hospital for an emergency, do we need our roads to be clogged up with trips to buy an ice cream?) Our heavy car-travel subsidies have nearly destroyed transit, which we also subsidize, but to a much lesser extent.[2] We as drivers don't receive accurate market signals about how much driving really costs, so without a second thought we drive across town to pick up a video during rush hour (a low-value car trip) and make nearly every trip by car—as if driving everywhere were human nature instead of behavior born of subsidized public funding. In other words, we suffer from an artificially high demand for low-value car trips (not to mention sprawl housing) because of market failure created by public subsidies.

So at the same time we discourage excessive driving, we need to make walking, bicycling, and public transit attractive and viable options. And that means establishing sufficient market and environmental signals to encourage a shift. We find this in many cities in Europe, where the public transit systems take an enormous number of car trips off the roads. Despite public transit that some would describe in such terms as dirty, overcrowded, and unreliable, a much higher percentage of people use public transit in Europe than in the United States. So what is Europe's secret?

Quite simply, European cities have the proper driver-discouraging, travel-choice-encouraging signals in operation: congestion, lack of free and abundant parking, mixed-use neighborhoods, higher residential density, expensive gas, and narrow streets. To discourage overreliance on cars, it must seem to us more rational to take public transit than to drive. Here, it is important to recognize that if our community objective is to replace overreliance on private car trips with higher public transit ridership, getting the signals right is much more important than providing quality public transit service (although we probably should provide that too).

But as long as we can get where we want to go faster and more comfortably and more conveniently by driving, most of us will drive. After 60 years of designing our cities for cars, most of us are a long way from the day when driving cars is irrational. But even if we all continue to drive everywhere, we can make our communities more pleasant *now*. For starters, we need to design streets that don't encourage driving at high, reckless speeds.

HOW WE GOT HERE (AND SO FAST)

Early in the twentieth century, on the theory that frenzied automobiles frightened horses and raised dust, many states followed British precedent and passed laws limiting self-propelled vehicles to four miles per hour and requiring that each be preceded by a man on foot carrying a red flag.

As one measure of how far we have moved from that view, on page 5 of the 1990 "Green Book," the American Association of State Highway and Transportation Officials' bible, whose formal title is *A Policy on Geometric Design of Highways and Streets,* the book tells us that the goal of roadway design is "to provide operational efficiency, comfort, safety, and convenience for the motorist."

There is a ruinous assumption here, as Burrington pointed out six years later in "Restoring the Rule of Law and Respect for Communities in Transportation" in the *New York University Law Journal:* "The interests of motorists and the public as a whole are implicitly assumed to be identical, even though it is well documented that the risks to which pedestrians are exposed, as well as noise levels and pollution emission rates, increase significantly with vehicle speed. . . . Traffic engineers . . . do not identify community interests such as children's safety and then balance motorists' interest in speed against those community interests. They merely seek to ensure that only 15 percent of motorists will be exceeding the speed limit."[3]

According to the Federal Highway Administration, to reduce the number and severity of car crashes, to improve conditions for bicyclists, pedestrians, and the environment, and to make roads safer for children, nothing is more important than slowing down motor vehicle traffic. (Stina Sandels, a world authority on children and road accidents, says that even the best road-safety education cannot adapt a child to modern traffic; traffic must be adapted to the child.)[4]

A road's "design speed," as defined by traffic engineers, is the highest speed at which a motorist can drive safely. The Green Book calls for the design speed on all but local, neighborhood streets to be as high as practicable.[5] A key strategy for restoring safer streets for us all is to construct a larger portion of our community's streets with *modest* design speeds. This means, essentially, going from wide, unlandscaped, pedal-to-the-metal streets to narrower, landscaped streets with on-street parking. "The tendency of many communities to equate wider streets with better streets and to design traffic and parking lanes as though the street were a 'microfreeway' is a highly questionable practice. Certainly the provision of two 11- or 12-foot clear traffic lanes is an open invitation to increased traffic speeds."[6]

Here's how a wide street influences us as drivers. First, it puts us farther from objects on either side of the street, which creates the illusion that our car is moving more slowly and prompts us to speed up. Second, it reassures us that we have a broad field of vision, which again induces us to drive faster. Third, more lanes can mean fewer vehicles in each lane and more distance between vehicles—another reason to speed up. Thus an urban arterial street with three 11- or 12-foot travel lanes or a broad, two-lane residential street can have a virtually irresistible effect: Even we who are not inclined to drive fast accelerate to highway speeds.[7] And "as the speed of traffic increases, the attitude of motorists to pedestrians becomes increasingly ruthless."[8]

Cutting down trees, removing other vegetation, taking property by eminent domain, and otherwise flattening terrain create what traffic engineers assume is the necessary "stopping sight distance." And the design speed of a road is the main determinant of the stopping sight distance.

Further, when we drive 25 mph or faster, we have difficulty perceiving that a pedestrian is ready to cross a street, deciding to slow down, and actually doing so. Typically, we decide instead to speed up, assuming that another car will stop.[9] At lower speeds, I have observed, we tend to be more courteous. "It's getting so only the elderly can remember the days when people actually spent time sitting on the front porch greeting people, or kissing good night after a date. Many homeowners have pretty much kissed off [their front yards]. The main reason is a lot more cars going a lot faster."[10]

How much will we need to slow down in our city driving to ensure safety, create an environment people find conducive to walking, socializing, and shopping, and minimize noise? To a maximum of 19 to 25 mph.[11]

FORGIVING STREETS

The traffic engineer's conventional approach to achieving "safe" streets is to widen them and remove from their shoulders obstacles and other forms of "friction." Doing so is conventionally expected to prevent even high-speed, out-of-control motorists from colliding with utility poles, trees, and other adjacent structures. This is also known as designing for the "forgiving roadway"—one that does not punish reckless driving.

A forgiving road design, which allows us to be less alert drivers (and be "forgiven" for driving recklessly), merely delivers faster cars and less safety for everyone. It is worst-case scenario planning because it gives us neighborhood streets wide enough for the rare huge truck. It assumes that drivers have poor driving skills. The forgiving road also fails to take into account our psychology as drivers. On a road designed for safe driving at 40 miles per hour, the average motorist will drive 40 miles per hour or faster, even if the signs say "Speed Limit 30." Our driving speed is determined by the maximum speed at which we feel comfortable driving. By encouraging high-speed driving, the forgiving-road philosophy gives us *less* traffic safety, not more.

There is an odd paradox at work here. A road newly designed to "improve safety," while it usually means fewer fender benders, generally leads to more serious accidents and more accidents involving pedestrians. Typically, the sole objective of "improving safety" is to make it safer to drive a car at higher speeds with less need to pay attention to the street.[12] This means a road less safe for pedestrians or bicyclists—and a road less hospitable to housing. "Increasing the safety of a car or road simply encourages drivers to take greater risks. Drivers are willing to take a certain amount of risk in exchange for the benefit of faster travelling time. . . . The new safety features lull the driver into a false sense of security. Vigilance, concentration, and attentiveness wane. . . . The most successful measures in reducing accidents may be those which force drivers to drive at speeds that are clearly below safety limits of the car and road."[13] Is it any wonder that decades of designing forgiving roads has given us so many drivers with declining driving skills, reckless behavior, and inattentiveness?

While research confirms that crashes are more common when roads are congested, studies have found that the crashes are less severe on the congested roads because of lower car speeds, perhaps resulting in fewer injuries or deaths on roads that are congested.[14]

THE RIGHT QUESTIONS TO ASK TRAFFIC ENGINEERS

If we want a more walkable lifestyle, we need to question traffic engineers who propose to modify a road, not meekly acquiesce to their roadway "improvement" plans. Too often, such plans are single-mindedly focused on improving conditions for high-speed car travel, which inevitably degrades the quality of life—particularly for compact, walkable areas. We can ask questions like these:

What is the *intent* of the road modifications? Is it simply to move a larger number of cars through our town at higher speeds (thereby degrading the viability of our in-town homes and small retailers)?

Will the new road be safer for pedestrians and bicyclists, or will it just improve motorist safety at higher speeds? (Usually, the unspoken intent is to create safer high-speed travel for cars, which provides the engineer with the moral high ground. Who could be against safety?)

What design speed is being used for the road? (For livability and people-first design, the design speed for in-town streets should be as low as possible.)

What design vehicle is being assumed? If it is to accommodate large buses, trucks, or emergency vehicles, how common will such vehicles be? (Designing for the typically rare large vehicle is worst-case-scenario planning that generally results in higher average vehicle speeds which, from a life-safety point of view, will cause more injury and death than a monster fire truck shaving a few seconds off an emergency call—car crashes are much more common than fires.)

What harm is being corrected? (A community may want to rethink a plan to spend large amounts of public dollars simply to save a few motorists a few seconds, particularly if the change will worsen livability along the street. Perhaps the community is more interested in a pleasant street than in addressing, say, congestion from a once-a-year sporting event "problem.")

CHANGING OUR SPEED EXPECTATIONS

To encourage us to be alert drivers (and stop chatting on our cell phones), streets need features such as trees, on-street parking, buildings at the sidewalk, and narrow travel lanes. "When [on-street] parked vehicles impede residential traffic, approaching vehicles often yield and then proceed with caution. In part, designs that encourage this kind of cautious driver behavior result in reduced speed, greater attention on the part of drivers to conflict, and, thus, safer streets."[15]

If we want drivers to slow down, we need to change the *expectation* that we should be able to drive fast. If we design the great majority of streets in our community for slow car travel, motorists over time will expect to drive slowly; a bonus will be a significant reduction in road rage (and related hostile driving) on these streets. So a critical strategy is to design nearly all streets for slow speeds, community-wide, especially residential streets—which are sensitive anyway, because they are the places where we most expect children, seniors, and pets to be, and where people in their homes are bothered by the noise of high-speed car travel. We need to slow cars on arterials, collectors, and local residential streets to change the motorists' expectations. Road rage and fast driving are not inevitable.

For several decades, American motorists have been conditioned to believe that streets allow safe high-speed driving, which encourages them to drive at higher speeds. If calming is applied only in portions of a community, the expectations will remain that most driving can be at high speed. When the expectation remains that high-speed driving is provided for, motorists tend to be enraged when they face the infrequent calming designs in a community. Only when the calming is applied community-wide can motorist expectations change so that slower speeds seem the norm, and the calming is therefore expected and accepted.

An emerging, exciting way to design communities for people instead of cars is through traffic-calming strategies.

WHAT IS TRAFFIC CALMING?

Traffic-calming designs, whose main goal is to reduce vehicle speeds, reduce drive-through traffic, and make motorists more attentive, give top priority to pedestrians, then bicycles, then public transit, and then autos—the reverse of the contemporary traffic-planning approach.

Livable cities strive to reduce traffic impacts to encourage social interaction, create a sense of place, reduce pollution and noise, create vibrant and festive pedestrian areas, and increase our comfort in public places—that is, to restore the pleasure of a quality public realm. Designing streets to reduce vehicle speeds and drive-through traffic is one traffic-calming strategy planners in Europe, and increasingly in the United States, are using. Another is redesigning streets to allow for more on-street parking, landscaping, and pedestrian activity. Further, planners are mixing land uses so that homes are close enough to shops, schools, and work sites to make cars less necessary. A final strategy gaining popularity is reducing the amount of, and increasing the charges for, auto parking.[16]

Now to specifics. The average speed of cars on many neighborhood streets and other minor roads is dangerously fast. Only in older neighborhoods with old-fashioned street designs and on major streets with traffic congestion do we still see lower—and safer—average speeds. We have been so good at providing for fast, unobstructed travel by car that we have seriously undermined the use of public transit, walking, and bicycling, not to mention the viability of in-town living. The reasons people frequently give in surveys asking why they don't ride bikes, for instance, are "danger," "road conditions," and "lack of facilities."[17]

The Federal Highway Administration identifies traffic calming as one of the more cost-effective ways to promote pedestrian and bicycle use in urban and suburban areas, where walking and bicycling are often hazardous and uncomfortable. By improving the quality of urban neighborhoods, traffic controls can also help reverse the flight of the middle class from the city.

Figure 6.1
Traffic Circle

Source: Photograph by the Author

To redesign streets or parking lots to slow down and "discipline" cars and make streets amenable for mixed use rather than for cars only, traffic-calming strategies include a number of physical designs. Some of the more common tools are traffic circles (figure 6.1), roundabouts (figure 6.2), speed tables (figure 6.3), on-street parking, narrow travel lanes, fewer travel lanes, traffic diverters, sidewalk bulb-outs, smaller turning radii at intersections, and elevated/textured/brick crosswalks that serve as speed tables.

Well known for its traffic-calming efforts in recent years, Portland, Oregon, has a "skinny streets" program for new residential areas: 20 feet wide with parking on one side, or 26 feet wide with parking on both sides. The city has found that such streets help maintain neighborhood character, reduce construction costs, save vegetation, reduce stormwater runoff, improve traffic safety, and make it possible to use scarce land for other than motor vehicle purposes.[18] The Portland Fire Department has discovered that skinny streets provide adequate access for emergency vehicles. (It has been noted that it would be more economical to purchase more modestly sized fire trucks that fit local streets than to build all streets to meet the needs of the largest size trucks.) Similarly, in California, studies in Berkeley show that traffic-control devices had little or no effect on police emergency response time, and Palo Alto found that bicycle boulevard barriers had not impaired police and fire emergency response.

Figure 6.2
Roundabout

Source: Photograph by the Author

Figure 6.3
Speed Table

Source: Photograph by the Author

Portland finds that traffic circles are most effective when constructed in a series; sometimes these are also located in the middle of a block. Circles not only have cut driving speeds but also have significantly reduced the number of accidents—by 50 to 90 percent when compared to two-way and four-way stop signs and traffic signals—because they reduce the number of conflict points. Seattle likes circles so much that the city has, in recent years, been building about 30 each year.[19]

Speed humps also reduce vehicle speeds and at the same time reduce accident rates, or at the least do not increase them, according to the Institute of Traffic Engineers (ITE).[20] Humps cause drivers little or no discomfort if we are going less than 25 mph, and they need to be spaced close enough to each other so that we cannot speed from one to the next. The ITE has found that despite concerns about liability, vehicle damage, and emergency vehicle impacts, these problems have not occurred or have been found to be insignificant when considering the positive effects of humps.

In fact, such modest physical reconfiguration of streets has proven the only reliable and cost-effective way to slow and control traffic.[21] Despite the conventional wisdom, neither stop signs nor posted speed limits affect overall traffic speeds or control speeding.[22]

However, humps—while effective in slowing motor vehicles—must be used with extreme caution. Humps are often excessively used because they are cheap yet effective. They can divert speeders to other streets, and can excessively slow emergency responders. They can be uncomfortable for transit users. Almost always, narrowing a street with bulb-outs, chicanes, raised medians, or traffic circles is preferable.

Our dangerously large intersections need to be redesigned. The traditional street corner has a modest 15-foot radius or less, which usually is enough to slow us down when we're making a turn[23] and also shortens the distance that a pedestrian must walk to get across the street.

Traffic-calming strategies also help reduce neighborhood noise pollution. This is because, at higher speeds, every 12 to 15 miles per hour increase adds another 4 to 5 decibels of noise.[24] From a distance of 48 feet, a car traveling at 56 miles per hour makes 10 times more noise than a car traveling at 31 miles per hour. Reducing average speed from 25 miles per hour to 12 miles per hour reduces noise levels by 14 decibels; that is, the car is 10 times quieter.

Opponents of traffic calming often pooh-pooh such changes. All we need to slow down speeders, they say, is more law enforcement. Yet a city cannot afford to put a traffic cop on every street; enforcement is nearly impossible, short of a police state. Perhaps doubters can find some solace in the popular label for such features as humps—"sleeping policemen."

For those who still question the worth of making such minor modifications in our community's street design, or who still think driving fast is their inalienable right as Americans, here is one final example. In the Berlin-Moabit area of Germany, 343 square miles with a 1990 population of 3.4 million, traffic calming produced these benefits: a 50 percent increase in bicycle use, along with reductions in child accidents (66 percent), fatal accidents (57 percent), severe accidents (45 percent), pedestrian accidents (43 percent), cyclist accidents (16 percent), and traffic accident costs (16 percent).[25]

A FINAL WORD

High car speeds breed uncivil behavior, disrespect, annoyance, impatience, and anger among drivers toward pedestrians, bicyclists, public transit, and each other. Traffic calming tactics, to be effective at reducing speeds and making our communities more livable, need to be applied *community-wide.* When we as drivers know that slower speeds are the norm, we can begin to appreciate our cities and neighborhoods as enjoyable places to drive *to,* not *through.*

CHAPTER 7

Ending Our Love Affair with the Car

It's true that Germans have always had a special love affair with the car, but there's no reason you have to remain trapped in a bad and unhealthy relationship.

—Pit Klasen, an architect in Bremen, Germany

Besides bringing traffic-calming strategies to our streets and allowing traffic congestion to regulate itself, we can consider a variety of other tactics for discouraging car dependence and for encouraging compact, walkable, mixed-use development and higher residential densities in our communities. These include other disincentives for overusing cars, especially for driver-only travel, that also encourage us to adopt other ways of getting where we want to go.

Not every tactic works in every situation, although virtually all of them can succeed at least to some degree in any community. (The common wet-blanket excuse that a community is somehow "different"—that a tactic might work for someone else but not for us—often springs from a fear of change.) Nevertheless, certain factors affect their usefulness, among them population density, urban design, and land use. These manifestations of growth and development are subject to government influence, given a sufficiently broad public consensus and strong enough desire to protect (or improve) the quality of community life. When planners, citizens, and elected officials understand how these tactical measures can interact with their particular circumstances, we have the best possible chance to see the quality of our community life maintained, even enhanced, despite what sometimes seems like a tidal wave of growth and development.

Because car travel is so heavily subsidized, we drive substantially more than we would if we bore the full cost of our driving, much of which the general public pays for in the form of uncompensated air, water, and noise pollution, crashes, sprawl, the decline of downtowns, and so on. Indeed, scholars in the field of transportation research indicate that we would drive one-third to two-thirds less if these "market distortions" or "underpricing" were eliminated and we had to pay our fair share for driving. Among the many tactics being used or considered for shifting these costs back to motorists are parking fees, ridesharing, guaranteed rides home, trip reduction laws, gasoline taxes, congestion fees, and high-occupancy vehicle lanes.[1]

PARKING: CASH-OUT PROGRAMS, PARKING ALLOWANCES, AND PARKING FEES

Excess parking promotes undesirable levels of solo car travel, makes communities less walkable and less safe, is more costly to businesses, promotes urban sprawl, and degrades an area's appearance. Our major parking problem today is that developers provide *too much.* Reversing the conventional approach of the past several decades—that local government require developers to provide *at least* "X" number of spaces per given building size—communities have begun instead to set a *maximum.* (We can counter concerns that a developer might provide insufficient parking if there were no minimum by pointing out that a business person, developer, or lending institution would not cut its own throat by providing too little parking.)

Cities such as Eugene, Oregon, Cambridge, Massachusetts, and Gainesville, Florida, have changed their zoning codes to establish maximum instead of minimum parking requirements for new development. Seattle is now thinking about expanding downtown maximum parking rules beyond downtown to promote transit-oriented development near transit stations for a new rail line.[2]

Many traffic analysts agree that "market-based pricing of parking would be the single most effective strategy for reducing parking," as a U.S. Environmental Protection Agency policy analyst states flatly.[3] "If parking were priced at market levels, a predictable reduction in demand is to be expected. This would result in both less driving and significantly lower building costs . . . less land would be devoted to parking." This is, of course, what we would expect, since when parking is free, we are happy to drive our car and park somewhere for even the most trivial trips. Therefore, when parking is priced, folks are less likely to drive and park at a drugstore a block away in order to buy a roll of film. They'll still buy the film, but they will give some thought to, say, walking or bicycling. So when we don't pay to park, lots of parking spaces are taken up by these kinds of low-value trips. No wonder it always seems so difficult to find a parking space! Estimates show that nationwide, priced parking would reduce auto commute miles by 76 billion miles per year, save 4.5 billion gallons of gas, and reduce the amount of parking needed by 17 percent.[4]

Studies in the mid-1990s indicated that 25 percent fewer drivers drive alone when parking at work is not free, and that car travel to work drops by 19 percent when employee-paid parking replaces free parking.[5] In other words, about one-quarter to one-fifth of those of us who drive to work are able to choose a different way to get to work, and that way to work is less costly than paying for a parking space. Free parking thus not only encourages car transportation by those who have travel choices but also is widely recognized as the main obstacle to ridesharing.[6]

Still, 94 percent of us who commute by car enjoy free parking, a tax-exempt subsidy worth $31.5 billion a year that increases car commuting by 15 to 25 percent.[7]

A free parking space represents an employee benefit worth about $1,000 per year, on average. Free parking has been called "an invitation to drive to work alone." In downtown Los Angeles, "employer-paid parking ... reduced the average variable cost of driving to work ... by 62 percent. Everyone would call it an environmental outrage if an employer offered all employees free gasoline as a subsidy for driving to work, but employer-paid parking provided these commuters an even bigger subsidy for driving to work."[8]

To move away from the enticement employees have to drive alone to work, employers can instead give employees a "transportation allowance" of, say, $100 per month; the employee can use that money to pay for a parking space or pocket most of it by commuting by bus or car pool, or keep it all and bike or walk to work. California legislation requires companies with at least 50 employees to provide this program.[9] When Los Angeles County in the early 1990s replaced free parking for its employees with a $70 per month transportation allowance, parking in county lots declined 40 percent. Studies that included thousands of commuters across the country found that a $30 per month allowance reduces parking demand by an average of 27 percent.[10]

For example, when CH2M Hill moved into new offices in the Seattle suburb of Bellevue, Washington, the engineering firm offered its 430 employees $40 per month if they walked, bicycled, carpooled or took transit to work, or free parking if they drove alone. "The firm's drive-alone rate declined from 89 percent to 54 percent and stayed there, while biking or walking increased from 1 percent to 17 percent. With parking demand down by 39 percent, the firm's problem of too many parkers for too few spaces disappeared. This approach reduced costs to the company and reduced traffic and pollution, while increasing tax revenue.[11]

Parking and transportation allowances accomplish the same goal: fewer car trips. The U.S. Department of Transportation estimates that we could save 4.5 billion gallons of gasoline a year if the IRS allowed employers to give each employee a tax-free $100 transportation allowance as part of a parking cash-out program, a savings significantly higher than that offered by a shift to alternative fuels such as ethanol.[12] A cash-out program can reduce auto commuting by 10 to 40 percent.[13] Parking cash-out programs and other forms of parking pricing programs tend to be the most effective tactics for reducing car trips—particularly drive-alone trips.[14]

And of course we can replace free parking with parking for a fee. One study found that employer-provided free parking convinces 27 percent of all commuters to switch from other forms of travel to cars, and that 41 percent of all solo drivers with free parking drive to work because of the free parking.[15] Only 2 percent of workers use public transit if their jobs are located beyond walking distance of a public transit stop and they receive free parking at work.[16]

There is some agreement that, if our goal is to encourage people to ride public transit, the most effective tactics are both making less free parking available and charging (or increasing) parking fees.[17] A case in point is Gainesville, Florida, where bus ridership fell yearly from 1990 through 1996, then rose by 74 percent in 1997 and 1998—September 1998 ridership was 184 percent higher than in September 1996. The main reasons for the increase: limiting, priced parking on the University of Florida campus. (Other reasons include providing more direct, frequent bus service to the campus, and including a bus pass in student fees.)

Charging meaningful parking fees, not raising residential densities, is the key to discouraging car trips and encouraging transit, walking, or bike trips, claims one civil engineer.[18] In San Francisco, 95 percent of workers whose employers charged for parking and offered public transit vouchers commuted by public transit.[19] Extremely high parking fees have been remarkably effective at the University of California–Davis in persuading commuters to ride bikes instead of drive.[20]

RIDESHARING AND CARPOOLING

A good example of the need for pairing tactics that discourage driver-only trips and encourage travel choice is the finding that financial parking incentives are essential to persuade the maximum number of people to share rides.[21] When a firm in California started charging $30 per month for parking, solo driving dropped from 90 percent to 45 percent, while car-pooling jumped from 6 percent to 48 percent.[22] Although rideshare incentives have a difficult time competing with free parking, a federal study of employer ride-sharing programs found that vehicle trips declined by an average of 20 percent when the program was introduced.[23]

In the mid 1990s, carpooling was much more common for shopping, recreation, and other purposes than for work; occurred mostly on multipurpose trips; and was most efficient when destinations were accessible to each other.[24]

GUARANTEED RIDE HOME

Communities that adopt "guaranteed ride home" programs assure employees a motor vehicle will be available should they have a trip need while at work, such as a family emergency, that they cannot make by walking, bicycling, or public transit.

"The Albuquerque SunTran's Guaranteed Ride Home (GRH) Program is offered to commuters that use any form of alternate transportation at least three times a week. Monthly bus pass purchasers are automatically registered for GRH. Commuters who use other forms of travel can register on-line [and the] service can be used up to five times a year for personal illness, family illness, unscheduled overtime or any other emergency that requires commuters to leave work or school." Similar programs exist in San Luis Obispo County, California; San Francisco; Montgomery County, Maryland; Denver; and Bellevue, Washington; and at Xerox in Palo Alto, California; Pennsylvania State University; and Hughes Aircraft in Tucson.[25]

In one university city survey, the "guaranteed ride home" service proved the most popular incentive cited for shifting from car trips to another form of travel—39 percent of employees and 28 percent of students chose this option.[26]

TRIP REDUCTION ORDINANCES

A community trip reduction ordinance usually requires employers, new residential developments, or both to reduce driver-only trips by means such as alternative work schedules, parking cash-out, employer-facilitated ridesharing (vanpools and carpools), bus fare subsidies, telecommuting, and "proximate commuting."

The most effective trip reduction ordinances—a form of transportation-demand management—include both incentives for traveling by other means and disincentives for driving alone, for example, increased costs for such driving, reduced parking space, and traffic calming. Disincentives last longer, as motorists who often lose enthusiasm for fleeting educational incentive campaigns are discouraged by the ongoing message from prices and travel conditions.[27]

Most of these ordinances set a trip reduction target and leave the choice of reduction tactics to the employer or developer. For example, Sacramento, California, assigns trip reduction credits to various tactics based on their estimated effectiveness, then requires the employer or developer to institute measures to achieve a minimum number of credits. Tucson, Phoenix, and many cities and counties in Washington and California have adopted car travel reduction programs that require larger employers to reduce the percentage of employees commuting alone. Most such ordinances don't fine employers or developers who fail to meet the target but levy fines only if they fail to submit a trip reduction plan or periodic performance report.[28]

In proximate commuting, an organization with multiple locations in a community allows employees to move to a work location closer to their home. In a recent Washington State demonstration project, only 17 percent of the employees at 14 branches of the organization worked at the branch closest to their homes. Employees were given the option of swapping jobs with employees who worked in a branch closer to home. At the end of the 15-month trial, the average commute distance for employees at the 30 branches had dropped 17 percent.[29]

GASOLINE TAXES

According to the federal Office of Technology Assessment, every 100 percent increase in the price of gasoline reduces car miles traveled by 10 to 50 percent. That the price of gas is connected to sprawl seems to be reflected in Western Europe: "It is no coincidence that European nations that exact high fuel taxes from motorists also have a balanced job and housing growth, limited sprawl, and heavily patronized public transit services."[30] Europe also uses gas tax revenue for a number of nontransportation social goods and services, unlike our practice in the United States.

In this country, gas taxes are the only tax revenue source dedicated to a special interest group: car owners. (Admittedly, there are a lot of us.) But gas taxes pay only a small fraction of auto costs. The rest is paid by all of us—driver and nondriver, and mostly by local governments, who routinely raid property and sales tax revenue to subsidize car travel. Among the losers are social services such as recreation, libraries, culture, landscaping, and fire services.[31]

Raising gas taxes would increase the equity between motorists and nonmotorists, especially the poor.[32] A gas tax that would cover all of the costs of car travel would be $5 to $14 per gallon.[33] Such an increase would be, to say the least, difficult politically—what official is going to campaign on raising gas taxes? Yet it could be made reasonably palatable by tax *shifting*—that is, reducing property and sales taxes proportionally and concurrently with the new tax increase.[34] (The tax-shifting concept supports moving more of our tax burden to things we want less of, such as pollution and resource depletion, and reducing or eliminating taxes for things we want more of, such as paychecks and business enterprises.)

In the 1980s, an elected official in California in fact called for a 50-cent per gallon federal tax to be phased in over five years. He argued that such a tax would help balance the federal budget, reduce oil imports, reduce the risk of economic recessions and high unemployment, reduce the trade deficit, reduce inflation, lower interest rates, provide an incentive for automakers to build more fuel-efficient cars, and reduce auto emissions.[35] The federal tax was never phased in. Harvard economist N. Gregory Mankiw has recommended a tax shift scheme where a 50-cent increase in the gas tax would be coupled with a 10 percent decrease in federal income taxes. He argues that such a strategy would increase economic growth, reduce traffic congestion, improve road safety, and reduce the risk of global warming. Mankiw says "this may be the closest thing to a free lunch that economics has to offer."[36]

There is statistical support, however, showing that because parking fees can take into account congested times of day or congested facilities, using them reduces the number of miles people drive much more effectively than raising gasoline taxes, which are unable to take such congestion into account.[37]

PLANNED CONGESTION AND CONGESTION PRICING

"Most people will not walk or bicycle or take the bus unless driving is too expensive or inconvenient or traffic is too frustrating," a Florida transportation study notes, and in Perth, Australia, "17 percent of all bus riders would shift to car use if road congestion declined."[38]

Among the benefits of "planned congestion" (that is, deliberately "doing nothing" in the face of congestion) we can count the money saved by not increasing road capacity, with which we can improve the transportation system for bicycling, walking, and public transit. Meanwhile, the "time tax" of congestion will encourage some motorists to switch to other forms of travel. At the same time, the higher trip costs due to congestion will discourage residents and businesses from locating in dispersed, low-density areas.

Furthermore, planned congestion is politically easier to implement than the preferred approach of congestion pricing. And with the improved quality of alternatives to driving alone brought about by planned congestion, it becomes politically easier to implement congestion pricing—the most efficient congestion management tactic.[39]

Congestion pricing imposes a fee for using congested roads during rush hour periods. The goal is to shift drivers to alternative times, alternative routes, or to noncar travel, and the fee varies depending on the time of travel and the location, which discourages low-value single-occupant travel rather than all travel. We have options: pay the fee at rush hour, avoid rush-hour periods, avoid congested roads, or travel by another means. "Motorists driving through city rush-hour traffic would be charged the highest congestion fees. The same trip made during the early hours of the morning in uncongested streets would be assessed a much smaller charge or no charge at all."[40] A congestion fee averaging 19 cents per mile during a congested period could reduce total vehicle trips by a little over 3 percent. Congestion delay, however, would decline 32 percent.[41] The fee is usually assessed using a bar code on vehicles and collected through the mail, a system much less costly than toll booths. To discourage single-occupant travel further, communities can promote other forms of travel with revenue from congestion fees.[42]

Charging motorists directly for road use and road modification sends a clear market signal that enables us to accurately assess whether it is worthwhile to make a car trip on a particular route, or at a particular time of day. With subsidized car use, we have no obvious economic incentive to avoid, say, low-value car trips on major streets during rush hour. Further, charging drivers congestion fees to pay for road widening is not only more economically efficient but also more equitable than indirect funding (such as property or sales taxes) because the process tests user demand. If we are unwilling to pay the fees necessary to fund the widening, it is fair to conclude that the widening is not justified. In addition, the fee means that those who do not drive (or who do not drive during congested times) avoid subsidizing those who do, through such revenues as gas taxes or property taxes.[43]

Looked at another way, if we choose to drive less, we typically receive only a tiny portion of the savings that result, the few pennies from reducing our per-trip fuel use.[44] Avoiding a $3 payment for not driving during rush hour is probably more meaningful to us as individuals than the benefit that the entire community shares from our choice.

A number of economists hold that urban traffic congestion is nearly impossible to solve without some form of congestion pricing. Yet advocating the use of this tactic, the most efficient and effective way to discourage low-value car trips, is political suicide in America, and unsurprisingly, the tactic is not in use anywhere in the country.[45]

HIGH-OCCUPANCY TOLL AND VEHICLE LANES

Reserving traffic lanes for cars occupied by more than one person reduces driver-only car trips when those lanes replace existing "general purpose" travel lanes. These high-occupancy vehicle (HOV) lanes cut peak-period vehicle trips on individual roads by 2 to 10 percent;[46] when a barrier physically separates the lane from others, trips drop as much as 30 percent. Nationwide, such lanes carry about half as many cars as regular lanes;[47] to use them more efficiently, some communities are considering opening them to single-occupant cars after collecting a congestion fee.

A variation on HOV lanes and congestion pricing is high-occupancy toll (HOT) lanes, which give us as drivers three options: drive for free on a congested lane, shift to a carpool or transit without being delayed by congestion, or pay a toll and drive without congestion.[48] Unlike "planned congestion" as a strategy to ration highway space, such lanes generate revenues that can be used for public projects such as transit improvements.[49]

Some commentators urge caution here, warning that HOV lanes increase auto dependence and car trips by temporarily reducing congestion and in fact support driver-only vehicle trips during rush hour.[50] Others caution that HOV lanes occasionally are "Trojan horses" for widening roads in the sense that supporters of widening may join with car pooling advocates in supporting the establishment of HOV lanes, knowing that such lanes will, in all likelihood, be little used, breed resentment in the minds of drive-alone travelers, and thereby result in political pressure to eventually convert the HOV lane into a general purpose lane.

TRAFFIC-UNFRIENDLY DESIGN

Some relatively obvious ways we can make our community's roads more unfriendly to low-value car trips are to stop adding travel lanes or turn lanes, to avoid increasing green-light time for congested roads, and to avoid synchronizing signal lights.

Adding travel and right- and left-turn lanes is clearly counterproductive if we're trying to reduce car trips.[51] They increase vehicle speeds and make car travel more convenient and comfortable, increase road width, and thus make walking, biking, and bus riding more dangerous, unpleasant, and inconvenient. Increasing green time on traffic signals has the same results.

That synchronizing signal lights helps improve air quality and reduce gas consumption, as commonly claimed, seems unsupported by studies. Research does seem to show that reducing delays for drivers (which synchronization achieves) increases both the number and length of vehicle trips to a degree that would outweigh any minor air pollution or fuel efficiency gains due to improved traffic flow.[52] A better approach is to time traffic signals to accommodate bicycle or public transit speeds to encourage these forms of travel. In addition, an all-red phase after green and yellow in the traffic light sequence gives walkers and slower-moving bicyclists time to clear the intersection.[53]

CHAPTER 8

Getting Back on Our Feet

A good sustainability and quality of life indicator: The average amount of time spent in a car.

—Paul Bedford

The paradox of transportation in the late 20th Century is that while it became possible to travel to the moon, it also became impossible, in many cases, to walk across the street.

—Joell Vanderwagen

To achieve a better community—a livable, walkable community—we need to not only end our love affair with cars but also move, literally and figuratively, to other ways of getting around. We need positive, effective incentives to walk, bike, or use the bus.

But a tactic that encourages travel diversity may succeed only if we simultaneously use multiple tactics that discourage car use (see chapter 7). For example, in suburban America, reduced bus fares attract a significant number of new riders only if some or all of the following occur at the same time: access to buses improves, residential density near bus stops goes up, traffic congestion grows, and free, abundant parking is converted to more modest amounts of market-priced parking—all tactics that elected officials can make happen.

The best way to get to the walkable community many of us strive for is to adopt the most effective tactics for reducing dependence on cars *in combination*. For many communities today, the important strategic, political issue is getting the bus, bike, and pedestrian infrastructure in place *before* they are both essential and substantially more costly to build or install.

ACCESSIBILITY FOR BICYCLING AND WALKING

Even when a community is compact enough to allow us to get around conveniently by bicycle or on foot, fences, walls, ditches, and cul-de-sacs may cancel out this proximity advantage, for example, separating a school or shopping center from nearby neighborhoods (figure 8.1). For this reason, some define sprawl as "any development pattern with poor accessibility among related land uses."[1] A development separated by barriers from nearby land uses, in other words, is a kind of sprawl even within the urban core, because it urges us to make all trips by car—even extremely short trips—and auto dependence is a key determinant of sprawl.

To combat this kind of dependence, pedestrian and bicycle path connections should be created between schools, shopping areas, parks, and neighborhoods, including connectors at the ends of cul-de-sacs. These connections substantially reduce travel distances for bicyclists and pedestrians, which increases the convenience of those forms of travel.

Because the main disincentives to bicycling, other than weather, are traffic safety and lack of bicycle routes, greenways are important as safe, cost-effective facilities to reduce car use. These popular bicycle/pedestrian paths, separate from the street and sidewalk system, typically follow a creek or an abandoned railroad right-of-way; because of the distance involved, most attract more bicyclists than walkers. The three keys to making such trails useful for transportation are accessibility from home to the trail (including its convenience to major destinations and a large

Figure 8.1
Putting Humpty Back Together Again to Create More Access

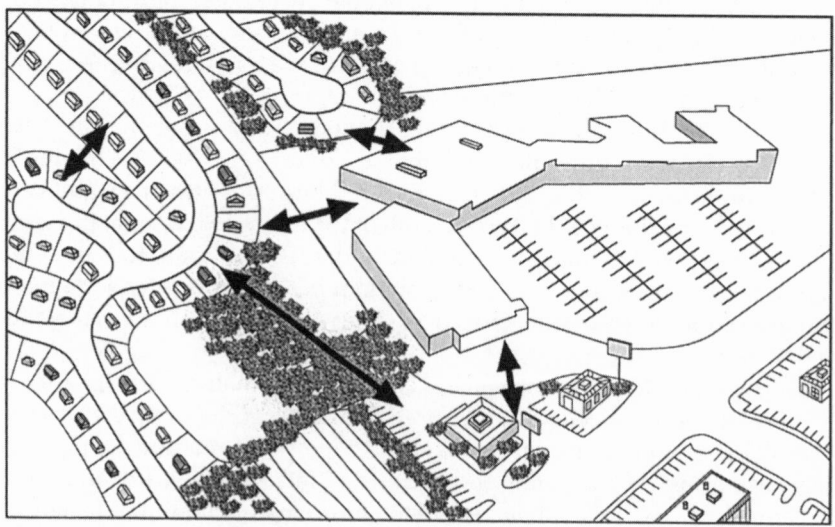

number of access points along the way), an on-going maintenance program, and trail safety.

Of the people who had bicycled recreationally at least once in the year before the survey was taken, 53 percent said they would commute to work by bicycle if safe, separate paths were available.[2] Separate paths such as greenways and rail trails may recruit new commuting bicyclists; the Burke-Gilman Trail in Seattle, for example, in 1992 saw greater recreational and commuter bicycle traffic, as did the city overall.[3] Along the urban-oriented Pinellas Rail Trail in Pinellas County, Florida, 30 percent of trips were for utilitarian purposes such as shopping or commuting to work; most or all of these would have been vehicle trips had it not been for the trail.[4]

Pedestrian-friendly streets and intersections also reduce car trips. City streets can again be places for casual socializing, transacting business, leisurely strolling, and recreation. Great streets are routes that invite us to walk along them comfortably and safely (see chapter 9).

BICYCLE FRIENDLINESS

In many cities, the most effective way to use bicycle travel improvement funds is to concentrate on projects that fill critical gaps in the bicycle system or provide connections between major trip generators. In Eugene, Oregon, a successful gap-filling project was adding a "greenway bicycle bridge" that cut car trips by at least 665 a week; 30 percent of the bicyclists surveyed said they would not have made the trip by bicycle if the bridge had not been built.[5]

We can make these kinds of improvements to complete bicycling corridors that have small sections where bicyclists feel unsafe. A small stretch of road without a bike lane, for example, can discourage bicyclists from using the streets at all, even if most streets are designed for safe bicycling.

Bike Lanes

Almost none of us (about 5 percent) will bike to work, to shop, or to a park unless we can travel on in-street bike lanes or separate bike paths, so it is no wonder that cities with higher levels of bicycle commuting have 70 percent more bikeways per roadway mile and six times more bike lanes per arterial mile than cities with lower levels of bicycle commuting.[6] Of the 46 percent of American adults who bicycled at least once in the past year, 46 percent would occasionally commute to work by bicycle if their communities had safe places to ride.[7]

A bonus for in-street bike lanes is their benefit to pedestrians. Bike lanes allow motorists more "swing turning width" onto and off of side streets, which means we can use less street space for turning at intersections and thus cut pedestrian crossing time and distance by 60 percent, in this case by keeping the intersection modest in size.[8] Downtowns and other neighborhood centers with speed limits of 20 to 25 mph have less need for bike lanes, and the need is minimal when speeds are 15 to 20 mph. At such slow speeds, bicyclists can safely share the lane with cars. (Indeed, the speed difference of various forms of travel on a route—the "speed differential"—determines their ability to coexist peacefully on a street or path. If bicycle and pedestrian speeds differ too widely on a path, pedestrians feel uncomfortable; high car speed on a street makes both pedestrians and bicyclists feel unsafe.)

PUBLIC TRANSIT AND TRANSIT-ORIENTED DEVELOPMENT

Generally, the intent of a transit-oriented development (TOD) or transit village is a transit stop or station surrounded by relatively high-density residential and commercial development, which transitions toward lower densities in concentric rings further from the center of the TOD. Examples of TODs include the Sunnyside Transit Village near downtown Portland, Oregon; TODs in Redmond, Renton, Seattle, and Shoreline, Washington; and SkyTrain stations in Vancouver, British Columbia.[9]

To promote use of transit, cities sometimes set a goal that strives to locate much of the region's new housing within a quarter mile of a transit route. To help create transit villages, former California governor Pete Wilson signed a bill allowing higher-density zoning around transit stations and use of redevelopment funds for nearby housing. Similarly, Portland, Maine, has adopted a plan calling for higher densities and mixed-use development in areas served by public transit.[10]

A Portland, Oregon, study found that compared to building a highway beltway, a TOD community would see 22 percent fewer home-based car trips; 20 percent of the workers in a TOD would use transit (compared to 9 percent in a conventional development); and the number of cars per household would be 11 percent lower.[11] A relatively large number of TOD workers would also walk or carpool.[12]

For TODs to be successful, it is crucial that they avoid common, auto-oriented design pitfalls. They must mix residences with offices, services, and retail; they must provide a compact, human-scaled, walkable ambience; they must be located to serve important destinations; and they must be good destinations in their own right—in other words, they must be a *place.* Deadly to creating a TOD that is a walkable place in its own right is the common blunder of creating a vast sea of asphalt parking, which usually deadens the TOD. With large parking areas, it is typically impossible to establish convenient walking distances from nearby residential areas to transit pickup points. In sum, the "three Ds" are important TOD ingredients. The TOD must have *diversity* of uses, sufficient *densities* of residences and commercial activity, and proper, people-oriented *design*. An important advantage that TODs provide over the suburban lifestyle is choice: unlike most suburbs, the well-designed TOD provides housing, shopping, and travel diversity.[13]

Bus Fares and Transit Passes

For cities with substantial highway systems, large subsidies for car travel, and dispersed, low-density development, "rubber-tire" public transit (including decentralized bus and van service) appears to be the only viable public transit option.[14] The question then becomes, How can we get people to ride the bus?

How about subsidizing the bus system to the extent that we can offer it free? Most riders who are recruited to the bus by nothing more than a free fare are low-income persons without cars and with little other transportation choice, that is, free fares alone do not go far toward reducing car trips. For fare-free service to reduce car ownership (or at least car use) and to encourage people to live in central locations, we have to pair high-quality bus service with car-parking supply restrictions or priced parking.

Fare-free bus service can be cost effective for some communities. For example, giving a free bus pass to University of Florida students would cost $235 per year each, compared to the $550 it costs the university for a parking space, including maintenance.[15]

When Boulder, Colorado, adopted a bus-riding incentive program, the $18,000 start-up cost in 1989 was less than the cost of building one downtown parking space. The city expected a 10 percent participation rate in the first year. It turned out to be 25 percent. New shuttle buses and discounted public transit passes helped increase bus ridership by 24 percent from 1992 to 1994. In 1992, during "Alternative Transportation Month," a local hospital saved 35,000 auto commuter miles using the program. University of Colorado students voted to increase their student activity fee by $10 so their student ID card would entitle them to free bus rides.[16]

When the city added an Eco-Pass program that gave free bus passes to employees of many employers in the city, regional bus ridership from 1994 through 1998 rose an average of 6 percent annually and an average of 4 percent for local ridership.[17] The program also includes a free package delivery service for downtown shoppers who use the bus, which encourages people not to drive to work even on days when they need to shop.[18] To induce businesses to subsidize public transit instead of parking, the Eco-Pass program reimburses 350 employers up to a quarter of their cost of purchasing annual bus passes for their employees. The number of Eco-Passes from 1996 through 2000 has remained stable at about 60,000 issued—Boulder's population in 2000 was about 100,000—over half to

University of Colorado students, faculty, and staff.[19] Vehicle miles traveled have increased in Boulder at less than one-fifth the rate of the region.[20] Other cities that have offered free employee bus passes include San Francisco, Milwaukee, and Denver.[21]

Unfortunately, IRS rules state that employers can provide only $22 per month tax free to employees who commute by bus. Free parking, on the other hand, is not taxed.[22] An IRS rule that assigned an income value to what is now free parking would help encourage commuters to switch to noncar travel.

CHAPTER 9

Designing for People

The 20th Century was about getting around. The 21st Century will be about staying in a place worth staying in.
—Jim Kunstler

The most important task of the urbanist is controlling size.
—David Mohney

As sociology professor and planning consultant Ray Oldenburg points out in *The Great Good Place: Cafes, Coffee Shops, Community Centers, Beauty Parlors, General Stores, Bars, Hangouts, and How They Get You Through the Day*, segregation, isolation, compartmentalization, and sterilization seem to be today's guiding principles for community growth and renewal. Desirable experiences occur in places conducive to them, Oldenburg claims, or they do not occur at all. When these places disappear, so do the positive experiences associated with them.

One way to ensure that such great good places continue to vanish is to adhere to the land development codes current in most American communities. These large, bulky, jargon-filled sets of regulations control the uses, size, siting, landscaping, and parking space for new buildings, their stormwater treatment, and the dimensions of the streets that serve them. These codes purport to contain the laws that ensure that new development projects enhance the community or at least not make it worse—in short, they seek to "protect the public health, safety, and welfare," to improve the community's overall quality of life. Yet nearly every community in America has adopted a land Development code that will, when used throughout the community for residences, offices, and shops, ensure that the community is afflicted with the worst aspects of auto-oriented urban sprawl found in Detroit, Los Angeles, Houston, or Atlanta. How can this be? Because our land development codes have come to embody the auto-oriented values we've developed over the past 50 years, and that assure a future paradise for cars and a hell for people. Nearly all of our codes, in other words, assume that there should be only one lifestyle choice: the suburban, car-oriented choice.

It is critical for us to recognize that the land development code best able to protect the broad categories of habitat—those for people, cars, and wildlife—needs at least three distinct sets of regulations for these three distinct habitats in a community. One size *does not* fit all.

It is as inappropriate to impose people-oriented, walkable standards throughout the community as it is to maintain auto-oriented standards for every setting. There will always be those who prefer the walkable urban lifestyle, the auto-oriented, suburban lifestyle, and the rural lifestyle. Each of these lifestyle choices should remain available, as long as they are made available equitably. And because each of these segments of our communities will persist, a political effort to impose one-size-fits-all standards community-wide would force elected officials to adopt watered-down, lowest-common-denominator compromises that leave no one happy— neither the car-based community, the walkable community, or the rural community.

Yet those of us seeking the walkable lifestyle are not necessarily doomed by our present land development codes to spend the twenty-first century isolated in our cars and in remote, cul-de-sac neighborhoods, victims of urban sprawl. What has begun to emerge across the country, in the face of the negative impacts of the ubiquitous suburban model, is a return to the timeless neighborhood design conventions that characterized development in the United States before World War II.

The most effective, desirable strategy is to establish *context-sensitive* community regulations that transition from walkable to auto-oriented to rural and wildlife preserve (a concept New Urbanists call a "transect" system).

For the walkable portion of the community, the leading design paradigm today is the New Urbanism. New Urbanism is a set of development practices that creates more people-oriented communities—attractive, efficient, sociable, and pedestrian friendly—at the same time that it significantly reduces car dependence. According to Duany, a leader in this design strategy: "Since its founding in 1992, New Urbanism has been the antithesis of sprawl, because it designs communities that are balanced in function; creates inclusive housing; supports home-based business; spatially defines the public realm; facilitates pedestrian accessibility; minimizes use of the car; supports transit; and builds on infill [in-town] as well as greenfield [newly developed] sites."[1]

ONE SIZE DOES NOT FIT ALL: THE TRANSECT SYSTEM

You can choose any color you want, Henry Ford notably told early car buyers, as long as it is black. (With regard to most of our communities today, Ford might say that you can have any lifestyle you want in America, as long as it is suburban.) New Urbanists are far more willing than Ford to appreciate individual taste. The transect system emphasizes lifestyle choice: land uses and building/street design are most urban, walkable, human-centered, and human-scaled at the center of a downtown or neighborhood center; the continuum becomes increasingly rural and naturalistic as the transect zones radiate out.

Each transect zone contains uses and designs that are, as New Urbanists would say, "immersive" within the zone category—that is, they mutually reinforce each other to create the transect zone character, be it urban, suburban, or rural. A transect "violation" occurs when features of different zones are mixed—an extreme illustration would be a skyscraper in a rural farming area.

Such violations point up an important problem with the "one size fits all" approach. For example, a large asphalt parking lot in the walkable downtown of a community represents a violation, because it creates unpleasant, unsafe, inconvenient, and uninteresting conditions for us as pedestrians. The same holds for a wide, high-speed street downtown. Sidewalks and street curbs might be a violation in an outlying neighborhood where most residents seek a more "rural" ambience that is degraded by such "urban" features. In other words, design features and dimensions must be matched to the lifestyle of each part of the community. Transect violations can not only tarnish an area's lifestyle but harm its property values. A location will lose potential buyers if it fails to deliver an unblemished version of the desirable qualities they seek.

What follows is an example of a transect that any community seeking to break out of the one-size-fits-all mode can embed in its development regulations. By identifying zones and their appropriate regulations, a community can protect and enhance the lifestyle sought for each zone.

First, a community must select its transect zones:

Transect Zone

TC: Town Center or Neighborhood Center Zone (community locations within the center, or heart, of a community, or near shopping or office concentrations)

SG: Suburban General Zone (residential areas surrounding the town center and neighborhood centers)

RR: Rural Reserve and Preserve Zone (outlying areas where ranchettes and farmhouses are found, as well as areas dedicated to the protection of wildlife habitat)

The transition zone between countryside and the urban city, the Suburban General Zone, encompasses the primarily suburban residential areas, the most rural parts of the city, and the countryside just beyond. Compared to the outer zones, SG, while mainly residential, has a more urban character and allows somewhat higher residential densities with a mix of housing types and a slightly greater mix of uses.

The TC zone at the urban end of the spectrum is primarily mixed use. The zone may be a small neighborhood center or a larger town center that serves more than one neighborhood.

In the TC Zone, the public realm—streets, sidewalks, and the space between facing building facades—is high quality and scaled for people, not cars. Characterized by a diversity of housing types and styles, a range of lot sizes, shade trees, public trails and sidewalks, and public parks and squares within walking distance of most or all homes, this zone creates neighborliness without compromising privacy. Distance to daily destinations is modest. Streets connect and integrate the neighborhood with the street system of the surrounding area, dispersing calmed car traffic and ensuring multiple connections to outlying destinations.

Suburban zones tend to contain single-family residences, without offices, services, or retail. Cars, fire trucks, and delivery trucks tend to be larger, as are streets, intersections, building setbacks, schools, and retailers. Back yards provide most of the social space, and garages and expansive front lawns punctuate the streetscape. These areas usually lack public open spaces where neighbors can meet and interact, and road design tends to encourage high-speed car travel. Designing for bicycles or pedestrians tends to be either overlooked or provided on a token basis for the occasional recreational bicyclist or pedestrian. Nearly all trips, no matter how insignificant, require a car. Roads are seldom connected and funnel most or all traffic onto a sparse network of collector and arterial roads. (Detailed specifications for an urban-rural transect regulatory matrix appear in Appendix A.)

THE URBAN, WALKABLE PORTIONS OF THE TRANSECT

For the urban portions of the transect, we can use the following catalog of timeless, people-oriented design principles as we restyle appropriate portions of our cities to become friendlier, more walkable, more human-scaled and livable communities.

People-Scaled Development

How big a community's features are—its buildings, blocks, signs, parking lots, and so on—indicates whether its designers had in mind mainly people or mainly cars. The large scale of billboards, for example, makes them easy to read by drivers speeding by. The same driver-friendly design holds for large parking lots, wide roads, tall street lighting, and enormous landscaped building setbacks.

People-scaled design includes building on smaller lots; mixing different types of housing with parks and commerce; keeping streets narrow, parking lots small, and light poles short; putting buildings close to the street, the sidewalk, and other buildings; having streetside entrances; and creating short street blocks and connected street networks. Such a design adds interest and character to a city's streets and keeps it from deteriorating into Anywhere, USA. When we design communities on the scale of people—pedestrians, bicyclists, shopkeepers, neighbors—a number of desirable features fall into place.

The principles of New Urbanism result in people-scaled communities. Noted architect and New Urbanist Leon Krier defined such a community in 1977 as "a neighborhood where I can buy a cup of coffee within five minutes of stepping out my front door."[2]

Neighborhoods are designed or redesigned with pedestrians in mind. (An example of this context-sensitive approach is the pedestrian-oriented "Traditional City" ordinance I drafted in 1998,[3] which establishes walkable development standards for the downtown area for the City of Gainesville—an area today recognized community-wide as pedestrian friendly.) Streets are interconnected, blocks are small, and almost any daily household need is no more than a five-minute walk away, about one-quarter mile. Homes, shops, schools, parks, workplaces, and civic buildings are interwoven; located for high visibility, civic buildings serve as landmarks, symbols, and focal points for community assembly and identity. A full range of housing types allows a mix of all age groups and income classes. Safe, pleasant, convenient bus stops discourage excessive trips to and from the neighborhood by car. This provides more transportation choices, enhances neighborliness, and reduces household transportation costs (every car a household can shed saves the equivalent of a $50,000 per year home mortgage payment, depending on interest rates).

Langdon believes a quality public realm is an essential ingredient in creating a sociable neighborhood. "Sidewalks and streets should be organized so that people will have incentives to explore their neighborhood. Houses need to treat the public areas as important, congenial places. Instead of glorifying interior and private spaces while leaving the public environment dominated by uncommunicative facades and garage doors, we need to reorient houses so that they dignify and enliven the places where neighbors and strangers come in contact with one another."[4]

In-town livability depends on a person experiencing a pleasant, walkable public realm when stepping outside. People attracted to an in-town lifestyle are looking for a high quality of life in the public realm.

Small, Defined, Accessible Neighborhoods

Neighborhoods without gates or walls represent the traditional American pattern. They are accessible, they are easy to walk or bicycle into and out of, and their residents share a desire to take responsibility for the whole community. Similarly, neighborhoods whose streets connect encourage not only walking and biking but a greater sense of community than neighborhoods whose streets end in cul-de-sacs (see chapter 2).

Since the 1950s, cul-de-sac neighborhoods have proliferated; many of us chose our homes *because* they are on a cul-de-sac. Yet connected streets significantly reduce trip distances and can reduce vehicle miles traveled within a neighborhood, compared to conventional suburban cul-de-sac designs. Connected street networks and give us more safe and pleasant routes to travel, distribute vehicle trips more evenly, and reduce congestion on collector or arterial roads. In fact, connected streets do away with the need for these high-traffic, high-speed roadways, dangerous to pedestrians and hostile to neighborhood peace of mind; connected streets reduce our use of major roads by 75 to 85 percent.[5]

In more recent years—since the late 1980s—gated subdivisions have joined cul-de-sac neighborhoods as the goal of many city dwellers, emblems of a desire for separation by income, race, economic opportunity, and land use, but motivated mainly by our fear of crime. Recent statistics suggest this fear is sometimes misplaced. "Traffic fatality rates represent dangers in the far-out suburbs that are much more severe than the danger of crime in central cities. . . . The prevailing view is that the outer suburbs are safer than cities and older suburbs, but evidence about traffic fatalities and murders suggests they are not. . . . In the 1990s, there were more than twice as many traffic fatalities across the country as there were homicides."[6] For example, "if you live in the Richmond-Petersburg metropolitan area, you are way more likely to be killed in a car wreck on a suburban/exurban road than you are to be shot by a stranger downtown."[7] In the Pacific Northwest, a 2000 study found that 1.6 percent of city residents were likely to be killed or injured by traffic accidents or crime versus 1.9 percent of suburban residents.[8]

When we live in a gated community, we are less likely to travel by bicycle, public transit, or foot because the wall or gate often substantially increases trip distances. And in such communities, because we often pay for some of our own services such as security and garbage collection, we may feel less inclined to support efforts to solve larger community problems.

One way to avoid gated streets is to forbid them in a city code. A more indirect approach is to require all streets to be publicly dedicated (except those serving limited "commercial only" areas). By default, gated streets would disappear, because it is not possible to gate public streets.

Mixed-Use Friendliness

Many of the reasons we decided, after World War II, that we must separate our homes from undesirable nonresidential activities have lost their urgency. Today, offices, shops, and industries are often unobtrusively housed in pleasantly landscaped, clean buildings rather than ugly buildings belching smoke, noxious odors, or foul sewage effluent. Today, Duany points out, if a commercial building *looks* like nearby residential buildings in terms of scale, disposition, and character, a mixed-use neighborhood can succeed without major objections from nearby homeowners.

Integrating homes, offices, and commercial development—something many cities accomplish with mixed-use zoning—adds vibrancy to communities by increasing the number of places people can meet, such as on the way to work, school, a civic event, a grocery store, a fitness center, and so on. The mix also gives children a more realistic idea of what goes on in a community apart from their usual familiar territory—parks, home, and school.

In terms of car dependency, mixed-use neighborhoods make it easier for us to accomplish a lot with just one trip; vehicle trips decrease by up to 25 percent in such circumstances, which also makes ridesharing and shared parking arrangements more feasible.[9] Walking, bicycling, and riding the bus are much more feasible for making a number of different types of trips.[10]

Along with mixing offices, residences, and stores, people-oriented design supports mixing types of housing and mixed-use buildings. Granny flats and similar ancillary dwelling spaces—carriage houses, outbuildings, and garage apartments—both provide affordable housing (especially for students and senior citizens) and encourage pedestrian and bus trips.[11] Mixed-use buildings, often with retail shops on the ground floor and offices and residences on the upper floors, add life to an area and, like granny flats and their kin, provide more affordable housing choices. Car dependency goes down, because employees of the retail establishments can live above the shops they work in. "Vertical mixing" should not place residences on the ground floor, because having users of the office or retail area walk through a residence would be, to put it mildly, disruptive. And putting shops at street level adds energy and interest for pedestrians. Mixing housing types that run the gamut of prices means a mixed-income neighborhood, and mixed-income neighborhoods reduce traffic problems: many of us can live close enough to our jobs to avoid car commuting.

Mixed-use neighborhoods, as opposed to residential-only neighborhoods, allow us to reestablish and rediscover what Oldenburg calls "third places," where people get together to develop friendships, discuss issues, and interact, in the process building a feeling of community identity. (The first and second places are home and work.) The disappearance of third places—a trend that began about the same time many of us took off for the suburbs—has been part of a decline in informal public life in the United States. Old neighborhoods and their cafes, taverns, and corner stores fell to urban renewal, freeway expansion, and newer neighborhoods zoned residential only.

Third places are the bedrock of community life, according to Oldenburg. Distinctive, informal gathering places, they make us feel at home; they nourish relationships and a diversity of human contact; they help create a sense of place and community; they evoke civic pride; they provide numerous opportunities for serendipity; they promote companionship; they allow people to relax and unwind after work; they are socially binding; they encourage sociability instead of isolation; they make life more colorful; and they enrich public life and democracy.

Here are Oldenberg's criteria for a well-functioning third place. Entry, and the food or drink inside, must be free or quite inexpensive. A great many people should be able to walk there easily from home; it becomes part of their routine, and a number of people regularly go each day. It should be a place where we feel welcome and comfortable, and where it is easy to enter into conversation. We should expect to find both old and new friends each time we go.

Contemporary examples of third places and other forms of social gathering spots are region-serving facilities such as farmers markets, governmental offices, major cultural facilities including performing arts centers, major walking and bicycling trails, convention centers, festivals, celebrations, outdoor concerts, large and active parks, post offices, and, increasingly, large retail establishments. These places are so effective in drawing people to a single place where they can interact with others, so essential to creating a sense of community, that the State of Oregon, for these reasons and others, now requires that state office buildings be located within a city rather than in outlying unincorporated areas.

One of the most visually appropriate community spaces for such important buildings is at the end of a street, an arrangement planners call a "terminated vista." Terminated vistas provide dignity and prominence to civic buildings such as post offices, libraries, city halls, churches, convention centers, and performing arts centers—the location signals that the building is a place the community values. Terminated vistas also make walking more pleasant by giving us a "goal" to walk toward, and a striking view on the way. Finally, such vistas help orient us physically in the community.[12] Nothing, according to Duany, is more satisfying in a community setting than a vista that terminates with a prominent civic building.

Like other third places, civic buildings in centrally located social spaces are usually highly accessible for the entire community, including its non-driving members, often the poor, the handicapped, children, and seniors. Also, a central location usually features a rich array of establishments that can benefit from its spillover effects, people who go to the concert or the civic center and then run other errands that are within walking distance, go to a restaurant or movie, or go shopping. Centrally located gathering places help keep downtowns from becoming irrelevant and dying ghost towns.

Absent these downtown social spaces, common quasi-gathering places for many contemporary communities are car-dependent, conventional shopping centers or malls, often ugly, sometimes failing. Before World War II, most retail and office buildings were set along tree-lined streets that featured on-street parking, with wide sidewalks that lent themselves to strolling—a pleasant, comfortable public realm where people went not only to shop or do business but also to socialize and relax. The shopping experience was vibrant, lively, and rewarding. Recently, Fred Kent, a nationally known urban designer, reported that in all his surveys of shopping districts, the biggest problems are not security issues but traffic issues—the speed of vehicles, the noise of vehicles, the congestion. "You realize that if you create less vehicle flow and slower vehicles, you create more of a sense of community and you increase the perception of safety and security."[13]

The encouraging news is that many communities today are retrofitting conventional, car-oriented shopping centers to resemble those traditional downtowns or walkable villages (figure 9.1).[14] (Appendix B, "Special Area Plan for Transforming a Conventional Center," is an example of regulations a community could enact to require such a retrofit.)

This transformation typically calls for a number of strategies: infilling buildings on the surface parking lots so that the buildings form more defined spaces, installing shade trees, retrofitting a connected grid of streets and sidewalks, and installing benches and pedestrian-oriented lighting. Some renovations include building residences in this new village or surrounding the village-type retail area with higher-density housing to enhance its vitality. Impressive retail sales in such retrofits have inspired many developers of conventional "power centers" to instead design places that mimic traditional urban main streets. ("Power centers" refers to the typical Big Box retailer strip center, anchored by a large store such as Wal-Mart or Home Depot.) When no nearby area features such urban, people-friendly amenities, a retrofitted center can outcompete other retail centers.[15]

A city that encourages the retrofitting of conventional shopping centers to function as quality walkable neighborhood centers reaps a number of rewards from the mixed uses found there (figure 9.2). Ideally, the rich mix of uses in such retrofitted centers and any important commercial core area such as a downtown create a setting that remains alive 18 to 24 hours a

Figure 9.1
Converting a Conventional Shopping Center

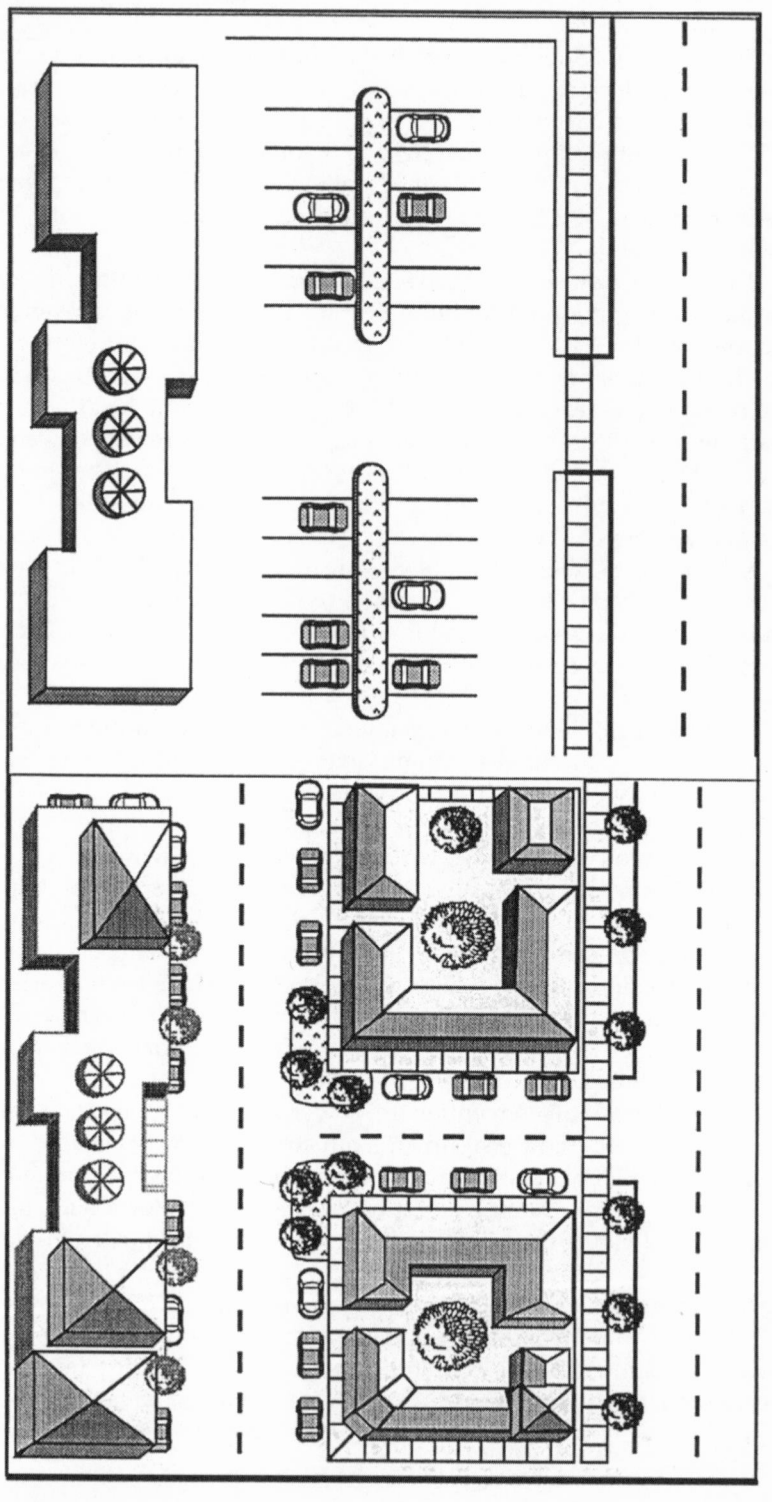

Figure 9.2
A Mix of Uses

- Encourages activities in the evening and weekends, enhancing the safety of visitors and security of homes, offices, and shops.

- Incorporates buildings at least 2 stories tall creating a pleasant "outdoor room" feeling.

- Includes places for work, residences, civic functions, and recreation within compact, walkable distances.

- Reduces the need for car travel, thereby lowering parking needs.

- Mixes uses vertically and horizontally.

- Makes transit efficient and makes smaller retail stores more viable.

day. Around-the-clock activity means vital and active streets that always seem fun, interesting, and enjoyable to visit or hang out in. Extending the life of an area beyond normal work hours encourages the use of such areas by students in school and employees around the city who work 8 to 5 jobs.

In addition, extending the hours of commercial operation can dramatically improve the perception of safety in a downtown or other central neighborhood area, because more "defensible space" and "citizen surveillance" exist, and less space is abandoned to gang activity.

Centrally Located Mixed Use

Not only our shopping areas and civic buildings need to be centrally located, but also our schools, parks, and squares. When all are within easy walking distance of most residents, our sense of community and neighborliness grows (not to mention we make fewer trips by car). When our children can walk to school or a park, these become social and recreational gathering places for students—they can get back and forth on their own, rather than depend on us or the school bus.

And children are not the only ones who need walkable, urban, neighborhood-based parks as part of their third-place network. These parks often make up for the smaller yards that come with higher densities. But to promote neighborliness and create opportunities for serendipitous meetings, such parks must be properly designed. Building facades and streets should front these spaces on all sides—particularly squares and plazas. A park should be small enough that walking across it isn't an ordeal. Ideally, these walk-to parks have good visibility from the street and are adjacent to a library, higher-density housing, a retail area, a civic building, or a bus stop.

Relatively large "activity" parks are generally best located at the periphery of neighborhoods and communities, where the space needed for ball fields and golf courses exists. Similarly, nature parks are best able to conserve natural features when they are large and remote from human settlements. Because of their size, activity and nature parks disrupt the walkability of an area and therefore serve a community best at the urban periphery.

Walkable Streets and Blocks

As designers have ignored the needs of pedestrians over the past several decades, the public realm—the streets, parks, sidewalks, and plazas—has become dangerous, uninviting, and undesirable. Pedestrians in such a community represent little more than inconveniences to motorists.

As Jane Jacobs noted 40 years ago in *The Death and Life of Great American Cities*, "lowly, unpurposeful and random as they may appear, sidewalk contacts are the small change from which a city's wealth of public life may grow" (p. 72). Yet many new residential and commercial developments either neglect to build a sidewalk along the frontage street or build one that is too narrow to be usable. For pedestrians to walk comfortably side-by-side, they need a sidewalk at least five feet wide.

And while we enjoy walking on these sidewalks, we don't want to have to walk too far to get where we're going, we don't want high-speed traffic flying past us, and we do want lots of interesting things to look at, such as engaging curiosities inside storefront windows.

How far is too far to walk? The experts—pedestrian and public transit planners—almost all agree that most people choose not to walk to a destination farther away than one-quarter mile, the distance that most of us can walk comfortably in five minutes at the typical walking speed of three miles per hour.[16] For community planning, this means we want to locate as many homes as possible within one-quarter mile of destinations we would like people to walk to—parks, schools, public transit stops, stores, civic and cultural buildings, and employment.

Usually, the shortest walking distance is a diagonal route. Curved sidewalks or sidewalks with right-angle turns may be attractive from the perspective of drivers, but pedestrians tend to feel patronized and inconvenienced when a sidewalk curves for no compelling reason. Because such sidewalk designs increase the walking distance, they also increase the likelihood of "cow path" shortcuts. Although curving sidewalks are appropriate for avoiding large trees or other important physical features, or when most pedestrians are walking strictly for recreation or exercise, most in-town trips have a practical purpose—we're trying to get somewhere. So to keep walking distances short, sidewalks (as well as streets) need to be straight and parallel to streets or on diagonal shortcuts.[17]

Also related to pedestrian pleasure and safety are raised, landscaped medians, refuges in the middle of the street as we cross.[18] From these vantage points, we need to look in only one direction for oncoming traffic and do not need as large a gap in the traffic flow as when we cross a street with no raised median. Medians landscaped with large street trees particularly add to a pleasant streetscape.

If our goal is short walking distances, our community is going to want short, walkable blocks, not longer than from 300 to 500 feet. When long blocks are unavoidable, they can be shortened with shortcut alleys or arcades or sidewalk paths that run from street to street in the middle of a block.[19] Short blocks mean a more dense network of streets, which disperses traffic—each street carries less vehicle traffic and can be scaled less like a superhighway and more like a livable space—which makes streets more pleasant for us walkers and easier to cross. More intersections give us pedestrians more freedom and control, because they offer us a variety of routes to get where we're headed. Shorter blocks also make a walk seem less burdensome, because we can set interim goals (such as intersections) and reach them more quickly.

One way to move toward shorter blocks is with narrower, smaller lots. "When buildings are narrow, the street length is shortened, the walking distances are reduced, and street life is enhanced.... Narrow street frontages mean short distances between entrances—and entrances are where the majority of [social interactions] nearly always take place."[20] Narrow, smaller lots encourage a more compact, walkable arrangement of houses, a more pleasing alignment of houses along the streetside sidewalk, and a cozier feel for a residential street. Smaller lots make homes in a subdivision more affordable. In addition, the higher, yet livable, density that smaller lots create makes public transit more viable.[21]

As for the streets themselves, again New Urbanism's goal is a less car dependent, more people-friendly design. "One of the most important—but least understood—aspects of architecture and urban design," write Michael Southworth and Eran Ben-Joseph in *Streets and the Shaping of Towns and Cities*, "is the extent to which the design and layout of residential streets determines the character and quality of communities—both urban and suburban, new and old." As we have seen in the case of gated and cul-de-sac communities, "some patterns create a sense of neighborhood and community, while others foster feelings of separateness and isolation. Some nurture social activity and children's play, while others lead to heavy traffic and degradation of the environment."

Great streets are places where we can comfortably and safely walk, where we find clearly defined boundaries and qualities that engage our eye, where buildings complement each other.[22] Narrow streets force cars and trucks to slow down, which significantly contributes to neighborhood safety, low noise levels, low traffic volumes—in short, neighborhood livability. Very wide streets are less safe for walkers because it takes longer to get across them and because vehicles travel faster on them.

Yet wide streets are often inappropriately justified by the need to accommodate the relatively rare larger vehicles, particularly fire trucks. A 1997 study of the safest street widths in Longmont, Colorado, looked at an eight-year period that included 20,000 auto accident reports and fire department records and discovered that the factors most significantly tied to injury and accident were "street width and street curvature. . . . As the street width widens, accidents per mile per year increase exponentially." The safest residential street width was 24 feet curb to curb; by comparison, "a typical 36-foot wide residential street [shows a] 400 percent increase in accident rates. . . . Some of the most dangerous streets turned out to be wide thoroughfares—36 feet to 44 feet, with relatively light traffic (less than 500 average daily trips)."[23]

What about those big fire trucks? The study paid specific attention to them. "One of the most common difficulties of gaining approval for narrow streets is objections from fire officials, who often predict dire consequences." But the study "found no increased fire injury risk due to narrow streets. By contrast, there were 227 car accidents resulting in injuries. Even if narrow streets did create a moderately greater fire injury risk, they would still be safer than wide streets," because the risk of car injuries is so much greater.[24]

Many others have reached the same conclusion.[25] Fire departments need to focus on *life safety*, not just fire safety. Significantly more city residents are hurt or killed due to car crashes on wide streets that encourage dangerously high speeds than die because a fire truck loses a couple of response-time seconds on a rare fire-fighting call.[26]

In line with such studies, people-oriented street design calls for a smaller curb-turning radius, that is, more acutely angled parking lot entrances and intersections that compel cars to slow to safer speeds to make turns. Designing street corners with smaller turning radii recognizes that the vast majority of vehicles expected to be traveling on neighborhood streets are small and slow moving. Larger radii, by contrast, take a worst-case scenario approach that designs for the extremely rare large or high-speed vehicle, an example of which is a fire truck. Such an overdesigned street results in higher vehicle speeds, less pedestrian and bicycle travel, and less livable neighborhoods. A larger radius also significantly increases the walking distance for crossing the street, which exposes the pedestrian to more danger from moving vehicles. The street best serves pedestrians if the radius requires car turning speeds of less than 20 miles per hour on left turns and less than 10 miles per hour on right turns, with crosswalk widths of no more than 48 feet.[27]

Turning radius is determined by the placement of the curb and is the size of the circle that will fit in the corner. The smaller the circle's radius, the sharper the turn. The sharper the turn, the slower one must drive. Typically, in a residential subdivision, the standard will be 25 feet. But by reducing this radius to 15 feet, the engineer still allows free auto movement but signals to the driver that a slower speed is appropriate. In addition, the narrower curve places the pedestrian closer to the goal: across the street.[28]

For example, a 10-foot curb radius creates a pedestrian crossing distance of 28.6 feet on a 28-foot-wide street—which creates a 7.9-second crossing time. In contrast, a 30-foot curb radius using the same street width creates a pedestrian crossing distance of 48.3 feet—which creates a 13.3-second crossing time. The safest radii for pedestrians require car turning speeds of less than 20 miles per hour on left turns and less than 10 miles per hour on right turns; crosswalks should be no wider than 48 feet.[29]

Pedestrian-Friendly "A" Streets

New Urbanists suggest that cities designate a discrete number of "A" streets—streets designed to promote the safety, comfort, and convenience of pedestrians in a relatively exceptional way. Such streets typically are narrow and feature sidewalks at least 5 feet wide, as well as—for starters—on-street or back/side parking, modest turning radii, buildings abutting the sidewalk, hidden mechanical equipment and trash receptacles, and pedestrian-scaled lighting. Ideally, of course, every street would be an "A" street. But experience suggests that a town effort to establish excellence for *all* streets in the community through regulation and public projects inevitably leads to mediocrity for all streets. There are two primary reasons for this. First, the regulations must be watered down for private developers to accommodate the needs of all hypothetical uses—in particular, the car-oriented uses. Hostile, car-intensive uses or uses that are otherwise visually unpleasant or harmful for pedestrians cannot feasibly be prohibited from an entire community, nor, perhaps, should they be. This being the case, certain streets should be "sacrificed" for the purpose of making the "A" streets truly wonderful. These "B" streets can take the pressure—particularly the political or judicial pressure—off "A" streets. "B" streets can accommodate the drive-throughs, the car washes, the parking lots, and the auto repair shops.

Second, most towns aren't wealthy enough to provide high-quality public projects for every street. This means that either some streets will get an inequitable amount of enhancement, or the enhancement will be equal, but equally mediocre. Designating a limited number of "A" streets means a smaller, more manageable, more realistic number of street miles will receive top-quality improvements.

On "A" streets and in other pedestrian-oriented areas of a city, landscaping can both soften the "hardness" of the urban area for walkers and help make us feel more comfortable by providing cooling shade, reducing glare, and helping form public spaces, "outdoor rooms," and street corridor edges. Trees also reduce energy consumption by cooling our asphalt roadways. Often, we need to plant street trees to correct livability problems—a too-wide street, buildings too low or set back too far from the street—that keep the street from feeling like a pleasantly enclosed outdoor room.

Aligning trees *formally* along the street and sidewalk to form a disciplined edge is one effective way to define such outdoor rooms. It helps to plant trees of the same species, although some may fear this would make the city tree canopy vulnerable to the spread of monocultural disease. Yet if we plan for tree diversity from one block to the next, rather than within one block, this is not a problem. If we find we need species diversity on a block, it's a good idea at least to choose trees of the same general shape and size. Whatever our species choices, formal landscaping adds dignity to the traditional areas of a city and inspires civic pride.

In addition to street trees, people-oriented street design encourages other "street furniture" that enhances the convenience and comfort of sidewalks—seating, bus shelters, drinking fountains, trash receptacles, people-scaled lighting and signs, and awnings tailored to various locations. Many of us like to sit where the most "action" is and watch people go by near major destination points, outdoor cafes, and entries to retail establishments. Seating should not be too high or low, should not be too exposed to harsh weather, and should fit the human contour.

Pedestrian-oriented street lighting means shorter and more numerous light fixtures and structures than we are used to as motorists. Human-scaled lighting that is neither too diffuse nor intense (glare can be unpleasant for both pedestrians and people inside their homes, as well as a danger to motorists) should be directed down toward the street and sidewalk where it is needed. Badly placed and high-intensity lighting can create a bleached-out atmosphere and can hide the nighttime sky completely.[30] As we move toward people-friendly cities, we can also discourage the emerging trend of businesses using lighting so that the building becomes a sign; this lighting draws attention to the building rather than providing for nighttime safety and security, and can strongly detract from the attractiveness and uniqueness of the community.

Street furniture should be low-maintenance and durable, and not so generous that it results in clutter and obstructs pedestrian circulation. The best furniture, whether lighting, benches, or signs, adheres to a unified design theme compatible with the character of the area—trendy designs, though tempting, quickly become dated.

Along with motorist-oriented towering streetlights, in people-oriented communities, we need to dispense with giant parking lots between the sidewalk and the front of a building and require parking at the rear or side of a building instead. This saves pedestrians from dodging cars as we negotiate a hot or snow-covered expanse, rewards us on the public sidewalk with building details and interior building activity to look at, and ensures us greater security from "eyes" in the building that provide street and sidewalk surveillance. David Sucher in *City Comforts* suggests that the location of parking lots is the major pattern setter of urban form, the most critical site planning decision and the most difficult to reverse.

On-street parking, another design option commonly urged by New Urbanists, works to the benefit of pedestrians rather than drivers intent on speeding through urban areas in a number of ways.[31] It buffers pedestrians from moving vehicular traffic, making the street safer and more pleasant for walking. The convenient parking along with an increase in pedestrian traffic helps businesses thrive, especially downtown. On-street parking usually reduces the number and width of travel lanes, thereby slowing vehicle speeds, easing street crossing by pedestrians, and reducing the number and severity of traffic accidents, in part by making motorists more alert to pedestrians. With on-street parking, we need fewer large parking lots, so businesses and residences need less off-street, on-site parking, which reduces the "heat island" effect. By contrast, off-street surface parking and first-floor parking in a parking garage create gap-toothed dead zones that detract from the urban vibrancy so attractive to residents of and visitors to a neighborhood or downtown.

Other sure detractors from urban vibrancy include multistory garages, overwide driveways, poorly located waste and recycling receptacles, prominent loading docks, and overhead utilities in full view of passersby. An essential solution to these often unsafe and obnoxious accoutrements?

Alleys.

Alleys give emergency vehicles another access to a building and offer children a relatively safe place to play. They eliminate the need for front-yard driveways (which reduces the number of curb cuts and cars crossing the streetside sidewalk), provide more space for on-street parking, and allow for narrower, and thus less costly, lots.[32]

Because we have abandoned our streets to cars, we too often allow them to become dumping grounds for unsightly outdoor heating, air conditioning, and ventilation equipment. Such features are best located at the rear or side of a building, or on the roof. Even in these locations, it is often necessary to screen such equipment from view, and thus also to minimize noise. Underground utilities dramatically improve the aesthetics of an area, are less vulnerable to trees that fall due to disease or storm, and reduce the need for severe tree pruning.

Moving from street design, parking, and street furniture to buildings themselves, pedestrian-friendly criteria include aligned building facades, buildings pulled up close to the street, articulated building walls, and building entrances on the street.

Sucher calls the relationship of the building to the sidewalk "one of the key architectural decisions in city planning for cohesive neighborhoods. This relationship is significant in residential areas but is of supreme importance in commercial areas. Indeed, it is the position of the building with respect to the sidewalk which makes a city. The good news is that the relationship is a very simple one: place the building at the sidewalk. That's it. Don't make it complicated."[33]

Buildings set far back from the street are inconvenient and unpleasant for pedestrians—inconvenient because they significantly increase our walking distance from the sidewalk, and unpleasant because they prevent us on the sidewalk from enjoying the building details and the activity within the building.[34] Buildings set off from the street by large front yards or huge landscaped areas create travel barriers for pedestrians, bicyclists, and bus riders. They tend to encourage higher vehicle speeds, because the road corridor has a more open, racetrack feel, as well as—for commercial buildings—large, obtrusive signs.

Buildings that front right on the streetside sidewalk will align to form a street wall that defines a comfortably secure public realm while allowing enough width for people to walk and enough space to allow shade-providing street trees. Human beings generally prefer defined spaces, which feel like cozy outdoor rooms and make the public realm seem less chaotic. In these spaces, we feel less exposed, and more as if we are "in a place."[35]

Similarly, homes with front porches set back a modest "conversational" distance from the sidewalk allow us to sit on our porch and interact and socialize with neighbors—intimate transition spaces from the public to the private realm. Front porches add to our enjoyment if we are walking and help deter crime by encouraging more "eyes on the street."

Citizen surveillance, or "eyes on the street," follows naturally when buildings, windows, entrances, and porches are near the street and side-walk and in areas designed for regular, frequent pedestrian activity. His-torically, we sat on our front porches or watched the street and sidewalk from our windows; neighbors often served as proxy parents when chil-dren were out of sight of their real parents. In retail areas, windows on a shopfront attract pedestrians, who act as a security system for the busi-ness. We have forfeited this natural citizen-security watch as we've moved our buildings and homes farther and farther away from the street and sidewalk. But we can choose to have it back.

The reassuring space formed by building facades and street trees feels even more secure with buildings two to five stories high. The building profile forms a comfortable street wall and the upper stories invite the establishment of the number of residences needed for a viable urban neigh-borhood. Low-slung, one-story buildings, appropriate in low-density resi-dential areas designed for car travel, reduce the density and commercial square footage needed to make public transit, walking, and bicycling viable, and typically are too low to form a desirable, intimate, comfortable public realm with the buildings across the street.

Another architectural feature with pedestrian appeal in residential areas is a recessed garage. Houses with recessed garages appear people-oriented and interesting for a pedestrian on the sidewalk, instead of sending a strong, unfriendly message that "a car lives here," or that the structure is a protruding garage with an attached house (called, not fondly, "snout houses"). When the garage is architecturally subordinate, the visually interesting features of the house can properly dominate the streetscape. Garages should be recessed at least 20 feet from the house facade because we so often park in front of our garage instead of inside it. A recessed garage keeps even these cars from sticking out in front of the building façade. Garage doors, too, should be hidden from view, as they are seldom additions to a lively streetscape.

For public retail and office buildings, a feature that plays an important role for walkers is an entrance on the street. Buildings that have only a rear or side entrance (usually, an entrance oriented toward a parking lot) not only make travel highly inconvenient for pedestrians and public transit users but also cut the building off from street life—the building turns its back on the public and reduces urban vibrancy.[36] As walkers in a walkable city, we want not only convenient, welcoming entrances on the sidewalk but also windows. What is more boring, deadly, and impersonal than a long expanse of blank wall?

Homogenized, banal "icon architecture" (also known as "cookie cutter" or "franchise" architecture), which immediately conveys a corporate image to the passerby—McDonald's golden arches, Kentucky Fried Chicken's red-and-white stripes—diminishes a city's unique identity and creates what Jim Kunstler calls the "geography of nowhere."[37]

A WOLF IN SHEEP'S CLOTHING

We should be on guard not to allow projects touted as New Urbanist that deliver New Urbanism's principles only in a skin-deep way, such as those that perpetuate car dependence, or that fail to provide a mix of housing affordability, even if the houses have front porches or other forms of window dressing.

NEW URBANISM AND THE POOR

I am always astounded when people attack New Urbanism as elitist and not in the best interests of poor people.

It seems as obvious to me that an auto-dominated community is as detrimental to poor people as it seems obvious that community design recommended by New Urbanism reduces the need for car travel and is beneficial. New Urbanism seems to be the best chance to reduce car dependency through urban design, which is an important reason why I am so enthusiastic about it.

Fundamental components of a New Urbanist community include inherently affordable types of housing that are usually not allowed by conventional land development codes. For example, New Urbanist projects nearly always include inherently affordable accessory units (granny flats), residences above offices or retail shops, and higher-density, smaller-lot residential units. These forms of affordable housing become increasingly affordable as the number of New Urbanist communities grows, which will lower prices as a result of competition.

Mixed-use and mixed-income housing units are allowable and acceptable in New Urbanist designs because they are properly scaled and detailed and do not generate as much car travel as single-use developments.

As Jane Jacobs noted in *The Death and Life of Great American Cities*, vibrant downtowns (which are hurt by an auto-based culture) provide important entry-level, low-capital job opportunities for low-income people—selling food from carts, providing personal services, selling specialty goods, and so forth.

And what do our auto-dominated communities offer the poor? They are expensive to live in. The average car costs the same as a $50,000 home mortgage, depending on the interest rates. If a household can live in a place where it can get by with fewer cars, it can save a great deal. Further, an auto-dominated city promotes segregation by income; wealthy people can choose to live in remote suburbs and send their children to schools there. At the same time, such a community perpetuates the demand for single-use, "protect the sanctity of my castle" pods by people who believe that mixed-use means noise, crime, and an overflow of undesirable car trips in the neighborhood. Along with this demand comes an ongoing push for wider roads and bigger parking lots, often at the expense of low-income neighborhoods, because it is politically and economically easiest to bulldoze low-income housing to expand the transportation system.

More? Auto-dominated communities often force poor people to live in places made affordable, and undesirable, by heavy traffic and its accompanying noise, danger, ugliness, and emissions, or places not well served by affordable public transit. In general, only the wealthy can afford to live in a pleasant place separated from the pollution, danger, and ugliness of the car. Such a design makes Big Box retailers profitable and hurts the small, locally owned, more accessible core-area retailers that are often important for low-income jobs and revenue. Finally, in these communities, walking is less pleasant and safe, and public transit less viable.

Quality New Urbanism promises and delivers a more affordable future.

CHAPTER 10

Toward Better Development Regulations

Successful City Planning: Public action that generates a desirable, widespread and sustained private market reaction.

—Alexander Garvin

As a community becomes more people-scaled and more concerned about making pedestrians happy, what happens to cars?

WHAT ABOUT CARS?

Communities intent upon establishing walkable environments will sometimes establish rules that restrict or prohibit businesses or activities that attract or cater to large numbers of cars. What kinds of businesses or activities are we talking about? Major car-repair services, drive-throughs, Big Box retailers, auto dealers, car washes, gas stations, and convenience store/gas stations are today especially prominent examples. Such businesses not only can be quite hostile to pedestrians, bicyclists, and public transit users, they make their surroundings unsafe, unpleasant, and inconvenient. These often noisy businesses tend to bristle with signs and bright lights.

A community can alleviate many of the problems of auto-intensive uses by requiring a modest scale, unobtrusiveness, and high-quality design. For example, regulations might require that a multistory garage be wrapped with offices or shops, or that a drive-through must be limited to one lane and cannot empty out onto an "A" street, that the building it serves must be at least two stories (to deliver sufficient pedestrian density and properly frame an "outdoor room"), and perhaps—in the best of all possible worlds—that the project be mixed use. In the case of large national chains, such regulations require strong political leadership, for their formulaic, car-oriented designs, typically mandated by the national office, usually call for huge parking lots out front, Anywhere, USA, architecture, and the like. Unwilling to abide by a community's unique, pedestrian-oriented design standards, these chains may start waving large property tax revenue or "lots of new jobs" in the faces of elected officials and threaten to back out and deny these benefits to the community if standards can't be watered down—here's where courageous political leadership is crucial.

Pedestrians are the lifeblood of a healthy city.[1] Instead of drive-throughs, a livable city can encourage or even require walk-in businesses (especially on "A" streets)—establishments to which we can walk from our parked car, a public transit stop, a bicycle parking space, or home. Walking encourages everything we seek in a neighborhood: sociability; human-scaled buildings, lighting, and signage; a quiet atmosphere; serendipity; retail health; and civic pride.

In Portland, Oregon, which has been moving toward a more pedestrian-friendly community for several decades, the average number of cars per household in areas hostile to pedestrians was 32 percent higher than in pedestrian-friendly areas. Downtown, car ownership has dropped and nonauto travel increased; carbon monoxide violations dropped from 100 per year to zero. The city has established a "pedestrian friendliness" index based on ease of street crossing, sidewalk continuity, and street character-istics (connected streets rank higher than cul-de-sacs).[2] Further, Portland put a permanent cap on downtown parking in 1972, stopped widening downtown streets, converted about one mile of streets into people-oriented public transit areas, widened sidewalks, and prohibited large blank walls along sidewalks. Portland's downtown today is widely recog-nized as economically healthy, vibrant, and livable.

WHAT ABOUT PARKING?

Portland is one of a number of cities that have curtailed parking in one way or another, both in established areas and new development projects (see chapter 8). "The more parking space, the less sense of place," com-ments Jane Holtz Kay.[3] Large, free parking lots invite us to leap into our cars instead of walking or using public transit. Surface parking lots take up valuable city land where there could be stores, offices, civic buildings, or plazas—uses that commonly add energy to a downtown, help provide the verticality needed to form outdoor rooms, and bring in more property tax revenue. Surface parking, by contrast, has a deadening effect. If Richard Ratcliff was right when he said that "[i]n a healthy city there is a constant replacement of less intensive uses by more intensive uses,"[4] a city with a growing proportion of parking is a sign of urban decay.

Until the recent past, the regulations in nearly all cities required *at least* "X" number of parking spaces per square foot of retail or office, which in fact far exceeded demand except on a few major shopping days. However, developers increasingly tend to oversupply parking—often exceeding even the generous requirements of most communities. For example, a study in the Seattle region found that even during peak periods, the parking supply for offices was 36 percent higher than average demand.[5] Today, it is typical to provide parking for the "20th busiest hour of use," but Donald Shoup notes that this leaves at least half of a shopping center's parking vacant for at least 40 percent of the year.[6]

Further evidence on the oversupply of suburban parking includes a study of east and west coast business parks. Here, 47 percent parking occupancy was found when the office buildings were well leased.[7]

Such parking requirements have only encouraged sprawl, for developers can adhere to them less expensively in land-rich suburbs than in downtown areas. To ensure that developers of sites do not offer excessive parking, more and more communities are capping the number of parking spaces that can be provided.

As a nation of parking lots and monstrous roads, we have been trained to believe that we can and must drive wherever we want to go and park within a few feet of the door of our destination. In a pedestrian-friendly community, this concept has less value when measured against a healthy, walkable, social vibrancy. More often we will choose to walk, bike, or ride the bus or subway. But it may be helpful to remember, as James Castle points out, that even today, "anyplace worth its salt has a 'parking problem.'" Most of us are willing to park far away and walk great distances if our goal is an exciting one—a football game, an arts festival, a county fair. Parking close to a destination is important only when the destination is dull or unimportant. Conversely and ironically, the more parking provided near an attractive destination, the less interesting the destination becomes.

"The effects of [minimum] parking requirements on urban form and transportation systems are self-reinforcing, yet they are rarely articulated in policy debates. These comments do not imply that a conspiracy has imposed minimum parking requirements on an unsuspecting populace. Far from it. The policies have been consistent with the social values of the time."[8]

Minimum parking requirements—that "X" number of parking spaces must be provided per given size of building—are law in nearly every American community. It is a testament to our love affair with cars, yet they tend to breed car trips that would not have occurred had there not been so much free parking provided. Indeed, Donald Shoup calls minimum parking requirements a "fertility drug for cars."

The relentless demand for more parking in many downtowns harks to the old Vietnam adage that "we must destroy the village to save it."

LEAVE THE DRIVING TO US: TRANSIT-FRIENDLY COMMUNITIES

Greyhound's slogan for years went something like "Take the bus . . . and leave the driving to us." Some development that incorporates features of New Urbanism—traffic calming, mixed-use development, and traditional neighborhood design—goes a step further by making public transit stations and transit stops a key design element. Communities incorporating this design, known to planners as "transit-oriented developments" (TODs) or "transit villages," strive to make pedestrian, bicycle, and drop-off trips to a transit stop convenient, safe, and enjoyable.

Such a design needs a critical mass of commercial, civic, residential, recreational, and school development within walking distance (one-quarter-mile radius) of the transit stop. To promote this critical mass, communities developing TODs are increasing residential and commercial densities near transit stops.

The design often includes street-front commercial buildings immediately adjacent to the transit stop, nearby housing for seniors, an open plaza, and other strategies that aim to create a 24-hour-a-day presence and a sense of place at the transit stop. The need for siting buildings conveniently near the transit stop is underlined by a survey that found the average walking distance between a traditional bus stop and buildings is four times greater than the walking distance to a building for the average parking motorist.[9] That is, we again find ourselves designing, quite often, for the convenience of the motorist and tend to overlook those who travel in other ways.

Another way to maintain this human scale—a walkable ambiance—is to avoid installing broad expanses of poorly located asphalt parking at transit points or park'n'rides —a common design mistake for transit centers. The advantage of surrounding transit stops with mixed-use development is the convenience of nearby retail and services for riders; we can easily take care of errands on our way home from work or school.

Calthorpe sets forth these seven principles for creating TODs. First, organize growth on a regional level to be compact and transit supportive. Second, place commercial, housing, jobs, parks, and civic uses within walking distance of transit stops. Third, create pedestrian-friendly street networks that directly connect local destinations. Fourth, provide a mix of housing types, densities, and costs. Fifth, make public spaces the focus of building orientation and neighborhood activity. Sixth, encourage infill and redevelopment along transit corridors within existing neighborhoods. And seventh, preserve sensitive habitat, riparian zones, and high-quality open space.[10]

To reduce car dependence and encourage such transit-oriented development, the state of Oregon in 1991 adopted the Oregon Transportation

Planning Rule, which required cities to reduce vehicle miles traveled by 10 percent over the next 20 years and 20 percent within 30 years. As a result, in that state, all land use design, densities, and design standards must be analyzed to determine if they support bicycling, walking, and transit. Codes had to be amended to allow higher residential density near transit lines and in new office and retail developments. Land zoned for neighborhood shopping must be easily accessible by foot or bike. New multifamily and commercial building entrances must be within 100 feet of a transit route.[11]

In a report published nine years after the rule's implementation, the authors note that the rule has had its "detractors . . . much of the opposition centered around specific planning requirements, such as building orientation and street connectivity." The result of negotiation,

particularly in the review stage, . . . is a softening of the Rule's requirements to what many feel is a more realistic level while at the same time retaining the overall goal of reduced reliance on the automobile. . . . Most implementing officials continue to work toward compliance. The persistence of 1000 Friends and the atmosphere of negotiation and compromise have been important factors in the progress that is being made. Even more important, though, is the sense that many have that the goals of the Rule constitute 'good planning' and that implementing the Rule is the 'right' thing to do. The Rule, if nothing else, serves as a catalyst to keep planners and policymakers moving in what many of them feel is the right direction—even if they remain skeptical that the ultimate goals of specific VMT or parking space reduction will ever be reached.[12]

Higher residential densities that allow people to walk, bike, or ride the bus or rail are an important foundation for transit-oriented development. The average density for TODs served by light rail is about nine dwelling units per acre; Portland, Oregon, strives for 15 per acre.

One effective way for communities to increase development densities and create a compact, walkable layout of buildings is to increase the amount of square feet that can be built on a given piece of land—what planners and developers call the "floor area ratio" (FAR). An FAR of 1.0, for example, would allow us to build a one-story building to cover the entire site, or a two-story building to cover half of the site. Setting a modest cap on the allowable FAR—particularly a cap below 1.0—encourages greater dependence on travel by car.[13] Low FARs tend to space buildings too far apart and create too much unused space that does little to create a human-scaled, enclosed ambience. Conventionally, FAR caps are based on the fear that buildings will cover entire parcels of land without them, thereby creating "overcrowding" and loss of landscaping opportunities. However, communities nearly always have code requirements for landscaping, parking, and setbacks, which, of course, reduce the amount of floor area coverage possible on a property, even if allowable FAR is high.

Fears that high FARs will create overly bulky buildings incompatible with neighbors can generally be addressed simply through use of building height limits.

In commercial areas, the FAR should be at least 1.0, and in office, industrial and mixed-use areas, at least 1.25 to 3.0.[14] Every 20 percent increase in floor space in commercial centers developed as nonoffice uses (often retail shops) brings a 4.5 percent increase in ride sharing and public transit use.[15]

In neighborhood centers, well-known urban designer Richard Untermann calls for FARs of 2.0 to 3.0. However, a FAR as low as 1.0 to 2.0 can be sufficient for encouraging transportation choices.

HOW DO WE GET THERE FROM HERE?
TRADITIONAL NEIGHBORHOOD DEVELOPMENT
AND STRATEGIES

A variety of strategies offer promising possibilities for we who yearn for walkable, people-friendly communities and neighborhoods, including traditional neighborhood development ordinances, overlay ordinances, parallel codes, and incremental code fixes.

Traditional neighborhood development (TND) ordinances prescribe many New Urbanist design features (chapter 9), including many of those described in this chapter. As their name suggests, TNDs allow a developer to incorporate the timeless design principles of traditional neighborhoods—self-contained, tightly gridded, and pedestrian-oriented to encourage socializing, walking, and other aspects of a vibrant outdoor urban experience. TNDs, in other words, make it legal to again build traditionally, often in ways that promote sociable, human-scaled communities.

To implement a TND, a community can allow the developer the option of adopting a "floating," or overlay, ordinance in one or more discrete locations where the goal is a relatively walkable, traditional character; the overlay trumps conventional, car-oriented regulations in place for that location. This regulatory fix tends to be the easiest option, as it needs to address only a relatively small yet crucial set of regulations, such as sidewalks or setbacks. Other regulations that already apply to the area, such as landscaping or stormwater, can remain.

An intriguing, recent idea is the use of people-oriented "parallel" ordinances or codes. Here, the community prepares a full set of ordinances (parking, landscaping, setbacks, allowed uses, signs, stormwater, etc.) that parallels the existing, conventional land development code. The parallel code must be able to stand alone without any supporting or underlying, in-place regulations, which means an enormous amount of work, as all of the development regulations the community uses must be "paralleled." The key strategy is to create incentives to make it easier for developers to use this people-oriented parallel than the existing and conventional code, since there may be a great deal of inertia tied to using the existing code, or developers and banks may be wary of using "untested" or "new" rules. A community can specify that applications submitted under the parallel code be moved more quickly through the approval process, or fees might be reduced or approvals made more likely.

Incremental code fixes are a variation on the overlay approach. In the case of code fixes, the community slowly, incrementally transforms its code of development ordinances to bring more people-oriented regulations gradually into community-wide use. For example, citywide commercial setbacks might be reduced, street standards made more modest, or sidewalk widths increased. More mixing of allowable uses might be allowed. While such incremental fixes can be made fairly easily, an important limitation is the "one size does not fit all" truism. For instance, applying modest, people-oriented, walkable regulations does not serve an entire community, because outlying areas tend to be less interested in walkable design. The sheer distances in these locations, alone, make walkable design impractical and at least partially inappropriate. Similarly, regulations that accommodate the larger dimensions required for cars are generally inappropriate in downtown areas. The solution is to establish "sliding scale" regulations, accommodating more modest dimensions at the walkable community core, and increasingly larger and car-oriented dimensions as one moves to the outlying areas of the community—a methodology illustrated earlier and in Appendix A by the transect.

Finally, a community can very usefully identify roads that can be put on a "road diet"—large, wide, "fat" streets from which travel lanes or turn lanes can be removed, or whose lane width can be reduced.[16] Most commonly, a community reduces a five- or four-lane road to a three-lane (two travel lanes and a turn lane/raised median combination).[17] Room gained through such diets can allow widening sidewalks, adding bicycle lanes, and adding on-street parking. Road diets have gained popularity across the nation, because they generally make the road more safe, attractive, livable, sociable, and healthy for retail, office, and residential uses.[18] And they enable a broader range of travel, accommodating not only cars, but transit users, bicyclists, and pedestrians.

SPACE

"The most important task of the urbanist is controlling size," writes David Mohney, dean of the University of Kentucky's School of Architecture.

In farm lands, forests, greenbelts, and prairies that have traditionally defined the outer edges of communities, space needs are relatively large. Healthy cornfields, woodlands, and savannas require lots of room to thrive. But such space is inherently unwalkable. It is fundamentally not human-scaled. The distance from the barn to the edge of the pasture, or the width of the prairie, are generally far in excess of a walkable, one-quarter-mile distance that humans can comfortably walk.

No, in these portions of the community, distances are relatively extreme and require motorized travel.

These relatively large space needs are a fundamental component of auto orientation. Cars require a great deal of space, which means that they thrive when buildings are far from each other, homes are at low densities, roads are very wide, and parking is nearly limitless.

Space tends to be abundant in outlying, remote areas of a community, and extremely scarce in walkable, in-town neighborhoods and downtowns.

This space difference is crucial to understand. Humans are most comfortable when distances and spaces are modest and scaled for walking. Buildings abut sidewalks, and are not pushed back behind vast asphalt parking fields, woodlands, or grass. Streets are modest in width and designed for slow car speeds. Large parks, schools and golf courses are at the edge of our communities, not in core areas. Parking lots are small. Homes, offices, and shops are clustered close together. These are the elements that create that cozy "hometown" feel—a "sense of place" that so many of us rightly seek out and work to protect in our towns. It is cars that require lots of space in a city, which means that in auto-oriented, sprawled communities, *open space is plentiful*—albeit used mostly for private yards, or roads and parking lots.

What is not compatible with auto-oriented sprawl is modest, human-scaled spacing and distances, because such places do not provide enough space for our Fords and GMCs.

A great many motorists and wilderness advocates have unintentionally joined forces in an unholy alliance.

For both the motorist and the wilderness advocate, vast amounts of space are necessary to optimize conditions for cars and nature. Large numbers of motorists and wilderness advocates have mistakenly concluded that, in cities, towns and neighborhoods, the interests of cars and wilderness are the same as the interests of people. Because of this, such advocates zealously crusade for the creation of enormous spaces inside human settlements. Given this objective, building setbacks are enlarged. City "open spaces" become gigantic. Parking lots become seas of hot, endless asphalt. Roads are widened into 8- and 12-lane monsters.

Unfortunately, while such large spaces help Bambi and our Toyota in the city, these big spaces degrade the quality of *HUMAN* habitat. Humans need *HUMAN-SCALED* space to thrive. To regularly go on pleasant walks. To be sociable with neighbors. To feel comfortable and secure.

The result of the campaign for big spaces is that the crusaders for cars and caribou compel us to create communities that make SUV's and bears happy, not people.

Increasingly, this downward spiral of a quality of life for humans in communities promotes a flight of people from cities to the remote, outlying suburbs. The call for inhumanely large spaces is yet another engine promoting communities to spread out into vast, low-density, sprawling megalopolises (which a number of motorists and conservationists are all-too-happy to support).

It is perfectly desirable and vitally important to create high-quality habitats for wildlife (and, to some extent, unhindered car travel) at the *PERIPHERY* of communities. But to return to the tradition of creating lovable, walkable, sociable neighborhoods and town centers, our design focus *INSIDE OUR CITIES* must return to the time-tested principle that quality human habitats demand *MODEST* spaces.

One size does not fit all. Nature (and car travel) needs large open spaces to thrive. Fine. But not within a city.

A walkable, in-town location must first strive for modest spacing and modest distances. That is our top priority for creating a quality human habitat. "Human scale," said Nancy Graham, the former West Palm Beach, Florida, mayor who led the revitalization of that downtown, "must prevail over the needs of motor vehicles."[19]

A TRADITIONAL NEIGHBORHOOD: EVERYONE BENEFITS

To recap, these are the advantages for communities of the New Urbanism, people- and transit-friendly development, and traditional neighborhoods (when they are done right): People without access to a car, such as children, the elderly, and the disabled, feel safer and more independent. A pedestrian ambiance and interesting pedestrian features make everyone on foot feel more secure, convenienced, and comfortable. The "citizen surveillance" of "eyes on the street" in public places is promoted; citizens watch over their collective security, and crime and public law enforcement costs drop. Government and household costs are lower, especially with the enormous savings in building and maintaining road infrastructure, and purchasing and maintaining cars. Per capita gasoline consumption and air pollution levels drop.

Further, public transit is more viable. Streets designed to slow traffic, increase travel choices, and reduce the length and number of vehicle trips vastly reduce the significant transportation impacts the neighborhood displaces to the larger community. Structures and the layout of lots and streets are built for permanence, instead of for a short-term "throw-away" life. Historic structures are retained, not replaced with parking or large suburban retail "boxes." Smaller, locally owned businesses can become established and operate successfully, at the same time that strip commercial visual blight is minimized.

Affordable housing options, such as residences above shops, granny flats, and carriage houses, encourage a mix of age groups and economic classes. Urban livability reduces the desire to flee to the suburbs, which in turn reduces the pressure for costly sprawl and strip commercial development. Neighborhoods are more memorable and dignified as community character is preserved and promoted. Nearby older neighborhoods gain stability, identity, and value. The neighborhood and community become self-sufficient and, therefore, sustainable.

In short, a sense of place, of community, and of belonging grow, along with civic pride and place-based loyalty. Traditional citizen hope and expectation for a better future are gradually restored with each new development in the city, and the extreme polarization between neighborhoods and developers lessens.

Conclusion

A community has to have the capacity to envision a future they want,
and not just the one they are likely to get.

—Unknown

Can we retain a sense of community? A sense of place? A satisfactory quality of life? Can we return to putting the needs of our community before the
demands of our cars? Forty years from now, will we be proud of where we
live?

Our love affair with cars is unsustainable for the environment, the economy, and quality of life in the twenty-first century. Car transportation is
truly a zero-sum game. Nearly always, when we make it easier to drive a
car, we make it harder to travel another way, and worsen our quality of life.

Fortunately, the emerging paradigm as we enter the twenty-first century includes the freedom of transportation choice for all of us—including
people who can drive a car, seniors, children, individuals with disabilities,
and the poor. Transportation choices will help our communities once
again become sustainable, unique, attractive, livable, and affordable—
places in which we can take pride. By contrast to the last century, the new
century can be one of moderation, equity, and adaptability, essential for a
stable, sustainable environment.

Yet it is not clear that many American communities will prosper in the
years ahead, given the gargantuan nature of the forces working against
them.

We need to stop buying into the self-fulfilling prophecy that we are all
doomed to lives of extreme auto dependence, forced to make every trip,

no matter how trivial, by car. And it is exceptionally important that we recognize that "good ideas" or "education campaigns" will be insufficient to overcome communities being destroyed by big roads for cars and sprawl. If we offer only timid incentives such as bicycle parking or public education advertisements or bus stops, in the long run, the auto-oriented sprawl will win.

OUR OWN WORST ENEMIES

Nearly every American adult has two things in common—citizenship and car ownership. Quite simply, nearly all of us are motorists first. Our lives center on car travel. Every day, we make 10 to 15 trips by car, giving us 10 to 15 daily opportunities to become enraged if we must slow down for anything or anyone. We are so intensely wedded to the welfare of our pickups and SUVs, our Fords and our Hondas, that driving at high speeds at all times comes before any other interest. As neighborhood residents, we put our cars before safety for kids. As businesspeople, we put our ability to speed down a street before the economic health of drugstores and restaurants. We are neither Democrats nor Republicans when it comes to motor vehicle promotion—all of us want more for our cars.

Despite overwhelming evidence of increased property values and safety for children and seniors, we regularly fight vigorously to oppose a local government proposal to install, say, a sidewalk on our neighborhood street. Most of us are, after all, using our car travel to isolate and wall off ourselves in suburbia from the in-town threat of "strangers," and sidewalks potentially attract unknown characters to our street.

Notwithstanding nationwide examples of how traffic-taming practices (such as narrowing roads) result in overnight improvements to the business climate of a street, businessperson after businessperson vociferously opposes local government effort to create a more livable street. Conservative and liberal alike, we join hands to support road widening and oppose road narrowing—to "ease congestion." (Ironically, in the face of efforts to restrain excessive, reckless car travel, which are actually in the best interests of the motoring public, our knee-jerk, "commonsense" conclusion is that such restraint is detrimental. Who understands, for example, that widening a road will *worsen* traffic congestion and increase road rage?)

Many of us, in a NIMBY-like way, oppose *any* new development. Who can blame us? For the past 50 years, nearly every development has worsened our quality of life.

We continue to fight the wrong battles. We battle to save Bambi in the city—where our focus needs to be not on wildlife habitat, but human habitat. We rail against population growth. We insist upon large landscaped buffers and setbacks. We oppose higher residential densities. We scream for bigger roads and giant parking lots when a large project is proposed.

Who among us recognizes that our single-minded effort to design for cars instead of people underlies our diminishing quality of life?

Among the many explanations for this dilemma, two seem especially telling to me. First, we have given up on efforts to rein in our overdependence on car travel. But the second, and possibly the most important explanation, lies in this: for the businessperson or the neighborhood activist to identify the auto-oriented causes of our difficulties is a form of *self-indictment*. Surely, it cannot be our fault. There must be some mistake. Let's blame the usual suspects. Big business. Developers. Government. Anyone but ourselves.

Transportation planning "choices" usually spring from *misinformed* community opinion. Opinion and demand is distorted by market failures caused by public subsidies. "Transportation surveys and models . . . essentially ask, 'If we build additional road capacity, will motorists use it,' which [in a distorted, subsidized travel market like ours] is equivalent to asking how many people would eat at a restaurant if meals were free."[1]

"If you ask people, 'Do you think that traffic congestion is a major problem?' most would probably say yes. If you ask them, 'Would you rather expand our road system or use pricing to solve congestion problems?' a majority might choose the road [widening] option. This is how transportation planning choices are typically defined. But if you present a more realistic choice by asking, 'Would you rather spend a lot of money widening highways to provide only moderate, short term congestion reductions, but which over the long term will increase personal, municipal, social and environmental costs, cause urban sprawl, and leave a legacy of automobile dependency, or would you rather start to create a more diverse transportation system?' the preference for roadway investments is likely to disappear."[2]

THE METASTASIS OF SPRAWL

It seems clear to me that sprawl is not possible without a transportation environment that encourages and *enables* excessive car travel. In my opinion, we need to identify auto-dependency as the culprit (not the loss of Bambi or the failure to stop overpopulation) if we are to effectively and efficiently control sprawl—particularly because we don't have the time or money to misidentify the critical causative agent over which we have some control.

It is much more feasible for us to control urban design, development patterns, and our transportation system than to control worldwide population. (I'm assuming that we must control *worldwide* population, because I know of no humane way to control immigration.) I believe that environmental and financial conditions will force us to establish an environment rich in transportation *choice* (as opposed to a "no choice" car-based environment) much sooner than worldwide population growth will force us to mend our ways. Both will inevitably be forced upon us. I just think auto dependency will stop long before worldwide population growth does.

Given all this, my work and advocacy focus on addressing transportation and development patterns. While I remain intellectually supportive of population control, I don't believe we can build a better future with that tool in my lifetime. I also worry that if we focus too much on population control, we'll waste time and money better spent on correcting bad urban design, whose results we see going on all around us each day.

We can look upon population growth as a bacterial epidemic that, uncontrolled, spreads across our landscape. But we can make this population-growth bacteria harmless and benign with the proper antibiotic: walkable design and transportation choice.

In contrast, an auto-dependent community will *inevitably* spread like a bacterial plague. THERE IS NO ANTIBIOTIC OR OTHER CURE for the auto-dependent bacteria. When we do everything we can to make cars happy, the sprawl plague spreads REGARDLESS of whether we control population. As a quality-of-life doctor, then, my prescription is to use walkable design and transportation choice, rather than population control, to cure my urban patient.

WHAT WE NEED

To assure a pleasant future, communities require characteristics that are extremely difficult to find: courage, leadership, wisdom, vision, and pride—exactly the sorts of attributes we find lacking in so many officials today, who increasingly cringe in the face of rising hostility and abuse from apoplectic citizens fed up with the character of community development over the past 50 years, mostly unaware of the real battles that need to be fought. The knee-jerk response, too often, is to revert to head-in-the-sand NIMBYism, or refuge provided by a counterproductive moral high ground.

We need visionaries able to imagine what could be. Without them, America's auto-oriented culture is on the road to ruin.

Without pride in our community or what it can become, we have no motivation to protect it from further degradation. A community without self-respect is a community willing to serve as a doormat to its economic development regime. While it may experience short-term economic gain, such a community guarantees its long-term economic decline. Courage and informed leadership are critical precisely because immense economic and emotional forces are aligned to drag a community into a downward spiral.

A great many dedicated, intelligent, vigilant people have seen their communities evolve into a nightmarish "auto slum," despite the best and most energetic citizen activism. Many throw up their hands and finally flee to remote, sprawling locations at the fringe of their community, or seek out a new paradise in a different part of the country.

As I have tried to point out, the tools we need to create a healthy, sustainable future are unpopular, largely because the car creates a self-perpetuating, self-promoting vicious cycle that drives us toward a point of no return. Each day, subsidized, sexy cars—and the far-flung, dispersed, unwalkable communities designed for them—recruit thousands more Americans to wage war in the interests of car travel. Every day, enraged by congestion or slowpokes driving in front of us, we find ourselves upping our resolve to create a community that is delightful for our Dodge. The values we motorists fight for are the values designed to make cars happy and, in the process, degrade the quality of human life, since the needs of cars and people inevitably clash.

Yet I am increasingly optimistic about our future. Eventually, our car dependency will hit a brick wall in terms of how much we can afford and how much we can stand the extreme auto orientation and deterioration of our quality of life—the mad dash to foul our own nest will eventually become both unaffordable and, partly for that reason, obvious to the majority of us.

Quality of life, originating from our returning to the tradition of designing for people instead of cars, is a powerful economic engine that will bring us lasting prosperity, a strong sense of community pride, and livable, sustainable cities. There are already signs of such a paradigm shift all over the country.

We can work *with* the market by insisting that at least one or a couple of development projects and road projects use modest, people-scaled design strategies described in this book—projects that can become enviable models. Such models can show citizens, developers, and property owners that there is a large latent demand for quality, people-oriented design—growing numbers of us will seek to be able to live in places that mimic such models, because their success—their attractiveness—is so obvious, and no longer seems like an impossible dream. To this end, we can seek out wise, courageous leaders with a vision—it is a daunting task, to guide a community toward a sustainable future.

A WORD ABOUT LEADERSHIP

We need more leaders of the courageous caliber of Nancy Graham in West Palm Beach, Joseph Riley in Charleston, John Norquist in Milwaukee. Does your community have the leadership essential for building a quality city? Here's a litmus test: pay attention to how your elected officials respond to a proposed public building project. When the project is announced, the deluge comes immediately: a tidal wave of citizen demands that elected officials revise the project's "too expensive" design, often from constituents paying enormous property taxes to subsidize auto-dependent services and facilities.

At this point, most elected officials fall all over themselves to cut all the "expendable frills"—the ornamentation, the building details, the features that give character to the building. After all, who walks anymore? Pedestrians don't matter. (No one mentions cars.) The result is another sterile, dreary, boxy public building—a dead zone in a downtown or other commercial area. When elected officials are offered an opportunity to "save tax dollars and make a development project more affordable," the mad dash toward mediocrity has begun—despite the fact that such a plain, featureless, characterless public building sends the unmistakable message that "we have no pride in our community (or our downtown). . . . Our community is not important." Furthermore, the so-called savings are, at best, short term because they will quickly be spent on the voracious roads and cars.

The lesson here? At times, we need urban development regulations to protect our communities less against private developers than against *public* officials desperate to avoid making *anyone* unhappy, even if such desperation means dishonoring the public realm with embarrassing, forgettable, built-on-the-cheap public buildings.

Similar worries, however, must be assigned to private development. Repeatedly, public officials without a vision are more than happy to have their community serve as a doormat—to let a developer "walk all over" the community by failing to request any form of locally appropriate design, to cheerfully accept a formulaic national chain building recipe which runs roughshod over community objectives and erodes a unique community character.

One glaring difference between mediocre and effective leadership is an unwillingness to compromise when it comes to designing for quality of life—indeed, true leaders insist on quality, even if it stirs up controversy. Elected officials who are not leaders typically have no vision and no agenda for what needs to be achieved, no long-range quality-of-life plan that they adhere to. They are indecisive and lack the courage to make a difficult, controversial decision—putting off the decision as long as possible, or hoping it can be passed on to the voters in a referendum. They are too often distracted by "applause meter politics," or the "squeaky wheel," which leads to a chaotic, rudderless, ad hoc approach to managing a community. Lowest-common-denominator efforts to "please everyone" is a recipe for mediocrity. "To achieve excellence," Charleston Mayor Joseph Riley once said, "should be a struggle."

Elected officials who show such an uncompromising attitude in achieving the objectives of the community instill confidence in their citizens and their staff. In such an environment, staff is more willing to be innovative. Citizens are more willing to be forgiving and patient.

Three fundamental elements create this kind of community leader. First is the courage to be steadfast in pursuit of an improved quality of community life, that is, to not cave in to multiple pressures toward compromise when a proposal is clearly in the public interest—from financial vested interests to misguided, misleading, smoke-screen concern about "poor people" and short-sighted calls for "penny-wise, pound-foolish" changes.

Second is the wisdom to recognize quality and timeless design in the public realm and not be swayed by spurious design arguments.

Third is the decisiveness to grasp the moment, to move quickly on a project while the vision is sharp in the minds of the decision makers (thus avoiding Death by Lowest Common Denominator, the nondecision that offends no one because it accomplishes nothing). This leader understands that putting off decisions or referring decisions to boards, task forces, or committees (which substantially increases the number of decision makers), almost invariably dumbs down or kills a proposal.

CRUCIAL STEPS

What follows is a short list of the crucial steps I believe we must take.

First, we must place a moratorium on any plans to widen or add capacity to urban streets. Urban streets that exceed three lanes and are under 25,000 car trips per day must be put on a road diet, reduced to no more than two or three lanes. Most all of our street intersections, similarly, must be shrunk in size and buildings pulled up to the intersection corners. A failure to put the brakes on big, multilane roads and intersections guarantees that the community will be unavoidably moving toward a future of urban sprawl, in-town urban blight, an increasing dependency on travel by car, and an overall declining quality of life.

An extremely common and terrible mistake made by communities across the nation is to insist that an enormous proposed project be accompanied by larger roads and bigger parking lots. Such advocates are either grasping at straws to try to make a project financially infeasible or, worse, are naively trying to avoid "gridlock" or congestion associated with the project. Too frequently, a large development is able to comply with this community demand. The result is not to reduce the undesirable impacts of the development, but rather exactly the opposite. The result of such "improvements" for a big project, as this book has urged, is to worsen the quality of life for the community because of an increased auto orientation and a reduced sense of place. Next stop: Anywhere, USA sprawl.

Second, even if road diets are not possible, we must at least revise our engineering "cookbooks" describing the design of our new and reconstructed streets. Instead of a one-size-fits-all approach, streets need to be *context sensitive*. That is, it may be fine for interstates and outlying rural roads to be wide and high-speed in their design. But once a road enters a community, the design must change. Lanes should be narrower and fewer in number, sidewalks must be installed, "superelevations" need to be avoided, curbs should be used. That is, *low-speed* street design specifications must be incorporated when a road enters a community. Inside a community, livability is the imperative, not high-speed car travel.

Third, we must institute traffic calming throughout the community to reduce both the travel speed of cars and the *expectation* of how fast one can drive. Anything less assures that our neighborhoods will continue to suffer and decline.

Fourth, we need to control the supply and location of auto parking. Too much parking, or parking located in front of a building, breeds car trips, reduces safety, and deadens the community.

Fifth, local and state government must adopt modest, human-scaled, context-sensitive design features in locations deemed by the community to be appropriate for walkability. In such locations, pull buildings up to streets and public sidewalks. Make parking lots smaller and place them in discreet locations away from the fronts of buildings. Make traffic lights, street lights, and signs more modest in size and height. Ensure that crossing streets is safe and convenient not only for adults, but for seniors and children. Designate other areas as suburban and rural, with development standards appropriate for such lifestyles.

Sixth, destinations must be within closer proximity to each other, near enough to make it easy to walk or bicycle to shops, offices, parks, cultural events, and civic activities.

Seventh, we need to increase residential densities in general—in appropriate locations. Since most American communities have developed at densities too low to make transit or walking possible, such compact, walkable residential development will need to be achieved incrementally in a great many locations—particularly in most in-town locations.

Last, our communities must move away from the "one size fits all" approach to design. Citywide standards for streets, buildings, setbacks, and parking represent a recipe for disaster because the needs of an outlying, car-dependent area differ radically from the needs of compact, walkable, in-town areas. By applying the same standards citywide, we lose housing and travel choices. Standards must be customized for various city neighborhoods, depending on their location. Those who prefer an auto-oriented lifestyle should be accommodated with larger setbacks, larger parking lots, and larger roads, as long as doing so is not paid by the entire community. Those who prefer a more compact, walkable lifestyle should be treated to more modest, people-scaled dimensions.

"Smart growth" strategies such as these may be smart for *people,* but they tend to be perceived as anything *but* smart for our old Plymouth or new Porsche. Which goes a long way toward explaining why city planners are so often surprised to see the full political spectrum of opposition arrayed against the use of such strategies. Because so many of us have been so wedded to car travel for so many decades, each of these essential community tactics is likely to face intense opposition from the great majority of citizens in most American communities.

In fact, the list of tactics represents both the most essential tasks *and* the most despised, highly opposed policies. While the vast majority of Americans openly oppose sprawl, they also happen to strongly support many of the elements that make sprawl more likely. We have spent decades designing communities to make cars happy, as Andres Duany has pointed out. If we are as interested in creating a more livable country as I believe we are, it is time to focus on making *people* happy.

That is where courageous leadership comes in. I agree with the person who said that if a policy maker is not making enemies, as well as friends, she or he is *not doing anything*.

It is time for us to start doing something.

It is time for visionary courage.

APPENDIX A

Urban-Rural Transect Regulatory Matrix

	TC	SG	RR
Max density	30–150 du/ac	3–8 du/ac[a]	?
Uses permitted	Mixed	Residential only	Farms, rural homesteads, preserves
Max FAR	2–10	1	0.4
Frontage parallel to street	Required	Optional	Optional
Frontage build-out	60–80% min.	40% min.	30% min.
Max lot width	24 ft	No maximum	No maximum
Front build-to (setback)	0–20 ft	20–40 ft	25 ft min.
Frontage build-to for parcel at street intersection	0–10 ft from each ROW. No parking, storm basins, gas pumps allowed on street frontage w/o at least 50 ft of building frontage at intersection corner along same side of ROW. Main entrance at intersection corner.	No build-to required	0–30 ft from each ROW. No parking, storm basins, gas pumps allowed on street frontage w/o at least 50 ft of building frontage at intersection corner of ROW. Main entrance at intersection corner.

(Continued)

	TC	SG	RR
Side setback	0 ft	7.5 ft	5 ft
Rear setback	0 ft	20 ft	24 ft
Height			
Minimum	Façade 20 ft, or two stories	None	None
Maximum	Four to five stories (none for civic)	Three stories (none for civic)	Two stories (none for civic)
Street design	Low speed (20 mph max)	Existing	Existing
Street intersection size	Max ped cross Medium. distance is 36–48 ft	Large	Varies
Corner radii	9 ft residential, 15 ft commercial	Existing	Existing
Max block length	500 ft	1,000 ft	N.A.
Street pattern	Connected, rectilinear	Disconnected curvilinear	Disconnected, curvilinear
Maximum no. of travel lanes	2	4	4
Sidewalks	6–10 ft[b]	5 ft	Optional, 4 ft
Fences	Max. 40 in. for front yards and side streets, 76 in. for rear and side not on a street. Wood, masonry, wrought iron, brick are allowed materials. Chain-link not allowed.	Chain-link allowed. Unlimited fence height. No restriction on material used.	Chain-link allowed. Unlimited fence height. No restriction on material used.
Parking	Max., number of spaces allowed not min. Rear and side location	Min., number of spaces required not max.	Min., number of spaces required not max.

(Continued)

	TC	SG	RR
Large trash receptacles, outdoor mech. equipment	Not allowed at front or near street, sidewalk	No restriction	No restriction
Orientation	Entrance faces street	No restriction	No restriction
Bldg articulation	No more than 30 ft blank horizontal façade, at least 20–50% first floor glazing^c	No more than 50 ft blank horizontal façade, at least 10% first floor glazing	No restriction
Street trees	Formally aligned, same tree species on block face	Picturesque clumping or aligned, diverse trees on block face	Picturesque clumping or aligned, diverse trees on block face
Lighting fixture	No higher than 20 ft	No higher than 40 ft	No higher than 30 ft
Prohibited uses	Auto sales, auto service, car wash, gas stations, principal use parking lots, outdoor storage, freestanding retail greater than 30,000 sf, gas pumps when accessory to food store	Nonresidential; multifamily.	Variable
Drive-throughs	Not allowed on "A" street, no more than one drive-through lane, must be at rear or side of building.	No restriction	No restriction
Curb and gutter	Required	Optional	Open swales allowed
Open space	Plazas, squares	Parks, meadows	Parks, meadows
On-street parking	Required	Allowed	Allowed

(Continued)

	TC	SG	RR
Alleys[d]	Removal not allowed	Allowed	Allowed
Balconies, porches	Can encroach into ROW	No encroachment	Variable
Signs	Wall-mount, projecting from wall, or above top of façade. No more than 10% of façade.	Conventional	Variable
Outbuildings	Allowed	Not allowed	Allowed
Residential garages	Recessed at least 10 ft from façade[e]	No restrictions	Variable
Parking structure	First floor must be office/retail	No restrictions	N.A.

[a]Density maximum (in dwelling units per acre) within this range based on underlying zoning district.

[b]On local streets, 6 ft for multifamily and industrial, 7 ft for commercial, mixed use, office, institutional. On collector streets, 7 ft for multifamily and industrial, 8 ft for commercial, mixed use, office, institutional. On arterial streets, 7 ft for multifamily and industrial, 10 ft for commercial, mixed use, office, institutional.

[c]30% glazing required for multifamily residential.

[d]Alleys must be retained if present.

[e]The garage must not be more than 40% of the length of the front façade of the house or 8 feet, whichever is greater, garage doors may be no more than 75 sf, and there can be no more than two individual garage doors.

APPENDIX B

Special Area Plan for Transforming a Conventional Center

With this Special Area Plan, the city calls for the retrofitting of the shopping center to function as a walkable town or neighborhood center.

(a) **Purpose.** The purpose of this plan is to accommodate redevelopment of the "XXX" Shopping Center that will gradually transform the Center into a walkable, mixed-use neighborhood center that features transportation choice, high-quality urban design, high levels of retail health, and interconnection to nearby neighborhoods.

(c) **Objectives.** The provisions of this plan are intended to accommodate redevelopment of the Shopping Center to:

    (1) Promote the development of both residential and nonresidential development.

    (2) Ensure that design gradually creates a walkable, "park-once" atmosphere featuring vibrancy, sociability, aesthetics, and improved retail health.

    (3) Create a connected grid of internal streets.

(d) **Effect of Classification.** This Special Area Plan is applied as an Overlay Zoning District. It shall operate in conjunction with any underlying zoning district in this area. The regulations of the underlying zoning district, and all other applicable regulations, remain in effect and are further regulated by the Special Area Plan. If provisions of the Special Area Plan conflict with the underlying zoning, the provisions of the Special Area Plan shall prevail.

(e) Specific Regulations.

    1. **Internal Streets.** Figure "X" [figure 9.1 in chapter 9] shows, conceptually, the internal, connected street grid that could be incorporated in

the shopping center. Owners of the shopping center shall be responsible for designating and establishing an internal street grid. The design speed for streets shall be no more than 20 miles per hour, and streets shall allow on-street parking.

2. **New Buildings.** New buildings constructed in the shopping center shall have a build-to of 0 feet. The building shall place its primary entrance to face the street and shall be at least two stories high. Buildings shall be aligned to form squares, streets, plazas, or other forms of a pleasant public realm. The first floor of new buildings shall have at least 30 percent transparent glazing. No more than 20 horizontal feet of unarticulated blank wall is allowed.

3. **Transit Stop.** The shopping center shall incorporate a strong, convenient, safe transit stop that is a short and easy walk from residential and nonresidential uses in the center.

4. **Connections.** When possible, cross-access between adjacent property and the shopping center shall be established so that travel can avoid the fronting major arterial street and provide travel choices by nearby developments and neighborhoods.

5. **Density Cascade.** Densities and intensities within the center shall cascade downward from the core of the center to the edges of the center.

6. **Sidewalks.** All front building facades shall front a sidewalk. The sidewalk shall be wide enough to permit 8 feet of clear width, street trees, and sidewalk furniture.

7. **Parking.** Off-street parking shall be to the rear or side of buildings. Parking lots shall be designed as plazas that sometimes happen to have cars parked on them. Multi-story parking garages are encouraged and shall be fronted by liner buildings having retail or office.

8. **Uses.** The shopping center shall not contain auto-oriented uses, as listed in Table XX in Sec. XXX of the Land Development Code or uses that generate significant noise, odor, visual blight, or dust.

9. **Gateways.** The shopping center shall create a sense of arrival and departure.

10. **Landscaping.** Considerable landscaping, especially in "bulb-outs," on balconies, and on rooftops, is encouraged.

Additional Encouraged Uses and Features. Community-serving public gathering facilities such as schools, libraries, residential, recreation centers, and child care are encouraged, as are public spaces with strong design features, such as water, benches, and public art.

Notes

INTRODUCTION

1. Gavin, *A Road Runs Through It*, 26.
2. Jackson, *Crabgrass Frontier*, 279–281.
3. Ibid.
4. Newman and Kenworthy, *Sustainability and Cities*, 83.
5. Schor, *The Overworked American*, 103, 109.
6. Transportation and Land Use Study Committee, "Final Report," 14.
7. Engwicht, *Reclaiming Our Cities and Towns*, 41, citing TEST (Transport and Environment Studies), *Quality Streets.*
8. Newman and Kenworthy, *Sustainability and Cities*, 64.
9. By making cars, not people, more comfortable, we *induce* more car trips (and more car problems) that otherwise would not have occurred.
10. Porter, "The Future Doesn't Work," 14.
11. The findings of many studies support this conclusion, among them Burrington, "Restoring the Rule of Law," 4, 7; Florida Center for Community Design and Research, *Integrating Community Design*, 222; Hine and Russel, "Traffic Barriers," 230–239; Surface Transportation Policy Project, *Mean Streets, 1998.*
12. "Nationwide Overhaul of Land Use Laws Needed," *New Urban News*, January–February 2001, 2.
13. Ibid. 7.

CHAPTER 1: DIRE STRAITS

1. richlaymandc@YAHOO.COM, "Rail Projects Are Sign of a Quiet Revolution," PRO-URB@LISTSERV.UGA.EDU. Accessed 6 June 2002.
2. Institute of Food and Agricultural Sciences, "Personal Transportation."
3. Newman and Kenworthy, *Sustainability and Cities*, 120, 122, 150–151.

4. Weissman and Corbett, *Land Use Strategies*, 25.

5. Newman and Kenworthy, *Sustainability and Cities*, 141–142.

6. Schwarzkopf, "Citizens Clean Air Project," http://www.houstonprogres sive.org/hpn/ccap-haq.html. Accessed 10 June 2002.

7. Stack, "Clear Houston Air Remains Elusive."

8. See Ewing, "Characteristics, Causes," 10.

9. Sayer, *The Costs of Sprawl*, 11.

10. Environmental Exchange, "Alternative Traffic Studies," Transportation Exchange Update, *What Works*, March 1994.

11. Conservation Law Foundation, *Take Back Your Streets*, 24.

12. U.S. Department of Transportation, *Traffic Safety Facts 2000*.

13. Spitzer, *The Roads More Traveled*.

14. Mitigation Panel, *Policy Implications*.

15. Chafee, "Driving home," 22.

16. U.S. Environmental Protection Agency, *Our Built and Natural Environments*, 8.

17. Hart, *The Elephant in the Bedroom*, 31.

18. Engwicht, *Reclaiming Our Cities and Towns*, 45.

19. U.S. Environmental Protection Agency, *Our Built and Natural Environments*, 66.

20. Dimitriou, *Urban Transport Planning*, 136. A person walking takes up about 6 square feet; biking, about 20 square feet; on a train, less than 5 square feet. A car in motion needs 500 to 1,000 square feet in addition to parking spaces (Bulley, "Personal Rapid Transit," e-mail to Pro-urg@listerv.uga.edu, re: "Personal Rapid Transit—Is It Viable?" Accessed 13 April 2002.)

21. McCann, *Driven to Spend*, 6, 9.

22. Segal, "What We Work for Now."

23. See http://www.seasonofsharing.org/autoexp.html. Accessed 15 June 2002.

24. McCann, *Driven to Spend*, 8.

25. Moore and Thorsnes, *The Transportation/Land Use Connection*. The authors' estimate includes road construction, maintenance, repair, emergency services, parking, costs to drivers (operation, capital, travel time, congestion), air and noise pollution, and accidents.

26. "Smart Pricing for Transportation Improvements," 82.

27. Goddard, *Getting There*, 252.

28. International Center for Technology Assessment, *Real Price of Gas*, 1.

29. Litman, "Fuel Taxes."

30. Goddard, *Getting There*, 251–55.

31. Surface Transportation Policy Project, *ISTEA Year Three*.

32. Schuster, "The Full Costs of Commuting."

33. U.S. Department of Transportation, *Federal Highway Cost Allocation Study*.

34. Goddard, *Getting There*, 250.

35. Litman, "Market Principles," *Online TDM Encyclopedia*, 1–7.

36. Krugman, "Reckonings: Nation in a Jam."

37. Campaign for New Transportation Priorities, *Transportation and Tax Policy*, 4.

38. Small, Winston, and Evans, *Road Work*, 57.

39. Miller, *Environmental Science,* 52.

40. Institute of Food and Agricultural Sciences, *Personal Transportation,* 1.

41. U.S. Department of Transportation, *Environmental Benefits,* 36.

42. Litman, "Parking Pricing."

43. Smith, "The Low-Rise Speculative Apartment," cited in Litman, *Parking Requirement Impacts.*

44. Litman, *Parking Requirement Impacts,* 11, 13.

45. According to the 1999 U.S. Census, of 103 million reporting households, 11 percent were bothered by noise, 8 percent by crime, and 4 percent by odor. *American Housing Survey for the U.S.: 1999,* table 2–8. Michael Phillip Wright, http://members.aol.com/mpwright9/noise6.html. Accessed 15 October 2002.

46. Conservation Law Foundation, *Take Back Your Streets,* 26.

47. Surface Transportation Policy Project, *ISTEA Year Three.*

48. Lockwood, "The New Urbanism's Call," 10.

49. Fulton et. al., *Who Sprawls Most?* 3.

50. Chen, "The Science of Smart Growth," 85.

51. Bookout, "Neotraditional Town Planning," 10.

52. Kasowski, "Suburban Sprawl," 3.

53. Harris, "The Need, Rationale, and Implementation."

54. Frank, *Costs of Alternative Development Patterns,* 5; Sayer, "Costs of Sprawl," 11.

55. Kasowski, "Costs of Sprawl, Revisited."

56. Dover and Poole, "Rediscovery and Process."

57. Hanson, "Automobile Subsidies," 62

58. Center for Urban Transportation Research, *Transportation, Land Use,* 13.

59. Rybczynski, "Rebuilding Los Angeles, *Gainesville Sun,* 11 June 1992.

60. Gottlieb, "One Who Would Like to See Most Architects Hit the Road."

CHAPTER 2: WE HAVE MET THE ENEMY . . . AND IT IS WE MOTORISTS

1. Ewing, "Characteristics, Causes," 7.

2. Transportation and Land Use Study Committee, *Final Report,* 5.

3. Cervero, "Unlocking Suburban Gridlock," 400.

4. Pew Center for Civic Journalism, "Top Local Problems"; Kollodge, " 'Transportation' cited."

5. Goddard, *Getting There,* 169. Owen, an economist, was the consultant to FDR's National Resources Planning Board, set up to plan America's future.

6. Hoyt, "The Influence of Highways and Transportation," 206.

7. Moore and Thorsnes, *The Transportation/Land Use Connection,* 2; see also Newman and Kenworthy, *Cities and Automobile Dependence,* 106.

8. Goddard, *Getting There,* 200.

9. Kunstler, *Home from Nowhere,* 30.

10. Goddard, *Getting There,* 197.

11. Ibid., 194.

12. Ibid., 68.

13. Forbes, "Vital Signs," 27.

14. See Levinson and Kumar, "Activity, Travel," 458–70; Manning, *The Journey to Work*; Neff, *Substitution Rates*; Pederson, *Transportation in Cities*; Stokes, "Travel Time Budgets," 25–36; Zahavi and Ryan, "Stability of Travel Components," 19–26.

15. Ewing, "Los Angeles Style Sprawl Desirable?" 107.

16. Newman and Kenworthy, *Cities and Automobile Dependence*, 106.

17. Goddard, *Getting There*, 199.

18. Kulash, "Traditional Neighborhood Development," 3–2.

19. Icon architecture includes McDonald's golden arches and other immediately recognizable corporate emblems.

20. Lincoln Institute of Land Policy, *Alternatives to Sprawl*.

21. Plowden, *Towns against Traffic*, 18.

22. Surface Transportation Policy Project, *Why Are the Roads*.

23. Goddard, *Getting There*, 178.

24. Downs, "Might As Well Enjoy It."

25. Surface Transportation Policy Project, *High Mileage Moms*, 1, 3.

26. McCann, *Driven to Spend*, 10.

27. Ketcham, *Making Transportation Choices*, 8.

28. Newman and Kenworthy, "Gasoline Consumption and Cities," 32, *Cities and Automobile Dependence*, 157.

29. Jackson, "Transportation Concurrency"; see also Cervero, *America's Suburban Centers*; Moore and Thorsnes, *The Transportation/Land Use Connection*.

30. Newman and Kenworthy, *Cities and Automobile Dependence*, 160, 163, 164.

31. See, for example, Litman, "Generated Traffic," *ITE Journal*, 38.

32. University of California Transportation Research Center, 2000.

33. Newman and Kenworthy, *Cities and Automobile Dependence*, 148, 152, 157, 158.

34. Holtzclaw, "New Emissions Assay."

35. Newman and Kenworthy, *Cities and Automobile Dependence*, 151.

36. Center for Urban Transportation Research, *Transportation, Land Use*, 17.

37. Richert, "Markets for Traditional Neighborhoods," 1.

38. Nathan R. Norris to pro-urb@listserv.uga.edu, 29 October 2002.

39. Lee, "Place Making in Suburbia," 73.

40. Freeman, "The Effects of Sprawl," 76.

41. Ewald, *A Concept*, 52–53.

42. Institute of Transportation Engineers, *Traditional Neighborhood Development*, 5.

43. Congress for the New Urbanism, Toronto, Ontario, Canada, 1997.

44. Longman, "Sprawl," 44.

45. Sayer, "The Costs of Sprawl," 11.

46. Heimlich and Anderson, *Development at the Urban Fringe*; Chen, "The Science of Smart Growth," 86.

47. Chen, "The Science of Smart Growth," 88.

48. 1000 Friends of Oregon, "The Debate over Density."

49. Litman, "Land Use Impacts," 10.

50. Langdon, *A Better Place to Live*, 48–49.

51. Cohen, "Anybody Home?"; Calthorpe, *The Next American Metropolis*, 9.

52. Surface Transportation Policy Project, *High Mileage Moms*.

53. Corless and Sprowls, *Beyond Gridlock*.

54. Surface Transportation Policy Project, *High Mileage Moms.*

55. Presentation at "Brytan Charrette," by W. Kulash, R. Gibbs, and A. Duany, Gainesville, Fla., 26 June 2000.

CHAPTER 3: FIGHTING THE WRONG BATTLES

1. U.S. Environmental Protection Agency, Our Built and Natural Environments, 19, 21.

2. U.S. Department of Transportation, Statistical Abstract of the U.S., 2001, table 1084, 680.

3. Center for Urban Transportation Research, Transportation, Land Use, 11.

4. Surface Transportation Policy Project, "Why Are the Roads So Congested?"

5. Ibid.

6. Florida Center for Community Design and Research, *Transportation, Land Use, and Sustainability,* 1.

7. Rusk, "Debate on Theories of David Rusk."

8. U.S. Environmental Protection Agency, *Our Built and Natural Environments,* 5, 6.

9. Ibid., 4.

10. Duany, Plater-Zyberk, and Speck, *Suburban Nation,* 142.

11. Ibid., 141.

12. For the quotation, see Chen, "The Science of Smart Growth," 86.

13. S. Hach, Sustainable Alachua County Listserve. Gainesville, Fla., 15 June 2000.

14. Goddard, *Getting There,* 193.

CHAPTER 4: MISGUIDED SOLUTIONS: THE
TENDENCY TO FOUL OUR OWN NEST

1. Newman and Kenworthy, *Cities and Automobile Dependence,* 71.

2. Webb, "What Cities Can Do," 50.

3. Ibid., 106.

4. Nozzi, "West Palm Beach."

5. "Highway engineers [during the Roosevelt and Eisenhower administrations] reflected happily that expressways increased values of suburban land adjacent to new interstates. What they never seemed to talk about was how urban land values often fell when impacted by highway projects" (Goddard, *Getting There,* 219).

6. Kulash, "Traditional Neighborhood Development," 5-2.

7. McCann, *Driven to Spend,* 22.

8. Downs, *Stuck in Traffic,* 27–30.

9. Ewing, *Pedestrian- and Transit-Friendly Design,* 14.

10. Presentation at "Brytan Charrette," by W. Kulash, R. Gibbs, and A. Duany, Gainesville, Fla., 26 June 2000.

11. Clarke, "Putting Pedestrians on a Pedestal," 165; also see Newman and Kenworthy, *Sustainability and Cities,* 140.

12. House Public Works Committee hearings, 1955–56.

13. Goddard, *Getting There*, 189.

14. Ibid., 58.

15. The goal of The Surface Transportation Policy Project (STPP) is to ensure that transportation policy and investments help conserve energy, protect environmental and aesthetic quality, strengthen the economy, promote social equity, and make communities more livable. The organization emphasizes the needs of people, rather than vehicles, in assuring access to jobs, services, and recreational opportunities. The work of STPP is made possible by individual donations and grants from a number of foundations.

16. Surface Transportation Policy Project, *An Analysis of the Relationship*, 1, 5.

17. Hansen and Huang, "Road supply," 205–218; Noland, "Relationships between Highway Capacity," 47–72.

18. Dorshner, "Road to Ruin," 16.

19. Porter, "The Future Doesn't Work"; Litman, "Generated Traffic," *ITE Journal*, 38.

20. Moore and Thornses, *The Transportation Land/Use Connection*, 56.

21. Conservation Law Foundation, *Take Back Your Streets*, 5.

22. Ibid.

23. Burrington, "Restoring the Rule of Law," 3, 4.

24. Longman, "Sprawl," 40.

25. Barnett and Klas, "Managing Growth," 70.

26. Ewing, "TDM, Growth Management," 10.

27. Transportation and Land Use Study Committee, *Final Report*.

CHAPTER 5: PUTTING THE BRAKES ON SPRAWL

1. Newman and Kenworthy, *Sustainability and Cities*, 187.

2. Taylor, "Public Perceptions," 46.

3. Florida Center for Community Design and Research, *Integrating Community Design*, 5.

4. U.S. Census Bureau. County and City Data Book: 2000. Table D-1.

5. Gainesville Department of Community Development, "Staff Analysis," 2000; *Florida Statistical Abstract*.

6. Weissman and Corbett, *Land Use Strategies*, 33.

7. Easley, *Staying Inside the Lines*, 14.

8. Moore and Thorsnes, *The Transportation/Land Use Connection*, 50, 113.

9. Richmond, "Comment on Carl Abbott's," 1.

10. Easley, *Staying Inside the Lines*, 11, 18.

11. Ibid., 80.

12. Moore and Thorsnes, *The Transportation/Land Use Connection*, 61.

13. U.S. Environmental Protection Agency, *Our Built and Natural Environments*, 78.

14. Cervero, *America's Suburban Centers*, 42.

15. U.S. Environmental Protection Agency. *Our Built and Natural Environments*, 61.

16. Newman and Kenworthy, *Cities and Automobile Dependence*, 42–47.

17. Ewing, "Characteristics, Causes," 7. Cervero, in *America's Suburban Centers* (46) recommends a ratio of jobs-to-housing units in a mixed-use neighborhood center of 0.75 to 1.50 (number of jobs divided by number of residences).

18. U.S. Environmental Protection Agency, *Our Built and Natural Environments*, 47.

19. Frank, "Linking Land Use and Transportation," 3.

20. Newman and Kenworthy, *Cities and Automobile Dependence*, 47, 129, 132.

21. Center for Urban Transportation Research, *Transportation, Land Use*, 21.

22. U.S. Environmental Protection Agency, *Our Built and Natural Environments*, 47.

23. Newman and Kenworthy, "Gasoline Consumption and Cities," 25.

24. Ibid., 29.

25. U.S. Department of Transportation, *Reasons Why Bicycling*, 24.

26. Holtzclaw, *Using Residential Patterns*.

27. Ibid., 69.

28. Ewing, "TDM, Growth Management," 24.

29. Holtzclaw, "Sustainability," 25.

30. U.S. Environmental Protection Agency, *Our Built and Natural Environments*, 48.

31. Ibid.

32. Morris, *Creating Transit-Supportive*, 41; Ewing, *Pedestrian- and Transit-Friendly*, 6.

33. Newman and Kenworthy, *Cities and Automobile Dependence*, 89–92.

34. Frank, *The Costs of Alternative Development Patterns*, 40.

35. Siemon and Zimet, "Public Places as Infrastructure," 4.

36. Smythe, *Density-Related Public Costs*.

37. U.S. Environmental Protection Agency, *Our Built and Natural Environments*, 41–43.

38. Ewing, "Is Los Angeles Style Sprawl Desirable?" 113.

39. Lucy, *Watch Out*, 14.

40. U.S. Environmental Protection Agency, *Our Built and Natural Environments*, 41.

41. "TODs in Oregon," *Urban Ecologist Newsletter*, 14.

42. Newman and Kenworthy, *Cities and Automobile Dependence*, 125.

43. Florida Center for Community Design and Research, *Integrating Community Design*, 217.

44. Burden, D. "Tower Road Charrette," PowerPoint presentation, Gainesville, Fla., 2000.

45. Downs, *New Visions*, 150.

46. U.S. General Accounting Office, *Community Development*.

47. McCann, *Driven to Spend*, 25; Earthword, "Transportation Planning."

48. McCann, *Driven to Spend*, 13.

49. Litman, "Location Efficient Development."

50. Litman, "Distance-Based Pricing."

51. Newman and Kenworthy, "Gasoline Consumption and Cities," 28, 29, 31.

CHAPTER 6: PROPERLY DESIGNING STREETS

1. Assuming eight miles of travel per day, the average car emits 1,609 kilograms of carbon dioxide, 141 kilograms of carbon monoxide, 4 kilograms of nitrogen oxide, and 11 kilograms of volatile organic compounds each year. Cars emit 551 grams of carbon dioxide, 48.2 grams of carbon monoxide, 1.33 grams of nitrogen oxide, and 11 grams of volatile organic compounds per mile (U.S. Department of Transportation, *Environmental Benefits*, 21).

2. Hart, *The Elephant in the Bedroom*, 48, 119.

3. Burrington, "Restoring the Rule of Law," 3.

4. Sandels, *Children in Traffic*.

5. Conservation Law Foundation, *Take Back Your Streets*, 7.

6. American Society of Civil Engineers et al., *Residential Streets*, 37.

7. Conservation Law Foundation, *Take Back Your Streets*, 6.

8. Stina Sandels, quoted in Engwicht, *Reclaiming Our Cites and Towns*, 50.

9. Untermann, *Accommodating the Pedestrian*, 175.

10. Conservation Law Foundation, *Take Back Your Streets*, 3.

11. Going from an average of 30 mph to 18.6 mph, there is a 13 to 17 percent decrease in carbon monoxide, a 10 to 22 percent decrease in hydrocarbons, a 32 to 48 percent decrease in nitrogen oxides, and a 7 percent decrease in fuel consumed (Newman and Kenworthy, *Sustainability and Cities*, 120, 122, 150–51).

12. Hoyle, *Traffic Calming*, 1.

13. Ibid., 5.

14. Shefer and Rietvald, "Congestion and Safety on Highways," 679–92.

15. American Society of Civil Engineers et al., *Residential Streets*, 28.

16. Lennard and Lennard, *Making Cities Livable*, 1987.

17. Conservation Law Foundation, *Take Back Your Streets*, 27.

18. Ibid., 32.

19. Ibid., 43.

20. Institute of Transportation Engineers, *Guidelines for the Design*, 3.

21. Hoyle, *Traffic Calming*, 1.

22. Ibid., 15.

23. Conservation Law Foundation, *Take Back Your Streets*, 37.

24. Ibid., 27.

25. U.S. Department of Transportation, *Traffic Calming*, 18.

CHAPTER 7: ENDING OUR LOVE AFFAIR WITH THE CAR

1. Litman, "Socially Optimal Transport Prices," 43.

2. Millard-Ball, "Putting on Their Parking Caps," 16, 18.

3. Dunphy, "No More Free Parking?" 10.

4. Ibid., 9, 10.

5. Shoup, "An Opportunity to Reduce Minimum Parking," 16.

6. Cervero, *America's Suburban Centers*, 3, 58, 205.

7. Shoup, "Congress Okays Cash Out," 2; Litman, "Market Principles," 7.

8. Shoup, "An Opportunity to Reduce Minimum Parking," 15.

9. California Environmental Protection Agency, "Parking Cash-Out Incentive."

10. Tumlin and Siegman, "The Cost of Free Parking," 7.

11. Litman, "Commuter Financial Incentives."

12. McCrea, "Preparing for the Post-Petroleum Era," 18.

13. Litman, "Potential Transportation Demand, 11.

14. Litman, "Commute Trip Reduction."

15. "Passes Help People," 2.

16. Land Use Digest, "Report Surveys Impact," 3.

17. Cervero, *America's Suburban Centers,* 58; Moore and Thorsnes, *The Transportation/Land Use Connection,* 74.

18. Hart, *The Elephant in the Bedroom,* 17.

19. Land Use Digest, "Report Surveys Impact," 3.

20. U.S. Department of Transportation, *Reasons Why Bicycling,* 55.

21. Shoup, "Congress Okays Cash Out," 4; Ewing, "TDM, Growth Management," 13.

22. Dunphy, "No More Free Parking?" 10.

23. Natural Resources Council, *Traveling Smart Handbook,* 17.

24. Lincoln Institute of Land Policy, *Making the Land use/Transportation/Air Quality Connection,* 6.

25. Litman, "Guaranteed Ride Home."

26. Gainesville Traffic Engineering Department, *Gator "Getting There" Guide.*

27. Litman, "Guide to Calculating," 3, 4.

28. Ewing, "TDM, Growth Management," 21.

29. Pryne, "Putting Shorter Commute on the Map."

30. Hanson, "Automobile Subsidies and Land Use," 67.

31. Hart, *The Elephant in the Bedroom,* 87, 88, 115.

32. Increased gas taxes are not necessarily harmful for lower-income groups. If the community is designed for transportation choice, low-income individuals can avoid the higher taxes by, for example, using the bus, bicycling, walking, or other means that reduce car use (Litman, "Evaluating Criticism," 4).

33. Hart, *The Elephant in the Bedroom,* 150, 151; International Center for Technology Assessment, "Real Price of Gas."

34. Hart, *The Elephant in the Bedroom,* 151; Durning and Bauman, *Tax Shift.*

35. Beilenson, "Either Raise the Gas Tax."

36. Castle, R. "Sustainability Tax—Not Income Tax," 31 May 2002, http://www.roncastle.com/writing/sustainability%20Tax%20%20Not%20Income%20ax.pdf., Accessed 16 July 2003.

37. Moore and Thorsnes, *The Transportation/Land Use Connection,* 73, 74.

38. Florida Center for Community Design and Research, *Livable Cities for Florida's Future,* 50.

39. Moore and Thorsnes, *The Transportation/Land Use Connection,* 76, 77.

40. Economist, "Jam Today, Road Pricing Tomorrow," London, 6 December 1997.

41. Litman, "Road Pricing," 5.

42. "Alternative Traffic Studies," 2; Plous, "Off the Road," 10.

43. Litman, "Road Pricing," 3–4.

44. Litman, "Market Principles," 5.

45. Litman, "Road Pricing," 1, 3; Moore and Thorsnes, *The Transportation/Land Use Connection,* 114.

46. Ewing, "TDM, Growth Management," 21.

47. Plous, "Off the Road," 11.

48. Litman, "Road Pricing," 6.

49. Hau, *Economic Fundamentals*.

50. Hart, *The Elephant in the Bedroom*, 139, 141, 144.

51. Downs, *Stuck in Traffic*, 27, 28.

52. Newman and Kenworthy, *Cities and Automobile Dependence*, 152.

53. U.S. Department of Transportation, *Measures to Overcome Impediments*, 47.

CHAPTER 8: GETTING BACK ON OUR FEET

1. Ewing, "Characteristics, Causes, and Effects," 2.

2. U.S. Department of Transportation, *The National Bicycling and Walking Study*, 30.

3. U.S. Department of Transportation, *Reasons Why Bicycling*, 45.

4. Personal Communication from M. A. Koos, State Trails Coordinator, Florida Department of Environmental Protection. Tallahassee, 5 December 1994.

5. U.S. Department of Transportation, *Measures to Overcome Impediments*, 43.

6. U.S. Department of Transportation, *Reasons Why Bicycling*, 59.

7. U.S. Department of Transportation, *The National Bicycling and Walking Study*, 30.

8. Burden, *Bike Lanes*.

9. Litman, "Transit Oriented Development," 5.

10. "Shorts."

11. Lincoln Institute of Land Policy, *Making the Land Use*, 4.

12. Corbett, *Portland's Livable Downtown*.

13. Belzer and Autler, "Transit-Oriented Development," ii, 4, 5, 8, 14.

14. Moore and Thorsnes, *The Transportation/Land Use Connection*, 72, 106, 112.

15. But excluding land, lighting, security, parking enforcement, increased air pollution, increased water pollution, increased noise pollution, reduced aquifer recharge, and discouragement of pedestrians and bus riders. "City Workers May Get RTS Passes, *Gainesville Sun*, 8 August 1994.

16. "Go Boulder."

17. City of Boulder, *Transportation Annual Report*.

18. "Free Ride."

19. Nataly Handlos (of Go Boulder! An organization promoting bicycling, walking and transit use), personal communication with author, Boulder, Colorado, 1 March 2001.

20. City of Boulder, *Transportation Annual Report*.

21. "Passes Help," 2.

22. Gordon, "Economic Incentives."

CHAPTER 9: DESIGNING FOR PEOPLE

1. Duany, "Our Urbanism," 37.

2. John Massengale, Congress for the New Urbanist listserver, 21 October 2000.

3. A copy of the Traditional City ordinance is available from the Gainesville, Florida, Department of Community Development.

4. Langdon, *A Better Place to Live,* xiii.

5. Institute of Transportation Engineers, *Traffic Engineering,* 5, 8, 13.

6. Lucy, "Watch Out," 14.

7. Ward, "It's Scary out There," 4.

8. Duany et al., *Suburban Nation,* 120.

9. Cervero, *America's Suburban Centers,* 42.

10. Institute of Transportation Engineers, *Traffic Engineering,* 13.

11. Morris, *Creating Transit-Supportive Land Use Regulations,* 45.

12. Institute of Transportation Engineers, *Traffic Engineering,* 6.

13. Gottlieb, "One Who Would Like."

14. Smith, *Planning and Implementing,* 29.

15. Presentation at "Brytan Charrette," by W. Kulash, R. Gibbs, and A. Duany, Gainesville, Fla., 26 June 2000.

16. Ewing, *Pedestrian- and Transit-Friendly Design,* 10, 13; Institute of Transportation Engineers, *Traffic Engineering,* 5.

17. Institute of Transportation Engineers, *Traffic Engineering,* 11; Florida Center for Community Design and Research, *Florida Pedestrian Safety Plan,* II–12.

18. Smith, *Planning and Implementing Pedestrian Facilities,* 4, 50, 61; Washington State Energy Office, *Municipal Strategies,* 12.

19. Ewing, "Beyond Speed," 11.

20. Gehl, *Life between Buildings,* 96.

21. Morris, *Creating Transit-Supportive Land Use Regulations,* 43.

22. Hochstein, "A New Urbanist Library," 81.

23. Swift, *Residential Street Typology,* 6.

24. Ibid., cited in *New Urban News* (Ithaca, N.Y.), November/December 1997, 9.

25. Duany et al., *Suburban Nation,* 67, 68.

26. Michael Wallwork told me in August 2000 that he was recently informed by a deputy fire chief that a new fire code is about to be implemented in Florida that requires, on new construction, 26-foot wide residential streets without parking, 30-foot wide street with parking on one side and 36-foot wide streets with parking on both sides. "It looks like the fire chiefs have got what they want and we have lost the battle to slow cars and make streets safer," he said.

27. Sucher, *City Comforts,* 130.

28. Ibid.

29. See Lagerberg, B., and Anderson, M., *Washington State Petroleum;* Florida Center for Community Design and Research, *Florida Pedestrian Safety Plan,* II-10; Metropolitan Transit Development Board, *Designing for Transit,* 12; Institute of Transportation Engineers, *Traffic Engineering,* 9, 10.

30. Institute of Transportation Engineers, *Traffic Engineering,* 11.

31. Ibid., 6, 12.

32. Ibid., 6, 8.

33. Sucher, *City Comforts,* 10.

34. Washington State Energy Office, *Municipal Strategies,* 16.

35. Florida Center for Community Design and Research, *Integrating Community Design,* 225.

36. Morris, *Creating Transit-Supportive Land Use Regulations,* 10.

37. Kunstler, J. H. *The Geography of Nowhere: The Rise and Decline of America's Man-Made Landscape,* New York: Touchstone, 1994.

CHAPTER 10: TOWARD BETTER DEVELOPMENT REGULATIONS

1. American Association of State Highway and Transportation Officials, *AASHTO Policy on Geometric Design,* 98–99.

2. Lincoln Institute of Land Policy, *Making the Land Use/Transportation Connection,* 11.

3. Kay, "Without a Car in the World."

4. Ratcliff quoted in Belmont, *Cities in Full,* 88.

5. Municipality of Metropolitan Seattle, *1991 Parking Utilization Study.*

6. Shoup, "An Opportunity to Reduce Minimum Parking," 19.

7. Gruen Gruen & Associates, *Employment and Parking.* Also see Willson, *Suburban Parking Economics,* 6.

8. Willson, *Suburban Parking Requirements,* 40.

9. Cervero, "Unlocking Suburban Gridlock," 391.

10. Calthorpe, *The Next American Metropolis,* 43.

11. Morris, "Oregon Transportation Planning Rule," 13.

12. Bianco and Adler, "The Politics of Implementation;" also available at http://www.upa.pdx.edu/CUS/.

13. Ferguson, *Transportation Demand Management,* Planners Advisory Service Report No. 477, Chicago: American Planning Association, March 1998, 36; Sno-Tran, *Creating Transportation Choices through Zoning,* Lynnwood, Wash.: Snohomish County (Washington) Transportation Authority, 1994, 12.

14. Sno-Tran, *Creating Transportation Choices,* 16.

15. Lincoln Institute of Land Policy, *Making the Land Use/Transportation Connection.*

16. For current information about road diets, contact Walkable Communities, Inc., at www.walkable.org.

17. In general, removal of travel lanes is feasible only when the volume of cars carried by the road does not exceed approximately 25,000 cars per day.

18. Evidence shows that diets can increase adjacent property values so quickly that the increased property tax revenue is able to pay for the diet in as little as one year. For more information about diets, see D. Burden, and P. Lagerway, "Road Diets," Walkable Communities, High Springs, Florida, March 1999 (unpublished).

19. Cunningham, "Main Street Successes in Florida."

CONCLUSION

1. Litman, "Generated Traffic," *Online TDM Encyclopedia,* 14.

2. Litman, "Transportation Cost Analysis," 12.

Bibliography

1000 Friends of Oregon. "The Debate over Density: Do Four-plexes Cause Canni-
balism?" *Landmark: 1000 Friends of Oregon* (www.friends.org/lndmrkwtr99.
html), Winter 1999.

Adler, J. "Bye-Bye, Suburban Dream." *Newsweek,* 15 May 1995.

"Alternative Traffic Studies Threaten Highway Project." *Transportation Exchange
Update,* March 1994.

American Association of State Highway and Transportation Officials. *AASHTO
Policy on Geometric Design of Highways and Streets.* Washington, D.C.: American Association of State Highway and Transportation Officials, 1990.

American Society of Civil Engineers, National Association of Home Builders of the
United States, and Urban Land Institute. *Residential Streets.* New York:
American Society of Civil Engineers, National Association of Home
Builders of the United States, and Urban Land Institute, 1990.

Arendt, R. *Rural by Design.* Cambridge, Mass.: Lincoln Land Institute, 1994.

Arrington, G. B. (1996). *Beyond the Field of Dreams.* Portland, Ore.: Tri-Met.

Barnett, C., and Klas, M. E. "Managing Growth: 10 Steps Toward a More Livable
Florida." *Florida Trend,* December 2000.

Beamguard, J. "Packing Pavement." *The Tampa Tribune,* 18 July 1999.

Beilenson, A. "Either Raise the Gas Tax Now or Pay OPEC Later." *Gainesville Sun,*
12 January 1989.

Belmont, S. *Cities in Full.* Chicago: American Planning Association, 2002.

Belzer, D., and Autler, G. "Transit-Oriented Development: Moving from Rhetoric
to Reality." Brookings Institution Center on Urban and Metropolitan Policy,
June 2002.

Bianco, M. J., and Adler, S. "The Politics of Implementation: Oregon's Statewide
Transportation Planning Rule—What's Been Accomplished and How." Dis-
cussion Paper 98–8, Center for Urban Studies, College of Urban and Public

Affairs, Portland State University, Portland, Oregon, November 1998, 22, 23.

"Bikes Not Lights Get CMAQ Funding in Chicago." *Transportation Exchange Update,* July 1993.

Blizzard, M. *Creating Better Communities: The LUTRAQ Principles.* Portland, Ore.: Sensible Transportation Options for People, 1996.

Bookout, L. W. "Neotraditional Town Planning." *Urban Land* 59, 2 (February 1992): 10–15.

Burden, D. *Bike Lanes: Improving Motorist/Bicyclist Behavior.* Tallahassee: Florida Department of Transportation, October 1994.

———. "Tower Road Charrette." PowerPoint presentation. Gainesville, Fla., 2000.

Burrington, S. H. (1996). "Restoring the Rule of Law and Respect for Communities in Transportation." *New York University Law Journal* 5, 3 (1996): 691–734. http://www.tlcnetwork.org/nyuart.html.

California Environmental Protection Agency. "Parking Cash-Out Incentive: Eight Case Studies." Research Note 98-3. June 1998. http://www.arb.ca.gov/research/resnotes/notes/98–3.htm. Accessed 15 May 2000.

Calthorpe, P. *The Next American Metropolis.* Princeton, N.J.: Princeton Architectural Press, 1993.

Campaign for New Transportation Priorities. *Transportation and Tax Policy.* Washington, D.C.: National Institute of Railroad Passengers, 1991.

Castle, R. "Sustainability Tax—Not Income Tax." 31 May 2002. http://www.roncastle.com/writing/sustainability%20Tax%20-%20Not%20Income%20ax.pdf. Accessed 16 July 2003.

Center for Urban Transportation Research. *Transportation, Land Use and Sustainability.* Tampa: University of South Florida Center for Urban Transportation Research, 1994.

Cervero, R. *America's Suburban Centers.* Berkeley: University of California Press, 1989.

———. "Unlocking Suburban Gridlock." *Journal of the American Planning Association* 52, 4 (1986): 389–406.

Chafee, J. H. "Driving Home a New Transportation Policy." *EPA Journal* 18, 4 (September/October, 1992): 21–23.

Chen, Donald D. T. "The Science of Smart Growth." *Scientific American,* December 2000.

City of Boulder. *Transportation Annual Report of Progress.* Boulder, Colo.: City of Boulder, September 1999.

Clarke, A. "Putting Pedestrians on a Pedestal: Ways to Rise above the Tide of Vehicular Chauvinism." In *Proceedings: Eighth Annual Pedestrian Conference.* Boulder, Colo.: City of Boulder Transportation Division, 1987.

Cohen, S. "Anybody Home?" *San Jose Mercury News,* 18 December 1994.

Conservation Law Foundation. *Take Back Your Streets.* Boston: Apogee Research, 1995.

Corbett, J. *Portland's Livable Downtown.* Washington, D.C.: Surface Transportation Policy Project, October 1992.

Corless, J., and Sprowls, S. *Beyond Gridlock.* Washington, D.C.: Surface Transportation Policy Project, May 2000.

Cunningham, R. "Main Street Successes in Florida." *Gainesville Sun* (Florida), 13 June 2002, G5.

Dimitriou, H. *Urban Transport Planning.* New York: Routledge, 1993.

Dorshner, J. "Road to Ruin." *Miami Herald Magazine,* 10 July 1988.

Dover, V., and Poole, S. "Rediscovery and Process." Presented at Florida Chamber of Commerce Growth Management Summer School Annual Conference, Marco Island, Florida, 1991.

Downs, A. "Might As Well Enjoy It." *Washington Post,* 1 January 2001.

———. *New Visions for Metropolitan America.* Washington, D.C.: Brookings Institution Press, 1994.

———. *Stuck in Traffic.* Washington, D.C.: Brookings Institution Press, 1992.

Duany, A. "Our Urbanism." *Architecture,* December 1998.

Duany, A., Plater-Zyberk, E., and Speck, J. *Suburban Nation.* New York: Farrar, Straus and Giroux, 2000.

Dunphy, R. T. "No More Free Parking?" *Urban Land* 52, 9 (September 1993): 9–10.

Durning, A. T. *The Car and the City.* Seattle: Northwest Environment Watch, 1996.

Durning, A., and Bauman, Y. *Tax Shift.* Seattle: Northwest Environment Watch, 1998.

Earthword. "Transportation Planning." Laguna Beach, Calif.: Center for Neighborhood Technology. *Eos Institute,* no. 4 (1992).

Easley, G. *Staying Inside the Lines.* Planners Advisory Service Report No. 440. Chicago: American Planning Association, 1992.

Economist. "Jam Today, Road Pricing Tomorrow." London. 6 December 1997.

Energy Outreach Center. *Redevelopment for Livable Communities.* Olympia, Washington: Energy Outreach Center, 1996.

Engwicht, D. *Reclaiming Our Cities and Towns.* Philadelphia: New Society, 1993.

Environmental Exchange. "Alternative Traffic Studies." Transportation Exchange Update. *What Works.* March 1994.

Ewald, W. R. *A Concept and a System.* McLean, Va.: Landscape Architecture Foundation, 1977.

Ewing, R. (1996). "Beyond Speed: The Next Generation of Transportation Performance Measures." In *Performance Measures for Growth Management,* edited by D. Porter, 31–40. Chicago: American Planning Association, 1996.

———. "Characteristics, Causes, and Effects of Sprawl." *Environmental and Urban Issues,* Winter 1994.

———. "Is Los Angeles Style Sprawl Desirable?" *Journal of the American Planning Association* 63, 1 (1997): 107–26.

———. *Pedestrian- and Transit-Friendly Design.* Prepared for the Florida Department of Transportation, Tallahassee. Chicago: American Planning Association, 1996.

———. "TDM, Growth Management, and the Other Four out of Five Trips." *Environmental and Urban Issues* 47, 3 (1993).

Ferguson, E. "Transportation Demand Management." *Journal of the American Planning Association* 56, 4 (1990): 442–56.

———. *Transportation Demand Management.* Planners Advisory Service Report No. 477. Chicago: American Planning Association, March 1998.

Florida Center for Community Design and Research. *Florida Pedestrian Safety Plan.* Tallahassee: Florida Department of Transportation, 1992.

————. *Integrating Community Design and Transportation.* Tampa: University of South Florida, November 1993.

————. *Livable Cities for Florida's Future.* Proceedings of a conference on energy efficient growth and transportation issues in Florida. Florida Department of Transportation. Gainesville, Fla., 2–4 May 1988.

————. *Transportation, Land Use, and Sustainability.* Tampa: University of South Florida, October 1994.

Florida Statistical Abstract, 1990–1998. Gainesville: University Press of Florida and U.S. Bureau of Census.

Forbes, G. "Vital Signs: Circulation in the Heart of the City: An Overview of Downtown Traffic." *ITE Journal* 68, 8 (August 1998): 26–33.

Frank, J. *The Costs of Alternative Development Patterns.* Washington, D.C.: Urban Land Institute, 1989.

Frank, L. D. "Linking Land Use and Transportation under Growth Management. *Land Lines,* January 1995.

Freeman, L. "The Effects of Sprawl on Neighborhood Social Ties." *Journal of the American Planning Association* 67, 1 (2001): 76.

"Free Ride Gets Boulder Workers on Bus." *PAS Memo,* February 1991.

Fulton, W., Pendall, R., Nguyen, M., and Harrison, A. *Who Sprawls Most? How Growth Patterns Differ across the U.S.* Washington, D.C.: Center on Urban and Metropolitan Policy, Brookings Institute, July 2001.

Gainesville Department of Community Development. "Staff Analysis." Gainesville Department of Community Development, Gainesville, Fla., February 2000. Unpublished.

————. "Staff Analysis." Gainesville Department of Community Development, Gainesville, Fla., March 2001. Unpublished.

Gainesville Traffic Engineering Department. *Gator "Getting There" Guide.* Gainesville, Fla., City of Gainesville, August/September 1994.

Gavin, J. "A Road Runs Through It." *American City and County,* December 2000.

Gehl, J. *Life between Buildings.* New York: Van Norstrand Reinhold, 1987.

"Go Boulder." *Urban Ecologist Newsletter,* Spring 1994.

Goddard, S. B. *Getting There.* House Public Works Committee hearings, 1955–56, Chicago: University of Chicago Press, 1994.

Gordon, D. "Economic Incentives for Changing Transportation Policy." *Urban Ecologist Newsletter,* Summer 1993.

Gottlieb, M. "One Who Would Like to See Most Architects Hit the Road." *New York Times,* 28 March 1993.

Gruen Gruen & Associates. *Employment and Parking in Suburban Business Parks: A Pilot Study.* Washington D.C.: Urban Land Institute, 1986.

Hanson, M. "Automobile Subsidies and Land Use." *Journal of the American Planning Association* 58, 1 (1992): 66–70.

————. "Do New Highways Generate Traffic?" *Access,* Fall 1995.

Hansen, M., and Huang, Y. "Road Supply and Traffic in California Urban Areas." *Transportation Research A* 31, 3 (1997): 205–18.

Harris, L. *The Need, Rationale, and Implementation of Wildlife Dispersal Corridors.* University of Florida, Gainesville, August 1991.

Harris, M. *Cultural Materialism.* New York: Random House, 1979.

Hart, S. *The Elephant in the Bedroom*. Pasadena: New Paradigm Books, 1993.

Hau, T. *Economic Fundamentals of Road Pricing*. Reports No. TWU 1 and TWU 2, Infrastructure and Urban Development. Washington, D.C.: World Bank, 1992.

Heimlich, R. E., and Anderson, W. D. *Development at the Urban Fringe and Beyond: Impacts on Agriculture and Rural Land*. ERS Agricultural Economic Report No. 803, June 2001, www.ers.usda.gov/publications/aer803. Accessed 15 March 2002.

Hine, J., and Russel, J. "Traffic Barriers and Pedestrian Crossing Behavior." *Journal of Transport Geography* 1, 4 (1993): 230–239.

Hochstein, M. "A New Urbanist Library." *Urban Land* 53, 10 (October 1994): 79–81.

Holtzclaw, J. "New Emissions Assay: Freeway Growth Pollutes; Traffic Calming Cleans." San Francisco: Sierra Club, 14 September 2000, http://www.sierraclub.org/sprawl/articles/hwyemis.asp. Accessed 10 August 2002.

———. *Sustainability: Where Cities and Cars Collide*. San Francisco: Sierra Club, 19 November 1993.

———. *Using Residential Patterns and Transit to Decrease Auto Dependence and Costs*. New York: National Resources Defense Council, 1994.

Hoyle, C. L. *Traffic Calming*. Planners Advisory Service Report No. 456. Chicago: American Planning Association, 1995.

Hoyt, H. "The Influence of Highways and Transportation in the Structure and Growth of Cities and Urban Land Values." In *Highways in Our National Life*, edited by J. Labatut and W. Lane. Princeton, N.J.: Ayer Company Publishers, 1950.

Institute of Food and Agricultural Sciences. "Personal Transportation: Cars." In *Energy Efficiency and Environmental News*. Gainesville: University of Florida Institute of Food and Agricultural Sciences, August 1993.

Institute of Transportation Engineers. *Guidelines for the Design and Application of Speed Humps*. Washington, D.C., Institute of Transportation Engineers, March 1993.

———. *Traditional Neighborhood Development: Street Design Guidelines*. Washington D.C., Institute of Transportation Engineers, June 1997.

———. *Traffic Engineering for Neo-Traditional Neighborhood Design*. Washington D.C., Institute of Transportation Engineers, February 1994.

International Center for Technology Assessment. *Real Price of Gas*. http://www.icta.org/ctanews/realpr.htm. Accessed 20 June 2002.

Jackson, K. T. *Crabgrass Frontier*. New York: Oxford University Press, 1985.

Jackson, T. T. "Transportation Concurrency: How It Can Be Achieved." *Florida Planning* 10, 10 (1990): 7–8.

Jacobs, J. *The Death and Life of Great American Cities*. New York: Vintage, 1961.

Kasowski, K. "The Costs of Sprawl, Revisited." *PAS Memo*, February 1993.

———. "Suburban Sprawl." *Florida Planning* 7, 1 (January 1995): 3, 5.

Kay, J. H. "Without a Car in the World," *New Colonist*, http://www.newcolonist.com/carfree_kay.html. Accessed 15 June 2001.

Ketcham, B. *Making Transportation Choices Based on Real Costs*. Presentation at the Transportation 2000 Conference "Making Transportation a National Priority." Snowmass, Colorado, 6 October 1991.

Kollodge, B. " 'Transportation' Cited as Top Problem Facing the Twin Cities Region." Metropolitan Council, St Paul, Minnesota. http://www.metrocouncil.org/news/news297.htm. Accessed 30 July 2002.

Koos, M. A. State Trails Coordinator, Florida Department of Environmental Protection, Tallahassee, Florida. Personal communication, 5 December 1994.

Krugman, P. "Reckonings; Nation in a Jam." *New York Times,* 13 May 2001.

Kulash, W. "Traditional Neighborhood Development: Will the Traffic Work?" Presented at the Eleventh Annual Pedestrian Conference, Bellevue, Washington, October 1990.

Kulash, W., Anglin, J., and Marks, D. "Traditional Neighborhood Development: Will the Traffic Work?" *Development* 21 (July/August 1990): 21–24.

Kunstler, J. H. *Home from Nowhere.* New York: Simon and Schuster, 1996.

———. *The Geography of Nowhere: The Rise and Decline of America's Man-Made Landscape.* New York: Touchstone, 1994.

Lagerberg, B., and Anderson, M. *Washington State Petroleum Markets Data Book.* WSEO 91-384. Olympia: Washington State Energy Office, January 1992.

Land Use Digest. "Report Surveys Impact of Transit-Focused Development." Washington, D.C.: Urban Land Institute, April, 1994.

Langdon, P. *A Better Place to Live.* Amherst: University of Massachusetts Press, 1994.

Lee, T. "Place Making in Suburbia." *Urban Land* 59, 10 (2000): 73.

Lennard S. H. C., and Lennard, H. L. *Making Cities Livable Newsletter,* Carmel, Calif., 1987.

Levinson, D., and Kumar, A. "Activity, Travel, and the Allocation of Time." *APA Journal* 61, 4 (1995): 458–70.

Lincoln Institute of Land Policy. *Alternatives to Sprawl.* Cambridge, Mass.: Lincoln Institute of Land Policy, 1995.

———. *Making the Land Use/Transportation/Air Quality Connection* (LUTRAQ). Cambridge, Mass.: Lincoln Institute of Land Policy, 1994.

Litman, T. "Commuter Financial Incentives." *Online TDM Encyclopedia.* Victoria Transport Policy Institute, 2001. http://www.vtpi.org/tdm/tdm8.htm. Accessed 17 July 2003.

———. "Commute Trip Reduction." *Online TDM Encyclopedia.* Victoria Transport Policy Institute, 2001. http://www.vtpi.org/tdm/tdm9.htm. Accessed 1 June 2003.

———. "Distance-Based Pricing." *Online TDM Encyclopedia.* Victoria Transport Policy Institute, 2002. http://www.vtpi.org/tdm/tdm10.htm. Accessed 15 June 2003.

———. "Evaluating Criticism of TDM." *Online TDM Encyclopedia.* Victoria Transport Policy Institute, 2002. http://www.vtpi.org/tdm/tdm49/htm. Accessed 14 January 2003.

———. "Fuel Taxes." *Online TDM Encyclopedia.* Victoria Transport Policy Institute, 2001. http://www.vtpi.org/tdm/tdm17.htm. Accessed 15 May 2003.

———. "Generated Traffic: Implications for Transport Planning." *ITE Journal* 71 (2001): 38–47.

———. "Guaranteed Ride Home." *Online TDM Encyclopedia.* Victoria Transport Policy Institute, 1999. http://www.vtpi.org/tdm/tdm18.htm. Accessed 10 June 2003.

―――. "Guide to Calculating Transportation Demand Management Benefits." Victoria Transport Policy Institute, 12 March 1999.

―――. "Land Use Impacts on Transport." *Online TDM Encyclopedia*. Victoria Transport Policy Institute, 2002. http://www.vtpi.org/tdm/tdm20.htm. Accessed 8 June 2003.

―――. "Location Efficient Development and Mortgages." *Online TDM Encyclopedia*, Victoria Transport Policy Institute, 2002. http://www.vtpi.org/ tdm/ tdm22.htm. Accessed 10 July 2003.

―――. "Market Principles," *Online TDM Encyclopedia*. Victoria Transport Policy Institute, 2001. http://www.vtpi.org/tdm/tdm60.htm. Accessed 2 July 2003.

―――. "Parking Pricing." *Online TDM Encyclopedia*. Victoria Transport Policy Institute, 2003. http://www.vtpi.org/tdm/tdm26.htm. Accessed 17 July 2003.

―――. *Parking Requirement Impacts on Housing Affordability*. Victoria, B.C.: Victoria Transport Policy Institute, 1999.

―――. "Potential Transportation Demand Management Strategies." *Online TDM Encyclopedia*. Victoria Transport Policy Institute, 1999. http://www.vtpi. org/tdmstrat.htm. Accessed 30 June 2003.

―――. "Road Pricing." *Online TDM Encyclopedia*. Victoria Transport Policy Institute, 2001. http://www.vtpi.org/tdm/tdm35.htm. Accessed 30 June 2003.

―――. "Socially Optimal Transport Prices and Markets." Victoria Transport Policy Institute, 12 March 1999.

―――. "Transit Oriented Development." *Online TDM Encyclopedia*. Victoria Transport Policy Institute, 2001. http://www.vtpi.org/tdm/tdm45.htm. Accessed 30 June 2003.

―――. "Transportation Cost Analysis for Sustainability." Victoria Transport Policy Institute, 24 July 1996.

―――. "Transportation Elasticities." *Online TDM Encyclopedia*. Victoria Transport Policy Institute, 2003. http://www.vtpi.org/tdm/tdm11.htm. Accessed 2 February 2003.

Lockwood, C. "The New Urbanism's Call to Arms." *Urban Land* 53, 2 (1994): 10.

Longman, P. "Sprawl." *Florida Trend*, December 1994.

Lucy, W. H. "Watch Out: It's Dangerous in Exurbia." *Planning*, November 2000.

Maine State Planning Office. *The Costs of Sprawl*. Augusta, Maine, Maine State Planning Office, 1997.

Manning, I. *The Journey to Work*. Sydney: Allen and Unwin, 1978.

McCann, B. *Driven to Spend: The Impact of Sprawl on Household Transportation Expenses*. Washington, D.C.: Surface Transportation Policy Project, November 2000.

McCrea, S. "Preparing for the Post-Petroleum Era." *Environmental and Urban Issues*, Winter 1994.

Metropolitan Transit Development Board. *Designing for Transit*. San Diego: Metropolitan Transit Development Board, July 1993.

Millard-Ball, A.. "Putting on Their Parking Caps." *Planning*, April 2002.

Miller, G. T. *Environmental Science*. 4th ed. Belmont, Calif.: Wadsworth, 1979.

Mitigation Panel. *Policy Implications of Greenhouse Warming*. Washington, D.C.: National Academy Press, 1991.

Moore, T., and Thorsnes, P. *The Transportation/Land Use Connection*. Planners Advisory Service Report No. 448/449. Chicago: American Planning Association, January 1994.

"More about Costs." *Transportation Exchange Update*, April 1994.

Morris, M. *Creating Transit-Supportive Land Use Regulations*. Planners Advisory Service Report No. 468. Chicago: American Planning Association, December 1997.

————. "Oregon Transportation Planning Rule." *Planning*, March 1993.

Municipality of Metropolitan Seattle. *1991 Parking Utilization Study*. Seattle: Municipality of Metropolitan Seattle, 1992.

"Nationwide Overhaul of Land Use Laws Needed." *New Urban News*, January/February 2001.

Natural Resources Council. *Traveling Smart Handbook*. Augusta, Maine: National Resources Council of Maine, 1993.

Neff, J. W. *Substitution Rates between Transit and Automobile Travel*. Presented at the Association of American Geographers Annual Meeting, Charlotte, N.C., April 1996.

Newman, P., and Kenworthy, J. *Cities and Automobile Dependence: An International Sourcebook*. Aldershot, England: Gower, 1989.

————. "Gasoline Consumption and Cities: A Comparison of U.S. Cities with a Global Survey and Its Implications." *Journal of the American Planning Association* 55, 1 (1989): 24–37.

————. *Sustainability and Cities*. Washington, D.C.: Island Press, 1999.

Noland, R. "Relationships between Highway Capacity and Induced Vehicle Travel." *Transportation Research A*, 35, 1 (2001): 47–72.

Northeastern Illinois Planning Commission. *1990 Land Use in Northeastern Illinois Counties, Minor Civil Divisions and Chicago Community Areas*. Chicago: Northeastern Illinois Planning Commission, 1995.

Nozzi, D. "West Palm Beach FL: Back From the Brink." http://user.gru.net/domz/palm.htm. Accessed 28 March 2002.

Oldenburg, R. *The Great Good Place*. New York: Marlowe, 1989.

"Passes Help People Hop onto the Bus." *Transportation Exchange Update*, April 1994.

Pederson, E. O. *Transportation in Cities*. New York: Pergamon, 1980.

Pew Center for Civic Journalism. "Top Local Problems." *Princeton Survey Research Associates*. College Park, Md. http://www.pewcenter.org/doingcj/research/r_st2000nat1.htm1#crime.

Pierce, N. "The Dawn of 'Civic Environmentalism.' " *Tampa Tribune*, 10 January 1994.

Plous, F. K. "Off the Road, Vehicles." *Planning*, September 1994.

Plowden, S. *Towns against Traffic*. London: Andre Deutsch, 1972.

Porter, D. R. "The Future Doesn't Work." *TR News*, December 1987.

Pryne, E. "Putting Shorter Commute on the Map." *Seattle Times*, 18 March 2002.

Puget Sound Water Quality Authority. *State of the Sound: 1992 Report*. Olympia, Wash.: People for Puget Sound, June 1992.

Richert, E. "Markets for Traditional Neighborhoods." *PAS Memo*, June 2000.

Richmond, H. R. "Comment on Carl Abbott's 'The Portland Region: Where City and Suburbs Are Free to Talk to Each Other—And Often Agree.' " Washington D.C.: Fannie Mae Foundation, 1997.

Rusk, D. "Debate on Theories of David Rusk." *Regionalist*, Fall 1997.

Rybczynski, W. "Rebuilding Los Angeles." *Gainesville Sun* (Florida), 11 June 1992.

Sandels, S. *Children in Traffic*. London: Elek Books, 1968.

Sayer, J. "The Costs of Sprawl." *Urban Ecology*, Spring 1993.

Schor, J. B. *The Overworked American*. New York: Basic Books. 1991.

Schuster, V. "The Full Costs of Commuting." *Bicycle Forum*, August 1993.

Schwarzkopf, D. *Citizens Clean Air Project*. http://www.houstonprogressive.org/hpn/ccap-haq.html. Accessed 30 June 2002.

Segal, J. M. "What We Work for Now," *New York Times*, 3 September 2001.

Shefer, D., and Rietvald, P. "Congestion and Safety on Highways: Towards an Analytical Model." *Urban Studies* (Edinburgh) 34, 4 (1997): 679–92.

"Shorts." *Urban Ecologist Newsletter* Fall 1994.

Shoup, D. "Congress Okays Cash Out." *Access*, Fall 1998.

———. "An Opportunity to Reduce Minimum Parking Requirements." *Journal of the American Planning Association* 61, 1 (1995): 14–28.

Shoup, D., and S. Stark. "The Parking of Nations." *Access*. Berkeley: University of California Transportation Center, Fall 2000.

Siemon, C., and Zimet, M. J. "Public Places as Infrastructure." *Environmental and Urban Issues*, Winter 1991.

Small, K. A., Winston, C., and Evans, C. A. *Road Work*. Washington, D.C.: Brookings Institute, 1989.

"Smart Pricing for Transportation Improvements." *Urban Land* 61, 2 (February 2002): 82–83.

Smith, S. A. *Planning and Implementing Pedestrian Facilities in Suburban and Rural Areas*. Transportation Research Board Report No. 294A. Washington, D.C.: Transportation Research Board, 1987.

Smith, W. *The Low-Rise Speculative Apartment*. Research Report 25. Berkeley: University of California Center for Real Estate and Urban Economics, 1964.

Smythe, R. *Density-Related Public Costs*. Washington, D.C.: American Farmland Trust, 1986.

Sno-Tran. *Creating Transportation Choices through Zoning*. Lynnwood, Wash.: Snohomish County (Washington) Transportation Authority, 1994.

Southworth, M., and Ben-Joseph, E. Preface to *Streets and the Shaping of Towns and Cities*. New York: McGraw-Hill, 1997.

Southworth, M., and Owens, P. M. "The Evolving Metropolis." *Journal of the American Planning Association*. 59, 3 (1993): 271–87.

Spitzer, C. *The Roads More Traveled*. Oak Ridge National Laboratory Annual Report. Oak Ridge, Tenn.: Oak Ridge National Laboratory, 1993.

Stack, M. "Clear Houston Air Remains Elusive." *Associated Press*, 2 February 2000.

Stokes, G. "Travel Time Budgets and Their Relevance for Forecasting the Future Amount of Travel." In *Transport Planning Methods: PTRC European Transport Forum Proceedings*. Coventry, U.K.: University of Warwick, 1994.

Sucher, D. *City Comforts*. Seattle: City Comforts Press, 1995.

Surface Transportation Policy Project. *An Analysis of the Relationship between Highway Expansion and Congestion in Metropolitan Areas: Lessons from the 15-Year Texas Transportation Institute Study*. Washington, D.C.: Surface Transportation Policy Project, 1998.

———. *High Mileage Moms*. May 1999. http://www.transact.org/report.asp?id=184. Accessed 18 July 2003.

————. *ISTEA Year Three.* 1994. http://www.transact.org. Accessed 30 July 2000.

————. *Mean Streets 1998: Children at Risk.* Washington, D.C.: Surface Transportation Policy Project, 1998.

————. *Why Are the Roads So Congested? An Analysis of the Texas Transportation Institute's Data on Metropolitan Congestion.* November 1999. http://www.transact.org/report.asp?id=63. Accessed 18 July 2003.

Swift and Associates. *Residential Street Typology and Injury Accident Frequency.* Longmont, Colo.: Peter Swift, 1997.

Taylor, B. D. "Public Perceptions, Fiscal Realities, and Freeway Planning: The California Case." *Journal of the American Planning Association* 61, 1 (1995): 43–56.

TEST. *Quality Streets: How Traditional Urban Centres Benefit from Traffic-Calming.* London: Greater London Council, 1988.

"TODs in Oregon." *Urban Ecologist Newsletter,* Winter 1994.

Transportation and Land Use Study Committee. *The Transportation and Land Use Study Committee: Final Report.* Tallahassee: Florida Department of Transportation, 15 January 1999.

Tumlin, J., and Siegman, P. "The Cost of Free Parking." *Urban Ecology,* Summer 1993.

Untermann, R. *Accommodating the Pedestrian.* New York: Van Nostrand Reinhold, 1984.

U.S. Bureau of the Census. *County and City Data Book:* 2000. Table D-1.

U.S. Department of Energy. *Transportation Energy Data Book: Edition 21–2001.* Oak Ridge, Tenn.: Oak Ridge National Laboratory, October 2001, chapter 11.

U.S. Department of Transportation. *1990 Nationwide Personal Transportation Survey* (NPTS). Washington, D.C.: Federal Highway Administration, August 1991.

————. *Benefits of Bicycling and Walking to Health.* National Bicycling and Walking Study, Case Study No. 14. Washington, D.C.: U.S. Department of Transportation, 1992.

————. *Environmental Benefits of Bicycling and Walking.* National Bicycling and Walking Study, Case Study No. 15. Washington, D.C.: U.S. Department of Transportation, 1993.

————. *Federal Highway Cost Allocation Study.* Federal Highway Administration. Washington, D.C.: U.S. Department of Transportation, 1997.

————. *Measures to Overcome Impediments to Bicycling and Walking.* National Bicycling and Walking Study, Case Study No. 4. Washington, D.C.: U.S. Department of Transportation, 1993.

————. *The National Bicycling and Walking Study: Final Report.* Washington, D.C.: U.S. Department of Transportation, 1994.

————. *Reasons Why Bicycling and Walking Are and Are Not Being Used More Extensively as Travel Modes.* National Bicycling and Walking Study, Case Study No. 1. Washington, D.C.: U.S. Department of Transportation, 1992.

————. *Statistical Abstract of the U.S., 2001.* Washington, D.C.: Federal Highway Administration, U.S. Department of Transportation, 2001.

————. *Traffic Calming, Auto-Restricted Zones, and Other Traffic Management Techniques: Their Effects on Bicycling and Pedestrians.* National Bicycling and Walking Study, Case Study No. 19. Washington, D.C.: U.S. Department of Transportation, 1994.

———. *Traffic Safety Facts 2000.* http://www-nrd.nhtsa.dot.gov/pdf/ nrd-30/NCSA/TSF2000.pdf. Accessed 17 July 2003.

———. *Transportation Potential and Other Benefits of Off-Road Bicycle and Pedestrian Facilities.* National Bicycling and Walking Study, Case Study No. 7. Washington, D.C.: U.S. Department of Transportation, 1992.

U.S. Environmental Protection Agency. "Environmental Benefits of Smart Growth." http://www.epa.gov/smartgrowth/topics/eb.htm. Accessed 17 July 2003.

———. *Our Built and Natural Environments.* Washington, D.C.: U.S. Department of Transportation, January 2001.

U.S. General Accounting Office. *Community Development: Reuse of Urban Industrial Sites.* GAO/RCED-95-172. Washington, D.C.: U.S. Government Printing Office, June 1995.

Ward, J. "It's Scary out There in Suburbanland." *City and County,* January 2001.

Washington State Energy Office. *Municipal Strategies to Increase Pedestrian Travel.* Olympia: Washington State Energy Office, 1994.

Webb, W. "What Cities Can Do: Revitalizing Denver's Downtown." *Brookings Review,* Summer 2000.

Weissman, S., and Corbett, J. *Land Use Strategies for Livable Places.* Sacramento, Calif.: Local Government Commission, 1992.

Willson R. W. "Suburban Parking Requirements." *Journal of the American Planning Association,* 61, 1 Winter 1995: 29–42.

———. *Suburban Parking Economics and Policy: Case Studies of Office Worksites in Southern California.* U.S. Department of Transportation, Washington, D.C.: Office of Technical Assistance and Safety, September 1992.

Wood, J. W. *Neotraditional Urbanism and Town Planning.* Belmont, N.C.: City of Belmont, 1996. (Wood is the city planner for Georgetown, South Carolina.)

Yuhnke, B. "Take a Deep Breath." In *Colorado Commons.* Longmont, Colo.: Spring, 1997.

Zahavi, Y., and Ryan, J. M. "Stability of Travel Components over Time." *Transportation Research Record* 750 (1980): 19–26.

Index

About the Author

DOM NOZZI is Senior Planner, Department of Community Development, City of Gainesville, Florida. His work has focused on long-range planning, urban design, and the preparation of land development regulations.